WHILE
THE GETTIN'S
GOOD

ALSO BY HERB GLUCK

Pro Football '73
Pro Football '74
Baseball's Great Moments

WHILE THE GETTIN'S GOOD

Inside the World Football League

THE BOBBS-MERRILL COMPANY, INC.
Indianapolis / New York

Library of Congress Cataloging in Publication Data

Gluck, Herb.
    While the gettin's good.

    1. World Football League.   2. Football.   I. Title.
GV955.5.W67G55   796.33′264′0973   75–6395
ISBN 0–672–52057–5

For Mary

Acknowledgments

There are so many people who have helped me that it would be impossible to express my appreciation to all of them. But I can make a start. First, I would like to thank my brother, Gerry Gluck, who took most of the pictures in this book. I think he is a terrific photographer, and the best brother who ever lived.

I would also like to thank Walter Myers and Gene Rachlis of Bobbs-Merrill, who had faith in the book.

Special thanks also to Peter Ildau of the Konica Camera Company for his excellent technical assistance, and to Ginger Sumner, who took that great picture of the author.

And finally, I would be incredibly remiss if I did not take the opportunity to state my sincerest gratitude to all of the players, coaches, front office personnel, public relations people (especially Vince Casey and Judy Coffin), and everyone else connected with the New York Stars/Charlotte Hornets. They patiently tolerated my intrusions and, hopefully, understood that I could never please all of them.

Herb Gluck
Whitestone, New York
August, 1975

WHILE
THE GETTIN'S
GOOD

While differences in temperament have no ethical significance, differences in character constitute the real problem of ethics.

ERICH FROMM

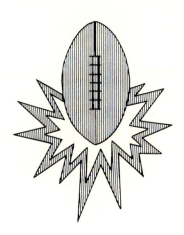

ON€

A sharp January sun glinted off gray rooftops; chimney smoke
rushed up into the wind, sirens wailed, children shouted—and in
the shuttered darkness of her basement apartment on Commonwealth Avenue, Dusty Rhodes slept.

Too many hours of talk and one drink too many had driven
her to bed in utter exhaustion. She was out of touch, floating
dreamlessly in a black void until the persistent jangle of her phone
started a fresh imprint. Reaching out to silence the piercing noise,
her hand crashed against a tall vase, sending it flying off the
nightstand in one direction while feather plumes went whirling off
in another. In a dulled rage, she grabbed the phone.

*"Hello. This is Dusty Rhodes. I am away from my office for a
short while, but I expect to be back soon. If you'd like, you may
leave a message when you hear the tone. This is the tone . . ."*

She vaguely recognized her voice on the Phone-O-Mate.
Suddenly, a human voice—male and resonant—interrupted the
machine.

"Hello, hello . . . What's going on?"

"Howard?"

1

"Yeah . . . What was that? Is there anything wrong?"

Howard Baldwin's voice immediately calmed her. Still, it all seemed so curious. She hardly knew the man. Their only meaningful get-together had taken place on a cold November evening in 1973—just two months before—in the insular atmosphere of a sports banquet. It was a typical affair, held at a fashionable hotel in downtown Boston. One of Dusty's clients, a New England Whaler hockey player, had been penciled in as a guest speaker.

During the pre-dinner cocktail prelude, Will McDonough popped out of the crowd, accompanied by a good-looking young fellow in a stunning tuxedo: Howard Baldwin.

Dusty was particularly happy to see McDonough there. He was her oldest and truest friend in town; a *Boston Globe* sportswriter who had given her sound advice in her first awkward days of employment with the Boston Patriots of the National Football League. McDonough was an indefatigable professional, and seemed to know everyone connected with athletics. Therefore, a flush rose to her cheeks when she heard him say to Baldwin, above the drone of the banquet crowd: "This young gal is going to make her mark in professional sports before very long. You can count on it, Howard."

Shortly after, Dusty and Baldwin fell into an extended conversation. How did she get into the sports agency business? he wanted to know. His question touched a nerve. It was as though he had asked her why she needed to breathe. It unlocked a floodgate of words. She started at the beginning and told him about her background in pro football. Baldwin, president of the New England Whalers hockey team, admitted he knew very little about football, but seemed genuinely fascinated when she discussed the Boston Patriot organization. He thought she was a walking encyclopedia of information. Dusty said she had to know the game in order to intelligently evaluate the best college players in a pro draft—and she had done just that in her two years with the Patriots. When the waiters began to set up servings of consommé, she shook Baldwin's hand and moved to a rear table. Even from that distance she could see him clearly—

seated on the dais—and sense in his bearing a strong, purposeful will.

Now she was talking to him again. Under totally different circumstances.

"No . . . nothing's wrong," she assured him. "I didn't get home until late. You know, business and all that. What time is it, anyway?"

"It's almost noon."

"My God, hold on while I see if there's a world out there!"

She carefully made her way to the window, using familiar objects like the top of a chair as guideposts, then opened the shutters. Sunlight flooded the room—a radiant sun that made her feel infinitely better. Returning to the phone, she felt cleansed.

"I'm sorry, Howard," she apologized. "What's up?"

"Well, I thought you might come over. Can you?"

"Sure. When would you like to see me?"

"Where do you live?"

"Oh, it's walking distance, really. I'd say about fifteen minutes from your office."

"Okay, can you make it in an hour?"

She could have made it sooner, but there was no hurry. After all, she thought, it was likely Baldwin just wanted to iron out an inconsequential matter concerning one of her Whaler clients—perhaps an availability conflict, or something of the sort. In less than a minute she was under the shower. The tingling sensation of warm water relaxed her muscles and did wonders for her spirits.

Refreshed, Dusty ducked under one of the many hanging plants that foliated the small apartment, swept up her last remaining pair of nylons from the carpet, rolled them up her long legs, then opened the clothes closet and removed a pair of knee-high leather boots, along with a brown wool suit and rabbit coat. Ten minutes later, with the front door closed behind her, Dusty walked out into the sunshine. The crisp, cold January air felt good against her cheeks.

At that moment, Boston never looked more dazzling. The new

3

buildings going up in startling number, the expensive boutique shops, and the elegant pedestrians along Commonwealth Avenue made life seem purposeful and challenging again. And yet, Dusty remembered reading somewhere that Boston was the third most expensive United States metropolitan area to live in, that an average family of four would need an annual income of $13,500 to live in moderate comfort. Hell, things could be a lot worse, she thought. And were. She didn't have twenty-five cents in her purse for a subway ride to the station nearest to Baldwin's office.

A car shot by as she crossed the street leading to Park Square. She noticed the driver was staring at her. Dusty didn't mind the eyes. Her clothes were flashy, her stride aggressive and her taut, six-foot frame worth at least one look.

She was born in West Chester, Pennsylvania, but part of her roots were in Canada. One of her uncles, Herb Gardiner, won the Most Valuable Player and Hart Trophy awards in the 1926–27 season while skating for the Montreal Canadiens of the National Hockey League. Another uncle, Charlie Gauer, was a star guard and then coach of the Philadelphia Eagles. That happy circumstance led Dusty to the pursuit of childhood pleasures transcending the games of hopscotch and "house." She attended hockey matches, cheered Eagle touchdowns from a seat alongside Bert Bell, commissioner of the National Football League, and was kissed by broad-shouldered athletes at numerous birthday parties given in her honor.

Dusty grew quickly. At the age of eighteen, taller than most boys, and anxious to compete in intercollegiate sports, she entered Penn State University. She played field hockey and basketball, ran the 440 and high jumped in track events. To earn money for her tuition, she attended the training table of the football team. In between, she studied to be a teacher. With a BA in sociology and a BS in secondary education, Dusty arrived in Boston, and on a rainy Monday afternoon in October, 1969, a fateful stroll past Fenway Park turned her young life around. The Boston Patriots hired her as a ticket office employee, and she worked in a cubbyhole room for three days until rescued by head coach

4

John Mazur. He assigned her to an administrative role and then, in 1970, to draft assessments. The following year she helped Rommie Loudd, director of player personnel, select Stanford's great quarterback, Jim Plunkett, as the number one pick in all pro football.

In 1972 John Mazur and general manager Upton Bell, the late commissioner's son, had a falling out. Mazur left. Dusty's loyalty to Mazur rankled Bell, and within days she was out, too. Dusty departed with the sinking feeling she had gone as far as she would ever go in sports. When Bob Woolf, the nation's most successful attorney-agent for athletes, asked her to work for him, she said there were too many things a woman couldn't do, was *not allowed* to do, in the business. Like what? Woolf asked. Like going into a locker room, she replied. But she finally accepted his offer and, in fourteen months with him, learned incredible things about the mores of athletes—when they weren't beating on one another with shoulder pads, bats, elbows and hockey sticks. While Woolf took care of all the contracts dealing with money management, licensing agreements, endorsements, and the like for more than two hundred athletes, Dusty dickered with landlords to find apartments and homes for her nomadic clients; bailed drunken halfbacks out of jail; wept with distraught wives on the verge of divorce; commiserated in personal tragedies and exulted in private triumphs. She became a fastidious counselor on money matters as well as on all things concerning the heart.

In late 1973 Woolf merged his company with a large New York concern and moved his office to Manhattan. Dusty remained in Boston to develop her own agency business.

It all seemed so far away now—the summers in West Chester, the crowded campus of Penn State, Patriot football at Foxboro Stadium. Now, walking toward Baldwin's office, she was uneasy. Most of her clients owed her money, and conflicting sentiments on work priorities had taken up too much of her time, as in the case of two state senators who had kept her out until the wee hours that morning, bantering endlessly about a publicity campaign for a forthcoming benefit tennis match. Worst of all, she was down to her last few pennies. Only a BankAmericard kept her one step ahead of famine.

A gusty wind whirled dust and old papers. Her eyes smarted, then focused on the Statler Hilton Building, an early-twentieth-century cement-gray edifice which stood on Park Square—on the ugly fringes of Boston's "combat zone."

Walking into the lobby, she recognized Eddie Andelman, who hosted a television talk show in town. Andelman was a charming guy and a good contact.

"Hey, Dusty, where are you going?"

"Up to the Whaler office."

Andelman removed his glasses. He blew at a speck and returned them to his pudgy face. "Funny thing, I just came from there. Baldwin's burning up the telephone. God knows on what. Do you have an appointment with him?"

"Uh-huh."

"Well, lots of luck, sweetie." She watched him go out the front door, smiling his way past a knot of lunch-crowd executives, then dawdled for a moment or two in the lobby, imagining all kinds of intriguing possibilities in Andelman's obscurant remarks. When the elevator door slid back on the seventh-floor landing, a veil lifted. She remembered the November sports banquet.

A forlorn Christmas tree stood inside the entrance—an artifact of the past holiday season. Cardboard boxes were piled up on a large wooden table. The stained walls were barren, except for a few lopsided glossies of grinning hockey players. Paper scraps and squashed cigarette butts collected on the floor. Baldwin's outer office looked like an interior decorator's nightmare.

The only chair in the room was occupied by a dumpy, pimple-faced teenager. She looked like a temporary, someone foisted on unsuspecting firms by a fast-talking employment agency. Dusty removed her coat, then folded it over her arm. There was no coat rack. She lit a cigarette. The floor was a huge ashtray.

"May I help you?" asked the girl. There were wide gaps between her front teeth.

"Yes, I'm Dusty Rhodes. I have an appointment with Mr. Baldwin."

Excusing herself, the girl waddled to the door of the inner office. Dusty half-sat on the table, looking mindlessly at framed hockey pictures. Her anticipation in the lobby and elevator turned to foreboding in the drab surroundings of the primitive reception room. The place would be more in character, she thought, if buffaloes were painted on the wall. Perhaps Baldwin himself sat cross-legged on the floor of his inner cave, hunched over a huge knuckle of flesh, eyes darting toward the door as though any intrusion would be met with a primal scream. Her fantasies were interrupted by the reappearance of the receptionist.

"Mr. Baldwin will see you now."

The abrupt change in mood amazed her. The room was meticulously organized, comfortable, with the look of soft leather and plywood. The walls were decorated with gleaming hockey plaques; framed pictures of Baldwin in the company of uniformed athletes; testimonials; school diplomas; a mahogany rack that contained expensive handguns and rifles. Truly, this was the refuge of a well-bred gentleman—a restful hideaway in the midst of chaos.

"Hi," he called out, getting up from his chair. "How are you?"

"Just great, Howard."

"Sit down. Relax." He pointed to a leather-cushioned sofa.

Why is he asking me to relax? she chafed. I *am* relaxed. But, in truth, Dusty felt a tightness within, a feeling of springs ready to uncoil.

"Here, take these." He handed her two thick notebooks. A pasted insignia on each cover hit her full in the face. The design was that of a stitched football enclosed by a circle, with the words WORLD FOOTBALL LEAGUE beneath. "I just came back from a meeting in California," said Baldwin. "As you can see, it had to do with football. A new professional league. I own the Boston franchise."

Dusty looked at him. Yes, he was serious.

"It was Gary Davidson's idea. He laid most of the groundwork

7

last summer. Ran his ass off in order to nail the heavy investors. The next thing you know, we've got a league with twelve franchises, all in major population centers. Now we're ready to kick off World Football League action *this season!* What do you think of that?"

Dusty worked her jaws free. "Terrific!"

"Okay, here's where you come in. I need your help. Here, look at this!" He held up a couple of manila folders stuffed with stationery. "One of these contains letters from prospective players, the other from high school, college and pro coaches. We're getting inquiries from all over the country. A lot of people want to hook up with us."

"Howard, what *exactly* do you want me to do?" she asked.

Baldwin came around from behind his desk, picked up one of the notebooks he had given to Dusty and opened it.

"This contains a rundown of the franchises, capsule biographies of the owners, things of that nature. Also, the WFL by-laws are included, along with some important rule changes. I guarantee, you'll be impressed.

"As for this one," he said with a wink, opening the other notebook for her inspection, "you can see it's a computerized printout of college players—hundreds of them—from every school in the country. A bitch of a scouting report. It's all there, the best and the worst of this year's crop. I figure you'll be able to spot some of the best. After that, I want you to go to New York for our first draft."

"When is the draft?"

"Four days from now . . . next Monday."

Four days? Cripes, it took longer than that just to draw a balance sheet on quarterbacks. She looked up at Baldwin, struggling to maintain her composure.

"Okay, I go to New York. Then what?"

"Then . . ." his voice trailed after her, ". . . I suppose you'll select the best damn players you can get your hands on. By that time, I hope to have a head coach down there with you. Maybe Babe Parilli. We've been talking, and Babe says he's interested in taking on the job."

To Dusty, everything felt just right. She knew she was out of the agency business and back in football.

"Actually," Baldwin said, grinning, "Will McDonough tipped me about Babe."

"Will McDonough? *Will?* Wow . . . that man's a real Santa Claus!"

"Yeah. Will's a fine fellow. I mean, he spelled it all out. Told me that Babe wanted to return to Boston in the worst way—that he was tired of always being on the move, away from his family and all that. And that he wouldn't hesitate if he could get a solid offer to coach in Boston. So I followed up, talked to Babe. I don't know what will happen, but I'm hopeful he'll say yes."

"Me too. He's a legend in this town. The Kentucky Babe back in Boston—can you imagine that?"

"I sure can. And I can imagine your helping me out as my main gal, Dusty."

"What does that mean?" She had heard vaguenesses like that before. Now was as good a time as any to confront Baldwin with the realities of her situation. "Listen, Howard, if I go along with all this, it means I have to phase out my agency business . . . get rid of my clients . . ."

"I wouldn't ask you to drop what you're doing after just listening to my side of things. That's why I want you to go through all this stuff, meet with some of the other WFL people in New York. I'm positive you'll be sold on the future of this league. If that's the case, I'll sit down with you and work something out. I give you my word."

"All right, fair enough." She picked up the notebooks. "I might as well start right now, Howard. You've got a deal."

But as they walked out of his office, Dusty realized there were a few details to cover.

"Where do you want me to work?"

"We have a small room down the hall that isn't being used. However, I think it would be best if you worked out of your place until I get it cleaned up."

"Okay, but I'll need some people to help me on the draft."

"Fine. Get anyone you want. As soon as you can tell me who

you want, call me. I'll take care of all the arrangements for your transportation, hotel, expenses—whatever. By the way, you'll be staying at the Essex House."

Baldwin helped her on with her coat, placed the two notebooks under her arm, then walked her to the front door. The receptionist looked up sadly, all the while poking Black Crow licorice candy into her mouth.

The elevator carried Dusty down to the lobby. By now, her stomach seemed to be floating between her kneecaps and ankles. She needed food, and lots of it. In a hurry. Thank God, she thought, it was still a credit card world. A number of fine restaurants in the Government Center area would gladly honor her plastic-molded bankroll. One such establishment, a colonial-styled, traditional seafood place, loomed invitingly in the near distance. As she swung the white-paneled door open, a muffled drone, sounding very much like the buzzing of politicians in a Back Bay clubhouse, rose up to flood her ears. The restaurant was a male chauvinist retreat, a haven for top business executives. Handsome, perfectly groomed men in hand-tailored suits sat at almost every table. Some turned to cast dull stares her way, distracted by her presence, as though she were an alien intruder in their midst.

A bulbous-nosed maitre d' escorted her to a small table near the front window, then slunk away after he had placed a finely decorated menu in her hands. Moments later she decided on the bouillabaisse. It was one of her favorite seafood dishes, a highly seasoned fish stew that always stirred a feeling of divine happiness. Perhaps, she speculated, there was something in the garlic. . . .

She glanced at the two notebooks, which rested on the edge of the table. Might as well get acquainted with the cast of characters and the franchises, she thought. Standing the organizational notebook upright, covers spread open, she began reading. But every now and then she noticed two men at a nearby table. One of them put on a pair of horn-rimmed glasses and actually stretched his neck in order to read the words on the cover. Dusty could have sworn he mouthed a confused expletive to his companion:

"What the fuck is the World Football League?"

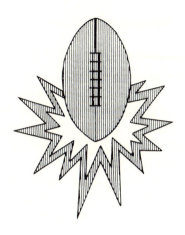

TWO

Four days before Dusty Rhodes sat down to her bouillabaisse luncheon in Boston, Howard Baldwin stepped out of an elevator and strode to a ballroom in the Marriott Hotel at Los Angeles International Airport. He was impeccably dressed. In behavior and movement, Baldwin mirrored his colleagues. Cool and perfunctory, they lined up at the ballroom entrance to be screened and admitted by a hotel security guard. In a few minutes the first board of governors meeting of the World Football League would be convened, and each of them knew their formal gathering would flabbergast the overlords of the National Football League. Baldwin was as sure of that gut reaction as he was that the date was January 14, or that he could hear the whine of jumbo jets over the hotel rooftop.

In less than two years he had climbed from relative obscurity to president of the New England Whalers—the most successful franchise in the World Hockey Association. Baldwin's organization, as well as the balance of WHA teams, was the brainchild of Gary Davidson and Donald J. Regan, California-based law partners who had the *chutzpah* to establish the league during the height of the salary wars which touched off the birth of the

11

American Basketball Association—another Davidson-Regan production.

Baldwin's true passion was hockey. He had played it well, hoping to become one of the few Americans to wind up in the Canadian-dominated National Hockey League. But after two years of rink competition as captain of the Salisbury School hockey team in Connecticut, he grudgingly allowed he didn't have the tools to make it in the pro ranks. Graduating from Boston University, he waited for an opportunity in the business end of the sport. An opening for a business manager developed with the Jersey Devils of the Eastern Hockey League. Baldwin took on the job. Then, in 1967, owner Bill Putnam of the NHL Philadelphia Flyers brought Baldwin up from the minors. For the next four years the frustrated hockey player worked as Flyer ticket and sales manager.

In early November, 1971, Baldwin met with Gary Davidson, who offered him a WHA franchise in New England, provided he could come up with $25,000 in front money, $10,000 in league expenses, and a $100,000 performance bond. Baldwin said he could manage it. He found a partner in Bob Schmertz, nationwide builder of retirement communities, owner of the National Basketball Association Boston Celtics—and millionaire sports fan. With Schmertz's money, he was able to graduate from sales manager of the Flyers to part-owner of the New England Whalers.

Now he was about to start a new pro football franchise in Boston, taking a precarious shot in a sport quite foreign to his taste and training. But Baldwin had faith, mainly because Gary Davidson was at the helm of the new league. It was Gary who had sharpened his smell for investors, who had helped him understand the intricacies of merging franchises with money people, who had handed him a WHA franchise in New England on a silver platter so that he could corral Bob Schmertz at a later date to finance the operation. Well, now he'd be able to use the same formula to launch his freebie WFL franchise in Boston. In this day and age, he speculated, backers would be falling out of the trees and at his feet within a few weeks. Leaning forward in his chair, scanning familiar faces in the Marriott ballroom, thirty-one-year-old

Howard Baldwin figured that life and Gary Davidson had treated him very kindly.

He cast a knowing smile at his old boss. Bill Putnam winked back. In his mid-forties—dimple-chinned, darkly mustached, and handsome in a sad-eyed sort of way—Putnam was a product of the Lone Star State, a Navy veteran and a graduate of the University of Texas. Armed with a business degree, he went to New York in 1961 to work for the J.P. Morgan Company. When he resigned in 1965, he was executive vice-president of their lending offices.

Putnam moved on to Los Angeles, joined Jack Kent Cooke Enterprises and, as executive vice-president, engineered the purchase of the NBA Lakers. Later, he located and negotiated the site for the Los Angeles Forum and worked out a deal which brought the expansion Los Angeles Kings into the National Hockey League. But Putnam wanted and *needed* ownership in a sports operation, so he left Cooke in 1967 to form his own expansion team in the NHL—the Philadelphia Flyers. Three years later he unloaded the club, taking out enough profit to glide leisurely through a period of reassessment in the sports consulting field. He also began to cultivate new friendships. One was with Gary Davidson.

In 1971 Putnam joined an investment organization called the Omni Group. In short order, he was able to put together a package that made him a part-owner and president of the Atlanta Hawks of the NBA and Atlanta Flames of the NHL. But once again, Putnam felt he had fallen just short of the *ultimate* reward.

In the summer of 1973 Gary Davidson told Putnam about a glittering Mother Lode that lay buried beneath an untapped pro football market. Come join me, said Davidson, the ore is everywhere. All you have to do is pick a territory. Soon you will find riches beyond your wildest expectations. Well, conjectured Putnam, Birmingham, Alabama, should be a healthy deposit. Okay, Birmingham it is, said Davidson. You've got it.

Putnam resigned from the Omni Group, divested himself of his interest in the Hawks and the Flames and nailed down territorial rights to the Birmingham Americans of the World Football League. Returning to Atlanta, he contacted a tall, shapely ex-secretary by the name of Carol Tygart Stallworth. He asked her if she would be willing to buy into his new WFL franchise.

"Are you kidding?" said the startled beauty, who had since become the wife of Ryder Trucking executive Jim Stallworth. Putnam assured her he was serious. Of course, he added, the franchise would have to be funded, but it wouldn't take much, certainly less than a million. Mrs. Stallworth surmised the investment would be like a dream come true, especially at those prices. So she put up some of the family cash and quickly ascended to the presidency of the Birmingham franchise, while Bill Putnam took over as chairman of the board. Now they were seated in a Los Angeles hotel ballroom, nodding to each other, shuffling papers, waiting for Gary Davidson to call the roll, thus officially launching the WFL.

Steve Arnold was in the room as a result of another pass handed out by Gary Davidson. The thirty-six-year-old San Francisco resident was a New York product who had spent much of his early youth following the bouncing ball and flying puck on board and ice at the old Madison Square Garden. He received a college education at Brown University in Rhode Island, then returned to New York to attend the Columbia Law School. After passing his bar exam, Arnold rededicated himself to his first love —sports. He went into the player agency business, at one time representing National Football League star Jimmy Brown. But Arnold eventually found greener pastures in the WHA, where Gary Davidson had orchestrated hockey franchises from Edmonton to New England. Like all things with men who share a special communication, Davidson and Arnold realized they could be good for each other. Davidson brought Arnold closer to his inner conclave and Arnold skimmed off dozens of WHA players as clients. Things worked out so well that, even as Davidson bowed out of the WHA picture, Arnold remained as a special advisor to the new league office.

Inevitably, the dark-eyed, bushy-haired Arnold (whose face resembled a mixture of Sandy Koufax and Ben Gazzara) was contacted by Davidson about the WFL. Do you want a franchise? asked Davidson. Of course, said Arnold. Okay, said Davidson, how about Memphis? The town should be ready for pro football, don't you think? Yeah, replied Arnold, the NFL isn't there yet, so maybe I can go down to Memphis and hustle up an angel or two. Which he did. Only, the angels told him that if they were going to invest their money, they'd rather do it in the NFL. Now, sitting in the Marriott ballroom, Steve Arnold figured he'd wait a little longer until something broke. After all, he thought, what did he have to lose? Memphis hadn't cost him a quarter.

Also in the room sat Nick Mileti, a chunky-framed man in his late forties who liked to dress in flashy, hip-bohemian outfits. Around his neck Mileti wore a chain of Indian beads; in his back pants pocket he carried his favorite leather accessory—a wallet stuffed to capacity with large bills. Mileti's life style was a frenetic romp. In business he maintained high visibility. With crackling voice and a well-greased propaganda mill working overtime, Mileti managed to find his proper niche as a sports entrepreneur. In the expansion years of the late sixties and early seventies, he became a packager of pro teams, a sports *toomler* who clowned, postured and laughed his way to part-ownership of baseball's Cleveland Indians, the Cleveland Cavaliers of the NBA and the Cleveland Crusaders of the WHA. However, Mileti's social life swung beyond the confines of Cleveland. He joyously traveled around the baseball, basketball and hockey circuits—where the Hollywood crowd, Golden Gate bluebloods, Windy City sharpies and Big Apple sophisticates became fodder for his voracious, fun-loving appetite. Along the way, Gary Davidson and he had a sit-down meeting to discuss the WFL.

Here, said Davidson, take Chicago. Find an investor. Sell the franchise. With Mileti's contacts, reasoned the WFL commissioner, it shouldn't be hard.

Mileti took it and waited for the right guy to come along.

The guy was Tom Origer, a youthful cigar-chewing business-man who at an earlier time had wanted to play football for the Chicago Bears. A heart murmur shattered that ambition while he was still in high school. In 1962 Origer went into the construction business with $15,000. Twelve years later his multi-family apartment houses had spread over Chicago, and he had enough money to keep him stocked in Havanas for the rest of his life.

But football was still deeply embedded in his mind. In late October, 1973, he read an item in the *Chicago Tribune:* Gary Davidson had started up a new sports venture called the World Football League; teams in the United States, Japan and Mexico would soon be in operation. Origer figured he'd fly out to Los Angeles to see how much it would cost to establish a team in Chicago. Davidson introduced him to Nick Mileti. The Cleveland dandy was willing to part with his territorial rights for a mere $500,000. It was worth more than that, said Mileti. Origer offered him $400,000. They settled for something in between. On October 23, Davidson (who sported a wispy mustache for the occasion) and Origer announced the Chicago entry into the new league from a dais in the Sheraton-Chicago Hotel. Davidson had his share of the front money, Mileti deposited his windfall in a Cleveland bank, and Origer floated on a cloud filled with rain.

Three months later, the new owner of the Chicago Fire franchise took his assigned seat in the Marriott ballroom. Smiling broadly at Davidson, shaking hands with his new clubhouse cronies, Origer vaguely remembered how it must have been for the legendary pro football pioneer, George Halas—owner of the Chicago Bears—who had gone to Canton, Ohio, on a warm September day in 1920 as representative of a Decatur, Illinois, starch company. Origer recalled reading that Halas and ten other inspired men from sleepy towns such as Muncie, Youngstown, Massillon and Rock Island sat on running boards in the Ralph E. Hay Motor Company and formed the American Professional Football Association, two years before it became the National Football League. It caused Origer to think: *Move over, George Halas . . . Here I come!*

For Louis R. Lee, twenty-eight-year-old leader of the Detroit delegation, it was an historic moment. He was well aware that early football pioneers had conducted their business in total

16

rejection of black aspirations, that tokenism in those days was reserved for a lone Carlisle Indian named Jim Thorpe. That's the way it was, Louis Lee knew, until the floodgates opened for black football players in the early 1950s. And now Lee was entangled in the labyrinth of a refreshingly new phenomenon in pro football history. Without a track record in sports management, without real or abstract wealth, he had come to Los Angeles as spokesman for thirty-one local men (including himself) and one woman. On his shoulders rested the task of buttoning up WFL rights to a Detroit franchise. But he didn't bring along the kind of money that surely rests in strongholds such as Grosse Pointe. Rather, his people were, for the most part, upper-middle-class professionals—doctors, lawyers, relatively minor industrialists—who had pledged limited financial support. But not one of Lee's backers came within distant range of a Nelson Rockefeller stockpile or even within reach of a Tom Origer bankroll. Scurrying around the inner city of Detroit and the manicured monotony of its environs, Lee collected a few thousand here, a few thousand there, then unloaded most of it on Gary Davidson in Los Angeles.

Lee's beginnings were in Abington, Pennsylvania. There he starred as an all-state football and basketball player. Recruited by the University of Michigan, he played in the 1965 Rose Bowl, then obtained a degree at the Michigan Law School. In 1970 he joined the Detroit law firm of Miller, Canfield, Paddock and Stone in an associate position. It gave him the contacts and credentials that would take him, four years later, on a journey to Los Angeles. Now he was standing proud in the narrow, restricted world of executive sports management. Louis Lee had *made it* as the first black president of a major professional sports team. Indeed, his liberal-minded associates would have doubled over with laughter had he chosen to answer the Detroit roll call with a rousing *Move ovah, Whitey . . . Heah ah is!*

In a room filled with Americans, a tall sandy-haired Canadian appeared singularly at ease. John Bassett, Jr., was an authentic Toronto millionaire, the possessor of enough cash to make him the trump card up Gary Davidson's sleeve. Bassett was no Johnny-come-lately to Canada. His family roots in the province of Ontario traced back to an age when the wilderness still flourished, when tall evergreens capped the landscape, when scenic waters sparkled clear and cold under pollution-free Canadian air. *Ut Incepit Fidelis Sic Permanet* is the motto of Ontario. *Loyal in the beginning, so it remains,* echo the Bassett progeny.

Square-jawed and determined, Johnny Bassett controlled Canadian television stations, newspapers and a film company. His interest in sports below the border led him to a rendezvous with Yankee peddler Davidson in the start-up days of the WHA. Securing the Toronto Toro franchise, Bassett insured his investment by teaming up with fellow owners to lure NHL hockey stars to the new league. Luminaries such as Bobby Hull, Gordie Howe and Derek Sanderson willingly signed multimillion-dollar WHA contracts, and the hitherto-complacent NHL shuddered with each signing. The raiding war brought about a predictable spiraling of salaries for hockey players in both leagues. Bassett could afford the price of inflation.

During the late autumn of 1973, the Canadian millionaire snapped up territorial rights to a WFL franchise in Toronto. His American buddy, Gary Davidson, offered him a deal he couldn't refuse—at bargain-basement rates. Circulating now about the ballroom, saying hello to old WHA friends, measuring his new friends in the WFL, Bassett felt sure Davidson's new toy would work—and amuse all those who watched it go. Already his mind spun with ideas on how to persuade Canada's minister of health and welfare to accept American football. Word had reached Bassett that his government was beginning to raise its hackles—that the entry of a WFL team within Canada's borders could very well destroy the Canadian Football League. Well, if necessary, Bassett reasoned, he was prepared to move his franchise to the States. But he preferred not to.

And somewhere deep in the recesses of his brain, he began to formulate a plan to drop a bombshell on the NFL. With almost unlimited resources, Bassett was prepared to dangle incredible sums at pro football's Big Three—O. J. Simpson, Joe Namath and Larry Csonka—in order to tempt one or all of them away from the NFL. The mere thought of such an eventuality caused him to smile contentedly. He could hardly wait for Davidson's gavel to descend.

Neither could Danny Rogers, who held territorial rights to the Hawaiian franchise. But unlike Bassett, Rogers could not dream of signing NFL superstars at the moment. The best he could hope for was to bring in some backers and grab off a few percentage points in the business, a fee for selling the franchise, and perhaps a high-salaried job in the front office of the unborn Hawaiian football team.

Actually, Ben Hatskin, another old pal of Davidson's, had first crack at the franchise, but the owner of the WHA Winnipeg Jets was taken ill, so the ball was tossed to Rogers, whose entrance into the Marriott ballroom caused heads to turn. Tall, lean, and suntanned, Rogers was by far the most handsome man in the room—and also one of the luckiest. It was his good fortune to have grown up in Southern California, the nesting place of Gary Davidson. Like Davidson, Rogers enjoyed surf and sun, played a mean game of tennis and, in his grasp of high-powered selling techniques, shared a common ground with the WFL commissioner.

Besides, he was a former jock. Davidson was unabashedly impressed with his background in sports. A University of Southern California basketball player, Rogers had earned all-America honors and became team captain and Most Valuable Player of the 1957 USC squad. Along the way, he broke all of Bill Sharman's lifetime scoring records. After graduation he went into coaching, first as assistant basketball coach at his alma mater, then at USC (Irvine) as head coach, a post he held for three years. But as much as Rogers liked coaching, he liked money more. So he left the college-campus life for a position as national sales manager of the Nutrilite Company, then ecstatically entered Gary Davidson's world. With the formation of the WHA, Rogers found his key to a gleaming treasure chest. The

19

first turn of the key ushered him into a plush job as licensing director for the WHA. Now the second door was about to be opened. In a couple of days he would be high above the Pacific Ocean, gazing down on Diamond Head and patting an attaché case that contained the names of some of the fattest cats in Hawaii. With a little more luck, he expected to be sitting in a leather chair facing Waikiki Beach, looking for all the world like the owner of a pro football team.

Still another Gary Davidson fan was Larry Hatfield, a thirty-eight-year-old ex-Mississippian whose conglomerate, Intersystems, totaled $23 million in sales in 1970. The following year Hatfield moved to Newport Beach, California, where he became president of the Big Brake auto repair chain, a subsidiary of Intersystems, then sold out to go into the trucking business. With Gary Davidson a close neighbor, the stage was set for Hatfield to focus his attention on something more glamorous than computers, photographic and printing equipment, trucks, and auto parts. Over cocktails, between tennis matches, and on sandy beaches, Hatfield and Davidson discussed the World Football League. The more he listened, the more Hatfield liked the idea. But Hatfield was no dummy. It would take millions, not thousands, to run a pro football team, and he wasn't about to use all of his hard-earned loot to gamble on the new league. Then one day Hatfield came up with an entry fee. He told Davidson that he had found a backer in Al Lapin, the founder of International Industries (an umbrella for International House of Pancakes and Orange Julius). As Putnam told it, Lapin whipped up a batter of green cash, then went back to his pancakes, leaving him to run the Southern California franchise.

Now Larry Hatfield was in the spotlight as a bona fide pro football owner. Now he could deal with warm-blooded athletes, not cold, unfeeling machines. Today, he thought, the Marriott Hotel. Tomorrow, the World Football League.

Not far from Hatfield sat Chuck Rohe, a balding forty-one-year-old graduate of the University of Southern Mississippi, former track coach of the University of Tennessee, and temporary caretaker of the Florida franchise. Rohe twinkle-toed into the board of governors meeting after a couple of meetings with Gary Davidson. He indicated to the commissioner that he could talk some people down south into picking up the tab for the operation of a pro football team, but was unable to follow through. However, he turned over some prospects to Davidson. High on the list was Fran Monaco, who ran a highly successful chain of medical laboratories in Florida. Monaco was a big football nut, close to a lot of NFL people, including Dick Butkus, who co-owned a restaurant with him in DeLand, Florida. A couple of days before the board of governors meeting, Davidson placed a call to Monaco, who was in Houston for the Miami-Minnesota Super Bowl game. Monaco told the commissioner he was interested in the Florida franchise, that he'd be able to work out some kind of deal if the price was right. In Gary Davidson's *Alice in Wonderland* world, all things were possible.

Although the Washington franchise was spoken for, its standard bearer was not present to enjoy the proceedings. E. Joseph Wheeler, Jr., owner of Wheeler Industries, a marine biology and engineering company, had put in his bid for the franchise—with regret that he couldn't attend the meeting. Davidson slipped Wheeler's letter and down payment into his Washington file and made a note to call the man in a day or two for the balance. Meanwhile, Wheeler's check for five grand served as a lock on the nation's capital—and all the territory within one hundred miles of the White House.

Three thousand miles from Los Angeles, Bob Schmertz looked down from the study window of his Manhattan duplex apartment on East 66th Street. In a short while, he would leave for his office in Lakewood, New Jersey. He had much to do. But for now the early-afternoon leisure suited him fine. He spent those moments thinking about Howard Baldwin and the WFL meeting that was probably just getting underway in Los Angeles. He checked his watch. It was a few minutes before one o'clock.

At five minutes to ten, Los Angeles time, Howard Baldwin busied himself with some of the material in his WFL organizational book, flipping pages back and forth, making penciled entries in the margins of particular paragraphs that caught his interest. In a short while he'd answer "Here" when Boston came up on the roll call. Then he would cover the New York entry as a surrogate for Bob Schmertz. Baldwin looked forward to standing in for his friend—who had put up the cash that enabled him to launch the Whalers.

But as far as *his* football franchise was concerned, Baldwin knew he had lots of work ahead once the meeting ended. The first WFL college draft was exactly eight days away, and he needed a staff to prepare for it. There was also the matter of hiring a coach, stocking the Boston team with players, finding a suitable stadium to play in—all of which needed his utmost concentration. More than *anything,* he needed a backer. Without someone like Bob Schmertz to pick up the tab on his new venture, everything else was academic. But then again, he suddenly chuckled to himself, he and Schmertz didn't have to worry about a franchise fee. In a country where NFL teams held a market value of $16 million, they both owned a WFL franchise for absolutely nothing.

Almost all the characters of the drama were in place. To Ken Bogdanoff, though, the charade he was going through seemed more like slapstick comedy. Bogdanoff squirmed in the Philadelphia seat, wishing Gary Davidson would get on with the meeting so that he could get out of Los Angeles and back to Philadelphia while he still possessed his senses.

Bogdanoff was an undergraduate at Temple University in 1967—a slight, blond-haired youngster with good study habits and flaming ambition. His thoughts lay beyond his father's world, which revolved around dentistry. Bogdanoff was sure he'd wind up pulling money out of business ventures rather than teeth out of patients' mouths. During one summer vacation period he had taken a job as a lifeguard at the exclusive Green Hill apartments in Philadelphia. Bill Putnam, then president of the Flyers, was a resident of Green Hill and often used the pool for a morning dip. Soon the young lifeguard and Putnam hit it off on a first-name basis. They exchanged jokes, talked about hockey, sometimes just sat quietly at poolside and dug each other's company. In the winter months that followed, Bogdanoff saw a lot of free hockey games at the Spectrum.

Two years later, now a Temple graduate, Bogdanoff applied for a job as assistant ticket manager with the Flyers. He did it on his own, never telling Putnam about his intentions, and was hired. One day Putnam saw him in the ticket office and asked him what he was doing there.

"I work for you," said Bogdanoff. They both had a big laugh over that.

The job was okay, but Bogdanoff became restless. He knew there had to be something better than selling tickets. When Putnam resigned from the Flyers, Bogdanoff figured he'd get out, too. By this time he was married, with added responsibilities. He went to work for his father-in-law, who owned a big knitting mill. Pretty soon the knitting mill seemed as unappealing as the inside of a dentist's office. After a year of unrelieved boredom, Bogdanoff began to search the want ads—just in case.

During Christmas week of 1973, he read an item in the sports section of the *Philadelphia Inquirer*. Bill Putnam had become the owner of a WFL franchise in Birmingham. Bogdanoff clipped out the article and carried it in his wallet until after the holiday season. Then, with another year of drudgery in the mill staring him in the face, he decided to contact Putnam and ask him for a job. Suddenly he was struck with a better idea. If Putnam could own a pro football team, why couldn't he? After all, he thought, he was young, ambitious, intelligent, and he liked football. So he called Putnam, who was living in Atlanta, and told him he was thinking of buying a WFL franchise in Philadelphia—if it was still available. As far as Putnam knew, Philadelphia was open. Come on down, he suggested; maybe he could help.

Bogdanoff saw Nate Gans that evening. Gans had been his best friend ever since grade school. In a sense they had always been partners when it came to important business matters. Gans felt the idea of owning a pro football team was so good he wanted to join Bogdanoff in the venture. On the second Monday in January they both sat in Putnam's Atlanta office. For three hours they listened as he told them such things as how to structure a sports franchise, how to raise money, how much was required to run a pro football team (Putnam guessed about $2.5 million the first year of operation), and how to always think positive. He gave Bogdanoff Gary Davidson's phone number in Newport Beach. On the plane ride back to Philadelphia, Bogdanoff and Gans cackled and roared like two schoolboys on an outing.

The next day Bogdanoff went to his father-in-law, asked him to make a list of his richest friends, then did the same with his father the dentist. They both scratched their heads, wondering what had come over the boy.

Young Bogdanoff was undaunted. He placed a call to Newport Beach, but was told Mr. Davidson was in New York on business and was staying at the Hotel Plaza. In the morning, Bogdanoff rode the train in to Penn Station, took a cab to the Plaza and called Davidson from a lobby phone.

"I'm a little jammed right now," said the WFL founder. "Television people are here . . ."

"I want to see you about buying a franchise for Philadelphia."

"Come right up."

A couple of Hughes TV Network representatives were in Davidson's suite. Bogdanoff heard them talk about percentage points and profits while he browsed through a tennis magazine on the other side of the sitting room. Fifteen minutes later, with the men gone, with only him and Davidson in the room, Bogdanoff asked about the price of the Philadelphia franchise. How much would it cost him? Nearly five hours went by before they arrived at a satisfactory figure. Bogdanoff could have Philadelphia for $400,000—and a $50,000 down payment would secure the rights.

Bogdanoff chewed on the end of a pencil for a moment. "That'll be no problem," he said, trying very hard to keep his voice from trembling. He started to mumble something about getting the money to Davidson in a few days, but the Californian said he was leaving for the WFL board of governors meeting the next morning. If Bogdanoff was serious about buying the franchise he'd better be at the meeting, too—with a certified check. While Bogdanoff thought that one over, Davidson began to remove his shirt. "You'll have to excuse me now," said the WFL commissioner. "I've got a date to play basketball."

When Bogdanoff reached the lobby, he felt his stomach flop. He was nauseous and famished at the same time. So he treated himself to an expensive steak dinner at the Plaza's Oak Room, then boarded a late train for his trip back to Philly, thinking of all the people he'd have to see in order to raise the down payment. He didn't bother to call Nate Gans that night, or his father, or his father-in-law. He just told his wife about his visit with Davidson. She said he had to be crazy to think of investing money in such a speculative venture. Then she turned off the bedroom light. Bogdanoff remained awake until he could see gray shafts of dawn steal into the room. He dozed off for an hour. The alarm clock woke him up.

Groggily, he got out of bed and called Gans while his wife slept. Sure, said his friend, he'd go into the deal, just as he promised. "Tell you what," Gans assured him, "I'll spend all day raising my half of the down payment. If I don't have it today, you can count on my having it by tomorrow." Bogdanoff felt better about things. By nightfall he had talked to his father, his sister, his father-in-law and everyone else on his list of potential backers. It finally boiled down to his father-in-law, who convinced himself he was really doing it for his daughter.

Before the banks closed on Friday afternoon, Bogdanoff and Gans had raised the $50,000. But around midnight Saturday, Gans called with sorrowful news: "Listen, I've changed my mind. I just can't take my family's money like this. I'm sorry, Ken." Bogdanoff twisted and turned under his blanket all night, got up early, kissed his wife goodbye and went to the airport with a certified check for $25,000 neatly folded in his wallet.

In the late afternoon, Bogdanoff attended a cocktail party in

Gary Davidson's Presidential Suite at the Marriott. Around a two-tiered table that easily seated twenty people, he rubbed elbows with his friendly competitors in the WFL, especially Putnam and Baldwin, who reminisced with him about *the old days* and seemed so pleased he had made the jump from assistant ticket manager of the Flyers to pro football owner in so short a time. Around ten o'clock, Davidson and Regan came over and asked him if he wished to join them for a late dinner. Bogdanoff suspected he had reached his Waterloo.

In the hotel restaurant, Davidson ordered a bottle of expensive French wine. When the menus arrived, Bogdanoff selected veal parmigiana, and the WFL partners opted for sirloin steak. Later, between bites, Davidson and Regan took turns telling Bogdanoff how rosy everything looked for the new league: their other two leagues were still surviving and becoming successful; it was a helluva opportunity for Bogdanoff to be the most talked-about young sports executive in America; and, finally, his $50,000 down payment was the best investment he could make toward a million-dollar future.

"I don't have the fifty," said Bogdanoff, by now too upset to touch his veal parmigiana.

"Oh . . . ?" chorused the partners.

"Well . . . I have half that. My friend decided not to go in with me. I only have twenty-five thousand."

Davidson and Regan thoughtfully chewed on the remains of their steaks.

"Tell you what, Kenny," Regan purred. "We can swing a special deal for you. Let's say we settle on twenty-five thousand, okay?" He smiled puckishly at Davidson. "That'll be okay, don't you think, Gary?"

"Yeah . . . but I think we should keep it quiet. I mean, we have a lot of people here all jazzed up, and if they knew we were giving Kenny a special deal . . ."

Bogdanoff assured them he had no intention of telling anyone —except maybe his father-in-law.

"Fine," brightened Regan. "I'll call the suite and have our

secretary make the changes while we're eating. Won't take more than a few minutes . . ."

Bogdanoff nodded lamely. When Regan returned to the table, Davidson was staring into space and Bogdanoff's eyes were focused on his plate, his dinner still untouched.

"Aren't you going to eat your parmigiana?" inquired Regan after he sat down.

"I'm not hungry."

"Well," Regan declared, "it's a shame to let it go to waste."

He leaned over, took Bogdanoff's veal parmigiana with a fork, cut it down the middle and proceeded to devour his half while Davidson ate the other half. What the hell is *this?* Bogdanoff said to himself.

A few minutes later, the secretary arrived with the agreement. Regan read through it quickly, handed it to Davidson, and both men affixed their signatures. Now, they leaned forward and asked Bogdanoff for his certified check. The youngster's head clanged. He had to call his attorney, he told them. After all, he suggested, the WFL partners wouldn't expect him to put his name on a contract without first going over the clauses with his lawyer, would they? Of course not, answered Davidson and Regan—they were lawyers themselves; they understood.

Later, in his room, Bogdanoff called his wife. He told her he had cold feet about the deal. "They not only want my money," he said, "they also ate my dinner."

In the morning, one hour before the scheduled board of governors meeting, Bogdanoff went directly to Davidson's suite. Regan opened the door. The commissioner was in the bathroom, said Regan with a big smile on his face. Once inside, Bogdanoff explained why he was going home; there was no way for him to handle the financing of a pro football team, not with only twenty-five thousand in borrowed money to his name. Regan asked him to reconsider, which made Bogdanoff feel even more sure of his decision. He remembered that Davidson was the guy who insisted an owner should be capitalized at $3 million, that the first year's budget alone figured to be between $2.3 million and $2.7

million, with a first-season loss estimated at upward of $1 million. Davidson had told him that at the Hotel Plaza just a few days ago. So what the hell was he supposed to reconsider?

Finally, Regan called into the bathroom: "Kenny's here, Gary. He's changed his mind. He's out."

Above the sound of faucet water: "Okay, Ken, thanks for coming by."

Bogdanoff shrugged, and then left. But at the elevator, Regan stopped him. "Listen," he said, "perhaps you could do us a favor. Sit in on the meeting and answer the roll call when Gary gets to Philadelphia."

At exactly 10:25 A.M., Bogdanoff obliged with a timid "Here." Philadelphia was accounted for, along with Memphis, Birmingham, Florida, Washington (by Regan), Boston, New York (by Baldwin), Toronto, Southern California, Hawaii, Chicago and Detroit.

Immediately after the roll call, the WFL commissioner's opening remarks to the assembled "board of governors" at the Marriott Hotel in Los Angeles were recorded by the Laurel Tape and Film Company. Under the direction of producer Richard Rubenstein, camera crews picked up the sight and sound of Gary Davidson:

"As you all know, the first meeting is being held by waiver of the original board of governors. As the first order of business I would like to say, first off, there's no way to keep secrets from the press. Therefore, I would suggest that when the meeting is over, we don't talk to anyone in the lobby, as there are many reporters around. Above all, don't leave documents around here once we leave. They may be snatched up by anyone and used for whatever purposes. I remember this happened at the founding meeting of the World Hockey Association. After that meeting, a lot of people came in and grabbed notes and whatever else they could find . . ."

Bogdanoff slipped a hand into his jacket pocket. The certified check for $25,000 was still there.

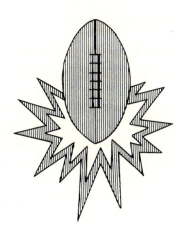

THREE

Rain clouds hung drearily over the streets of Boston during the early-morning hours of January 21. In the Park Square section of the city, a solitary light from the seventh floor of the Statler Hilton Building cut into the fog, indicating that people were up and about, working through the night—even as a Monday dawn pushed against the black skies.

The eerie illumination came from a tiny room down the hall from the New England Whaler office. Under a hideous glare, Dusty Rhodes, red-eyed, stared at a scouting report, while Tom Beer and Ken Beatrice rummaged through a cardboard box filled with college football media guides. There, in frazzled concentration, they had worked for thirty-six straight hours. Barring a collective heart attack, they would be at the Essex House in New York the next day for the first WFL college draft.

But now they had to finish the predictably awesome task of collecting the names, positions and college affiliations of literally thousands of players throughout the country, feed all the information into a computer, then into their brains, in order to come

29

up with a handful of talent who might or might not play for the newly established WFL franchise in Boston.

Dusty ran a finger over the offensive tackle list. There were check marks next to some of the names: Claude Minor, San Diego State; Tim Guy, Oregon; Gerry Sullivan, Illinois; John Hicks, Ohio State; Al Oliver, UCLA; Henry Lawrence, Florida A&M; Bart Purvis, Maryland—and Matt Herkenhoff, Minnesota. Herkenhoff was checked, double-checked and underlined.

"Okay," said Dusty to Beer and Beatrice as they sifted through the cardboard box, "I have Herkenhoff down for a number eight or nine pick. Do you still go along with him over Hicks?"

Both men nodded, and Beatrice stopped what he was doing to emphasize a point. "We'd be wasting our time with Hicks. He's NFL-bound, no question about it. Anyway, Herkenhoff is just as good. Let's see," he muttered, wiping sleep away from one eye with the back of his hand, then concentrating like a swami over a crystal ball. "Matt Herkenhoff . . . big . . . quick . . . comes in at two hundred and sixty-five pounds and stands six-five in his socks . . . hits like a sonamabitch . . . uhh . . . coach calls him the most valuable lineman he ever had . . . was the best line-man in the North-South game . . . all-conference and all-state in football and basketball at Melrose High School in Minnesota . . . Uhh . . ."

The amazing thing was that Beatrice always seemed to be right. The New England Patriots, as an example, had benefited considerably in the past few years by going with his scouting reports at draft time. Beatrice certainly knew his business. He could also tell a good computer system from a lousy one.

"Forget this crap. It's nothing more than a limited, haphazard guide," he told Dusty after examining the WFL scouting book. "Do you know where it comes from?" he asked.

Dusty hadn't the foggiest idea.

"It's an NFL book, but it doesn't matter, because anybody could have gotten the same information out of *The Sporting News* for seventy-five cents."

A registered psychologist and an assistant director of training in the mental health and public welfare field for the Commonwealth of Massachusetts, Ken Beatrice was a thin, pale-faced, bespectacled young man who ran a nationwide computerized scouting organization of twenty-four behavioral scientists—all of them volunteers, all of them football fanatics like Ken Beatrice. Because of their training, Beatrice and his buddies weren't just interested in the physical assets of college players. They were also concerned with "heart and psyche"—the emotional factors which prevent eighty percent of college football players from making it in the professional ranks. Obviously, Matt Herkenhoff was well within the percentile group who figured to succeed, according to Beatrice's calculations.

Tom Beer also believed in Herkenhoff, although he didn't know much about *psychological patterns* and *motivational capacities*. Beer's sole occupation since his graduation from Houston University in 1967 was that of a tight end in the NFL. After six years of service with the Denver Broncos and the New England Patriots, plus ten days in camp with the Miami Dolphins in 1973, Beer returned to Boston with nothing going for him except a lot of free time to write a book. He did. It was a dedicated effort called *Sunday's Fools,* the saga of one man's experiences while being stomped, tromped, kicked and chewed in the NFL. He completed the manuscript, then waited around for another team to claim him for more stomping, tromping, kicking and chewing. But late in December, with the NFL season practically over, he sadly came to the conclusion he wasn't "one of the boys" anymore. Only a morbid curiosity led him to phone Will McDonough to check on an intriguing item he had read about a brand new football league that was being formed by Gary Davidson. "The WFL means business," McDonough assured him.

So did Dusty Rhodes, who called Beer late one night with a rundown of her plans to draft college players for a WFL team in Boston. Beer was friendly with Dusty, had had many interesting chats with her while the two worked for the Patriots. But he needed reassurance. What if he helped her? he asked. What then? She told him to stand by. Howard Baldwin would get in touch with him, work something out if Beer decided to pitch in for the draft. The next morning he got the call. Now, working out of the Whaler closet—running down all-America names from Ohio State, Notre Dame and Ole Miss, matching the statistical charts of obscure hotshots from Maine, Furman and Slippery Rock—Beer felt completely unperturbed about his future. Taking the assignment meant that he would be signed to a player contract and, perhaps, an administrative job in player personnel. The scars and bruises he had received in the NFL, Tom Beer felt, would be worth it after all.

So the beleaguered trio sweated and strained, each for his own reasons: typing; correlating profiles on quarterbacks, running backs, guards, tackles, receivers, centers, defensive ends, linebackers, cornerbacks, safeties, kickers and punters; filing the rejects and placing the "most wanted" list in active folders; writing press releases; listening to the crackling sounds that came from a pre-transistor radio . . .

Gary Davidson was in town. On a talk show late Sunday night, he spoke glowingly of the budding WFL and said further progress would be announced at a Monday-morning press conference.

Later, around midnight, the phone jangled. Dusty answered. It was Howard Baldwin. "Prepare a press release," he instructed her. "The Boston franchise has just signed Babe Parilli as head coach."

She located Parilli's bio in a Pittsburgh Steeler guide book. Then, beneath a New England Whalers Hockey Club letterhead, she began to type:

FOR IMMEDIATE RELEASE

Howard L. Baldwin, president and general manager of the Boston franchise of the World Football League, announced today that he has signed Vito "Babe" Parilli to a multiyear contract as head coach of Boston's newest entry to the sports scene, the Boston Bulldogs.

Baldwin had given her the new nickname on the phone. She didn't think much of it. However, she continued to bang out the release.

Babe will be perfect for the job, combining his very successful tenure as quarterback coach in Pittsburgh, his practical knowledge from sixteen years as a quarterback, and the overwhelming appeal he has regionally and the respect he has nationally.

After filling in the details on Parilli's playing career, his statistics, and his awards in college and the pros, Dusty added two final paragraphs:

The immediate goal is selecting the best college prospects in the draft, and then in turn signing the draftees and the protected players on the Bulldogs' list. With this foundation, Baldwin and Parilli will be working to put together the best possible roster of thirty-three players for the World Football League's opening game in July. The site for the midweek games is not yet decided, with several of the area stadiums being considered.

The New England Whalers' championship in the World Hockey Association climaxed a year in which the organization Baldwin assembled was hailed as one of the most dynamic in pro sports. It is thought to be the most successful first-year franchise in professional sports history. With Babe Parilli as head coach, and Dusty Rhodes as assistant to the president, Baldwin has already begun to build a winner. Howard Baldwin and the Boston Bulldogs will be looking for a repeat performance.

That was Baldwin's gift to her at midnight. She was now *assistant to the president.*

By nine o'clock—as Monday-morning workers rolled off buses and trains to begin earning their wages in the Park Square compound—Dusty had rolled off two hundred mimeographed copies of the Parilli signing. Five minutes after the ink was dry, the door to the Whaler closet opened.

"Listen," Howard Baldwin said. "We changed the name. We're going with the Boston Bulls. Has a nice ring, doesn't it?"

"Oh, my God!"

For the next thirty minutes she worked on a new release, changing the team name wherever needed, then ran off two hundred more copies. It was close to ten o'clock; just enough time to get to the Howard Johnson's "57" Restaurant to launch the first Boston Bulls press conference.

A barrage of tough questions exploded from all over the crowded room. The reporters were cocky. Perhaps dubious was a better word for their mood. They asked Gary Davidson how he thought the new league could survive without any established stars to compete against the known NFL talent; how the Bulls expected to draw crowds when they didn't even have a stadium to play in; why the new league was risking a 1974 opening at a time when the economy was down and prices were up; and *when* would overexposure of the product finally catch up to the game and kill it altogether?

Davidson gave a flawless presentation. He answered all the questions as if he were Einstein instructing students in basic math. His bravura performance left the press with lots of copy but scant personal satisfaction.

Babe Parilli satisfied everyone. The press knew him well. He was the kid who came out of Rochester, Pennsylvania, to play for Bear Bryant. He was the quarterback who had led the Patriots to the American Football League's Eastern Division title in 1963. The new head coach of the Boston Bulls was the nicest, most considerate athlete they had ever cornered in a locker room.

Blinking at the flash bulbs, Babe Parilli looked somewhat like the protagonist of a Frank Capra movie: humble, shy, trusting, naive, honest-as-rain. It showed in his dark brown eyes, on his smooth, square-chinned face. It came from the way he moved his shoulders and the manner in which he listened to questions. And it radiated in the refracted light that sparkled from a huge diamond on his 1969 Super Bowl ring.

Flanked by Davidson and Baldwin, a slightly nervous Parilli expressed his appreciation for an opportunity to coach in the WFL, promised to do his best to recruit and sign good football players—and to win a championship for the people of Boston. He seemed like the same old Babe. In the noisy, restless crowd, he looked over his line, set up in the pocket, then hit his targets with short, snappy answers. No rollouts. No scramble. No desperate bombs. When he stepped down to be congratulated by the well-wishers, Parilli knew he had scored his first victory as a Boston Bull.

Outside, the weather had turned ugly. Fog crept along the streets and settled in crusty layers over the runways of Logan International Airport—creeping, crawling, wheezing fog that slowed or halted virtually all transportation into and out of the city.

The rawness of the day was further acerbated by the beginnings of a light rain which splattered against the restaurant windows, leaving dirty splotches as large as coal dust to gather on the panes. Staring into the grubby whirlpool, Dusty felt an urgency to check on the scheduled 5:00 P.M. shuttle flight from Logan to LaGuardia Airport—a flight that would take Davidson, Baldwin, Parilli, Beatrice and herself to New York for the draft. Too bad Tom Beer wasn't going, she thought, but somebody had to mind the store.

A busy signal kept her waiting for twenty minutes or so. When she finally reached the reservation desk, she was told the plane was grounded. Logan International was fogged in and rained out. Dusty picked her way through a cluster of newsmen to Parilli's side. "Let's get out of here," she whispered at his ear. "We've got problems."

At 3:30 P.M. a thoroughly chilled Boston Bull staff and WFL commissioner sat in Howard Baldwin's paneled Whaler office, looking constantly at their watches while Dusty's finger spun the phone dial. At last she connected with an alternate mode of transportation. If they hurried, they could catch the 4:20 P.M. Amtrak out of South Station. "It'll get us in around eight-fifty!" she trumpeted.

"Good," said Baldwin. "Gary and I will grab a cab. See you all on the train."

At 3:40 P.M. Dusty, Parilli and Beatrice dashed out of the Statler Hilton. A hissing, roaring downpour swept over them, beating on their heads and backs, before Tom Beer could open the door of his car at curbside. Into the dry interior they piled— overnighters pushed to the floor, a cardboard box containing the draft selections propped on Beatrice's lap.

As Beer's car sliced through the torrent to South Station, Beatrice slumped down in his seat, suddenly tired to the death, numbed from three straight days of picking the best college players he could find for the Boston franchise—as well as for the New York franchise.

It was simple enough. Bob Schmertz had needed someone to represent New York in the draft.

"Who can you recommend?" the Whaler money-man had asked junior partner Howard Baldwin.

"Well, we've got Ken Beatrice working on our draft. Maybe he could double up . . ."

Ken Beatrice accepted the dual assignment. For three days and nights he wavered between quarterback Gary Marangi of Boston College and Mike Boryla of Stanford; cross-checked his printout on linebackers Randy Gradishar of Ohio State and Ed O'Neil of Penn State; weighed the pros and cons of tight ends Keith Fahnhorst and J. V. Cain, Minnesota and Colorado speedsters—then split them into two opposing camps. With still more positions to go over, with only a few more working hours left before the draft, Beatrice could finally look out of the car window, look beyond the rain, and feel reasonably satisfied he had done his best.

The car slowed. Parilli cleared a small circle on the side window. He squinted into the traffic and imagined they were trapped in a graveyard of junked autos. It was close to four o'clock, and they were still some distance from South Station. Only a helicopter would be able to lift them clear of the mess. Just then, Beer saw a break in the endless lineup of shimmering metal. He swung his wheel to the right and went down a side street. Cutting past dawdling motorists, running his radials up on sidewalks to skirt wide-bellied trucks, he somehow managed to keep the nose of his vehicle pointed toward daylight, away from brick walls, trees and apoplectic traffic cops. With a final burst of speed—spraying gutter water in its wake—the car swung around to the front of South Station and came to a halt. It was exactly 4:17 P.M.

Beatrice was the first to stagger out, hugging the cardboard box containing the draft picks firmly to his chest. Parilli and Rhodes grabbed the luggage. They followed him on the run, past the portico into the high-ceilinged station.

"Where's the train to New York?" Parilli shouted at a sour-faced attendant.

Before he could answer, a booming voice from above incanted: "TRAIN NUMBER 179 . . . THE MERCHANT'S LIMITED . . . WITH STOPS AT BACK BAY STATION, DEDHAM, PROVIDENCE, NEW LONDON, NEW HAVEN, STAMFORD AND NEW YORK . . . NOW DEPARTING ON TRACK 12. ALL ABOARD . . ."

Sweating, gasping for breath, they reached the grimy stall, in time to see steam curdle up from the train's underbelly; in time to hear the shrill scraping noise of wheels over steel track.

"Sonofabitch," screamed Beatrice, "the friggin' train is moving!"

With a mighty effort they caught up with the clanking monster and jumped aboard like fleeing desperadoes.

"The dining car," said Parilli. "Let's go to the dining car. We can work there . . . and get something to eat. I'm starved."

It's a tangled, twisted evening, and later Parilli remembers the train ride as a kind of madness played out in an atmosphere of smoke, dust, fumes, heat rays and crewcut guys yelling, "Hey buddy, over here . . . grab a seat . . !" and chocolate-colored waiters in white jackets with uptight attitudes, and wheels clicking over polished track, and, in the middle of all the craziness, a rectangular dining room table with Dusty, Beatrice and himself endlessly spouting phrases like "He seems to have all the tools . . . For a big guy he can really move . . . For a little guy he can really hit . . ." Meanwhile, they eat stale cheese sandwiches, potato chips, fig newtons, Oreo cookies. They drink Cokes, milk, lukewarm coffee, water. At one point Gary Davidson works his way through the suffocation as a relief man. He chomps on a Baby Ruth while Dusty slides out to spend some time with Baldwin in one of the coaches up front. All the while their waiter keeps saying, "It ain't right for the other folks," and once he explodes so that the whole dining car can hear him: "I hope you have a rotten draft!" And as they ride past Stamford they finish their business, put all the sheets with all the scribblings in the cardboard box and stand up in one of the coaches until the Merchant's Limited labors through the grimy tunnel and comes to a squeaky, jolting stop in Penn Station.

Around nine o'clock the next morning, bright sunshine filtered through layers of gray slate sky, easing the New York City temperature to a pleasant forty-four degrees. At that hour, a yellow cab pulled up to the Marriott Essex House on Central Park South. A tall, heavy-browed fellow in a camel's hair coat emerged, paid his fare, then shuffled crab-backed into the hotel. Taking a sharp right at the head of the lobby, Howard Cosell pushed open a glass door. He paused momentarily for a quick, questioning glance at a paneled mirror, patted his hairpiece, then stepped down from the reception area to the main ballroom. The best-known sportscaster in the nation—the grand mufti of Monday Night Football—jammed a cigar between his million-dollar lips and moved into the crowd. Under crystal chandeliers, framed by red drapes, anchored by plush red carpet, Cosell shook hands, tossed out clever *bon mots,* blessed the WFL gathering with a wave here and a wiggle of his finger there. All things considered, nearly every writer, jock, official and gate-crasher greeted him as though he were a distant cousin or long-lost uncle who had sprung unannounced from the bush country.

A few minutes later, circulating, Cosell walked over to Babe Parilli. Seated at the draft table, writing on a sheet of paper, Parilli appeared suspiciously like someone emerging from a hangover.

"Vito Parilli." The nasal, kvetchy voice was unmistakable. Parilli didn't bother to look up.

"Hi, Howard."

"An historic moment, indeed," Cosell said, grinning, his eyes narrowed for the ultimate thrust. "Ah yes, Vito, how well I remember you as the magnificent Kentucky Babe . . . the exemplary quarterback of the Boston Patriots' past . . . and then as a mere shadow of your former self in those drab, lusterless years with the New York Jets . . . the crouching, anonymous ballholder for field-goal specialist Jim Turner. And here you are today, a disparate member of the Boston Bulls, the field leader of an untested World Football League franchise . . ."

Parilli chuckled and responded with a mild expletive.

In his tiny enclosed room in the New England Whaler office, Tom Beer sat behind a scratchy metal desk and waited for the phone to ring. He was aware of the reporters who circled around him—Gil Santos, the voice of the Patriots on WBZ; Mike Lupica of the underground *Phoenix;* Ron Hobson of the *Patriot Ledger;* and Jack Craig of the *Globe.* In a matter of moments they would be jotting down the name of the Bulls' number one pick as soon as Parilli called it in from the Essex House. Meanwhile they waited, while Beer's fingers drummed against the armrest of his chair, jaw muscles tightened, his long legs pinioned under the desktop. What a helluva dump to be sitting in, Beer thought.

A few seconds later Parilli's call came through. The first pick in the first round went to Memphis. They selected all-America quarterback David Jaynes of Kansas. "Okay, Babe," Beer quickly calculated, "that clears us for Marangi." His voice assumed a commanding bite. His eyes remained glued to his worksheet. His mind shaped, framed and fixed names and positions with the speed and efficiency required of an artillery officer at a command post behind the battle lines.

Quarterback Gary Marangi rated way up on the Bulls' computer scale in almost every category. He was physically sound and strong. Statistically, he had a sixty-percent pass completion record in his senior year. Psychologically, he tested out as a good mental risk. And geographically, Marangi was a natural for the area because his school was Boston College. The only thing left to check on had been his interest in the new league. So Parilli had called him from his suite at the Essex House the night before the draft. Marangi assured him he was definitely interested in the WFL. Okay, Parilli said, in that case the Bulls were going to pick him first in their draft. "Wow, that's great," Marangi exclaimed. "Now it'll be difficult for me to consider an NFL offer

39

unless a team picked me either one, two or three." The NFL draft in New York was still one week away, so the Bulls took their shot and hoped for the best.

Florida had the next pick after Boston and drafted running back Woody Green of Arizona State. Fourth up was Toronto. They went for fullback Bo Matthews of Colorado. Birmingham picked fifth and selected Wilbur Jackson, the Alabama running back. Then came New York.

In the Casino on the Park ballroom of the Essex House, Ken Beatrice leaned forward, placed his elbows on the bright red tablecloth, cleared his throat and announced: "New York selects Stanford quarterback Mike Boryla."

Beer chuckled when Parilli informed him of Beatrice's pick. But he wasn't about to let the Boston reporters who hovered around his desk in on the secret. At least, not then. It would take too long to explain.

Southern California exercised its territorial rights (granted before the draft by Gary Davidson) by choosing running back James McAlister of UCLA. Rumors at the Essex House intimated that owner Larry Hatfield had actually signed McAlister, Kermit Johnson, his college running mate, and Booker Brown, the all-America offensive tackle from USC. Parilli relayed the information to Beer. "If it's true, Babe, the draft is already a success."

Heisman Trophy winner John Cappelletti became the eighth pick in the first round. The sensational Penn State fullback went to the Philadelphia franchise. Linebacker Fred McNeil of UCLA was claimed by Hawaii, and Chicago followed by taking Bill Kollar, defensive tackle from Montana State. Washington-Baltimore, on the strength of Joe Wheeler's $5,000 deposit with Gary Davidson, picked Richmond running back Barty Smith. Detroit completed the first round with the selection of Michigan tight end Paul Seal.

And then they started all over again. Through six rounds—until seventy-two college players were drafted. Grinning broadly, Tom Beer slammed the phone down in its cradle.

"Well, fellas, the shit's hit the fan. Now we'll see how much of it is going to stick."

Six days later, at the propitious moment, Commissioner Pete Rozell of the NFL leaned into a microphone and made an announcement: "The Dallas Cowboys, on their first-round pick, select Ed Jones, defensive end, Tennessee State."

The scene was the Georgian Ballroom of New York's Americana Hotel. With measured indifference to the WFL challenge, somewhat like sleeping lions flicking at flies, twenty-six NFL teams began an electric scoreboard countdown that would end the following evening with 442 players selected in seventeen rounds. It was a peculiar draft. The NFL snubbed every quarterback in the first round—and the second—until Danny White of Arizona State became the first pick in the third round by Dallas. The Kansas City Chiefs also waited until the third round before drafting David Jaynes as a quarterback hopeful. The Buffalo Bills picked Gary Marangi in the same round. One round later the Chiefs decided to draft Matt Herkenhoff for a tackle position. Surely, thought the Kansas City strategists, Herkenhoff would turn his back on the WFL Boston franchise, which had selected the University of Minnesota lineman ninth in its draft. The Cincinnati Bengals, on the other hand, figured Mike Boryla would rather be a fifth-round player candidate in the NFL ranks than a first-round pick in the WFL. Almost lost in the shuffle, buried deep in the 1974 grab bag of college talent, University of Missouri running back Tommy Reamon became the theoretical property of the Pittsburgh Steelers. Lazily, one of the Steeler reps scanned a list of the seventy-two WFL initial draft picks. Reamon's name was missing. Before the end of the season, Pittsburgh would be kicking itself for allowing the Missouri back to join the WFL. But for now, very few of the assembled NFL teams at the Americana were necessarily disturbed by a number of developments going on in Gary Davidson's league.

Even before the doors to the Georgian Room opened on January 29, the NFL learned of the signing of UCLA's James McAlister and Kermit Johnson and USC's Booker Brown to long-term contracts by Southern California president Larry Hatfield. The announcement rated headlines in the morning editions, causing one NFL official to comment: "That's probably the biggest news those humpty-dumps will make all year—but don't quote me." Another pinprick in the NFL side came from Bob Woolf. The player agent-attorney, upon learning of the Southern California signings—estimated to be a package at close to $1 million —predicted that NFL salaries would go up one hundred percent, and maybe much more. "All it takes is one WFL owner to say, 'I don't care what it costs; I'm going to buy a winning team,' and that will blow the roof off as far as money is concerned," said Woolf.

Adding fuel to the fire, word filtered into NFL draft headquarters that Jack Pardee, a veteran of fifteen years as a linebacker in the NFL and a Washington Redskins player-coach under George Allen, had resigned from the Redskins to become head coach for Washington-Baltimore of the WFL. Also, revolutionary rule changes adopted by the WFL on the eve of its draft undoubtedly annoyed the NFL more than it wished to admit. Although the NFL Rules Committee opened the running game somewhat in 1972 by moving the hash marks three and one-half yards closer to the center of the field—representing the first significant movement since facemasks became mandatory in 1954—the WFL listed ten rule changes designed to place "action and entertainment" into its brand of football:

> The ball will be kicked off from the thirty-yard line to ensure more runbacks.
>
> The goalpost will be moved back to the rear of the end zone.
>
> Missed field goals will be returned to the line of scrimmage except when attempted inside the twenty-yard line.
>
> A two-point conversion attempt (passing or running) will be optional.
>
> Receivers will need just one foot in bounds for a completion.
>
> There will be a fifth quarter, split into two seven-and-one-half-minute segments, to break ties.
>
> Fair catches will not be permitted on punts.

An offensive back will be permitted to go into motion toward the line of scrimmage before the ball is snapped.

The hash marks will be moved in toward the center of the field.

Any incompleted pass on fourth down will return the ball to the line of scrimmage. This replaces the rule that states any fourth-down pass inside the twenty-yard line shall be returned to the twenty.

In addition, the WFL would start its first year of operation with a multicolored football, somewhat akin to the ABA colors that replaced the drab brown of the NBA. Davidson also stated that league play would start on July 10. There would be no exhibitions, he said. The league would play twenty regular-season games, and a championship World Bowl game between the top divisional leaders would determine the WFL equivalent to the NFL Super Bowl championship team.

Thus, in a direct probe at NFL tranquility, the WFL began a battle for survival. The first salvos were fired by Gary Davidson's legions in a bidding war for players; the first signs of NFL defections were duly reported by the press; and a new approach to wide-open football was dangled before the fans. It was reminiscent of the glorious days of yesteryear, of 1960, when the American Football League crept uncertainly from darkness into light to challenge the supremacy of the NFL. Ultimately, the ragamuffin pretenders grew in stature and began to match the older league in quality of play, in money reserves and in fan support. Ultimately, it all ended with the AFL-NFL merger in 1966. And now history was repeating itself. But a superficial examination of WFL stirrings did not, however, enable the NFL to conclude that reality was identical to perception.

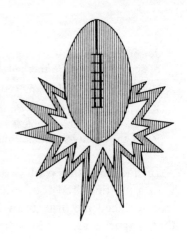

FOUR

So passed January into February. Under wet, gray skies that covered the eastern seaboard, WFL owners moved about in a mounting hum of activity. Joe Wheeler beat on the doors of JFK Stadium in Washington but could not obtain permission to field a team there. Meanwhile, he planned a first-come-first-served postcard campaign for team ticket purchasers. The earliest postmarks would govern seating priorities. To make sure he'd have a bull's-eye view of the fifty-yard line, Wheeler disclosed he was going to be the first to send in a card. Later in the month he scouted Annapolis, midway between Washington and Baltimore, but the naval academy fired a broadside his way. Memorial Stadium and its 28,000 seats were off limits—with or without Wheeler's postcards.

Down in Jacksonville, pint-sized Fran Monaco set up shop at a reported $650,000 purchase price to Davidson. His team was nicknamed the Sharks; New Smyrna Beach High School Coach Bud Asher was brought in to coach on the professional level; Monaco secured the 70,000-seat Gator Bowl as the team's playing facility; and the little woman behind Fran's throne was his blond, blue-eyed vice-president, treasurer and wife—Douglas!

Above Jacksonville and Washington, Gary Davidson did some fancy juggling in Philadelphia. Having lost Ken Bogdanoff and his $25,000, the commissioner used his floating franchise in the following manner: he sold it to a corporation in which he was a minority stockholder. In turn, the corporation sold it to a group fronted by Jack Kelly, Jr., brother of Princess Grace of Monaco —no connection to Fran. Davidson bit heavily on the Kelly group, extracting an agreement which called for a $690,000 entry fee. Thus, the Philadelphia Bell Football Club came into being. It set up offices at 220 South Broad Street, hired former Los Angeles Rams player Ron Walker as head coach and rented waffle-shaped John F. Kennedy Stadium (a 102,000-seater located in the Philadelphia Sports Complex) for its home games. Without fanfare, Ken Bogdanoff joined the Bell as business manager. Davidson helped him get the job under one condition —he'd never tell Jack Kelly about their previous financial nego-tiations during the board of governors meeting in Los Angeles. Bogdanoff kept his word.

Bill Putnam returned to Birmingham after the WFL draft and found the city in a veritable dither. The mere thought of having a major league football team led Birmingham editorial writers, newscasters, politicians, and even local DAR chapters to extol Putnam for his great humanitarianism. As a burnt offering, civic leaders placed the 70,000-seat Legion Field at Putnam's feet, and he handed up to the multitude a head coach—Jack Gotta. A forty-two-year-old native of Bessemer, Michigan, Gotta was Coach of the Year in 1972–73 with the Ottawa Rough Riders of the Canadian Football League. Now he was coming south to take over as general manager and head coach of the Birmingham Americans.

Memphis stood cold and unyielding on high bluffs on the east bank of the Mississippi River. In the early February frost, Steve

Arnold met with Mayor Wyeth Chandler, the City Park Commission, grain millionaire E. W. Cook and others in an effort to establish a WFL franchise in the city in 1974. But Memphis leaned toward the NFL, which held out a thin promise it would consider expansion into the city in 1977. Sensing the obvious, Arnold turned his attention to the southwest, where potential backers lurked in the shadows of their sprawling oil fields. And before a spring sun moved into position, before Memphis could further weigh its pro football options, Arnold took off for Houston.

On the balmy West Coast, approximately thirty-five miles southeast of Los Angeles, 47,000-seat Anaheim Stadium became the new home of the Southern California Sun. Owner Larry Hatfield moved into the multipurpose facility with high expectations. In his first official act to develop a winning team in Orange County, Hatfield hired Tom Fears as his head coach. Fears was an all-America end at UCLA in 1946–47, then spent nine great years as an all-pro receiver for the Los Angeles Rams. In 1968 he became head coach of the New Orleans Saints, led the team to the best expansion record in the NFL, then bowed out under pressure in 1970 to join the Philadelphia Eagles as an assistant coach. Four years later, with added weight on his once-svelte frame, sporting a graying mustache and Vandyke beard to distinguish the change from carefree youth to aging executive, Fears was counted on by owner-president Hatfield to field a winning team, put points on the scoreboard and induce paying customers into the seats of Anaheim Stadium. However, even as Hatfield boasted that as many as 35,000 faithful would be on hand for the Sun's opening game in July, local cynics were predicting in February that Disneyland would be a stronger gate attraction.

Three thousand miles west, on the beach of Waikiki, Danny Rogers felt ocean spray on his face and a swell inside his tanned chest. Moving swiftly, Rogers successfully lured thirty-four-year-old Sambo Restaurant chain entrepreneur Sam Battistone and equally youthful Honolulu hotel-condominium magnate Chris Hemmeter into splitting co-ownership of the Hawaiian franchise. In the transaction, Rogers became general manager of the team; Mike Giddings, an assistant coach with the San Francisco 49ers for six years, was brought in as head coach of the Hawaiians; and Honolulu Stadium, a sagging stone-and-wood edifice containing 25,000 seats, was selected as the temporary playing field. In another year, according to construction plans, the Hawaiians would be playing in the ultramodern 50,000-seat Halawa Stadium. So it was arranged. What began as an undefined blur had now become a sharp vision of reality. Smiling with deep satisfaction, Rogers looked into puffy patches on the Pacific horizon and wrinkled his nose at a passing plane. Soon, he thought, there'd be lots of trips back and forth to the mainland, and good times would roll in every one of the twelve assorted cities of the WFL.

Tom Origer wasted no time in getting his football operation started in Chicago. He was the first owner to shell out cash for a franchise, the first to sign a pro player—wide receiver Jim Seymour on January 8—and the first to hire a head coach. The job went to Jim Spivital, a forty-seven-year-old Oklahoman who had played halfback for the Baltimore Colts in the early fifties before going over the border to play for and eventually coach the Winnipeg Blue Bombers of the CFL. Now, as icy winds buffeted Chicago streets in early February, most of the administrative groundwork had been laid. In June the team would check into training camp at Lake Forest College, twenty-eight miles north of Chicago, and starting in July the Chicago Fire of the WFL would be playing its home games at Soldier Field, stomping grounds of the NFL Chicago Bears. Facing the future with as much enthusiasm as he had ever given to the construction field, Origer set about to build a winning football team in the biggest crapshoot of his career.

Meanwhile, John Bassett came back from the New York draft to the beginnings of a controversy in Toronto. Canadian Football League Commissioner Jake Gaudaur shuddered over the prospects of WFL player raids, while Toronto Argonaut general manager John Barrow claimed the WFL had already begun its scheme to bury the CFL. And at the highest level of government, Health and Welfare Minister Marc Lalonde issued a terse statement that he would make a determined effort to keep all United States pro football teams out of Canada—then took his case to the federal justice department in Ottawa. While Canadian mouths flapped and Canadian legal wheels turned, Bassett declared that the whole issue had unraveled because Canada was afraid of the NFL. "What Lalonde is really concerned about," said Bassett, "is the possibility of the NFL coming to Montreal, because the French community prefers the NFL to the CFL."

It was such an assumption that led Bassett to press even harder to operate a franchise in Toronto. He looked over a few small stadiums, including the Canadian National Exhibition Grounds, and laid plans to have a major league facility built to house his new franchise. His first administrative appointment was to bring in Leo Cahill as general manager. A native of Utica, Illinois, Cahill began his pro football career in Canada in 1960 as coach of the Montreal Alouettes. In 1967 he took over the head coaching job of the Toronto Argonauts, led the team to a Grey Cup championship and was named Coach of the Year in 1971. Bassett then looked around for a head coach, got ready for the WFL pro draft in New York on March 19, and scoured the CFL ranks to sign "futures," meaning that his team (now nicknamed the Northmen) might obtain the services of Canadian players after their option year ran out. He also kept a list of superstar NFL players locked away in his mind as targets for hire. As long as he was in a shooting war for survival, John Bassett figured he'd have to level his sights at everything that moved.

A bridge and two tunnels connect the city of Windsor, Ontario, to the city of Detroit, Michigan. Detroit is the automobile capital of the world, the largest city in Michigan, and one of the leading sports centers in the United States—with the baseball Tigers of the American League, the Pistons of the NBA, the Red Wings of the NHL and the Lions of the NFL. Armed with a piece of paper that declared himself and thirty-one associates as co-owners of a WFL franchise in Detroit, Louis Lee began to shape an administrative staff. By early February, Everett "Sonny" Grandelius— former New York Giant runner and head coach of the University of Colorado—was named vice-president and general manager of the club. Dan Boisture, former head coach of Eastern Michigan University, was selected to run the team on the field, and Louis Lee assumed his post as president of the new Detroit Wheels of the World Football League. In the team press guide particular attention was paid to Grandelius's statement that the Wheels "can make an honest, qualified run at the WFL title in our first year."

The New York franchise, in the person of Bob Schmertz, spent the first two weeks in February waiting for good news. Unfortunately, it never came. Howard Baldwin had not been able to find backers for his franchise in Boston.

Nevertheless, the Boston Bulls made a major announcement on February 5. George Sauer, a wide receiver with the New York Jets from 1965 to 1970, had signed a multiyear pact with the club, thus ending a three-year period of contemplative retirement from pro football. In doing so, Sauer declared his intention to return to the same forces that created, as he termed it at the time of his withdrawal, an "unhealthy, dehumanizing spirit of competition." Now he was in the same system again, and Bulls coach Babe Parilli was elated. "With George's great hands and tremendous deceptive tactics," said Parilli, "he will be a nightmare for any secondary in pro ball."

The days in San Francisco were long, stretching out into longer nights, with soft winds whistling outside while Sauer read Camus and Sartre and Blake in his apartment down near the bay. In the spring he would ride his bicycle over to a park alongside the bay, feeling the wind on his face. It stirred memories of other days when the wind was at his back and his hands were into the wind, reaching high for the ball that glided on a descending arc toward his fingers.

And he jogged. In his sweatpants and sneakers; pumping his legs, feeling the strength in his thighs. Alone. Running into the wind, feeling the pressure, hearing the sounds beyond the bay, beyond all distance: a hum, a roar, the sound of brass and reeds and drumbeats; a whistle; a tumult of noise, louder louder LOUDER! A pistol report. Silence. The wind carried it all away while he jogged.

In his apartment he looked out the window and thought of Pam, who flew out of San Francisco on schedule and smiled cheerily as she waved goodbye each time. One day he turned away from the window when he saw a plane heading east. Cold sweat broke out on his forehead even though the day was warm and beautiful.

A novel was born in his head, a story of wreckage and renewal, of annihilation and rebirth. He wrote a thousand words a day, sometimes more. Oftentimes less. When summer faded to autumn in 1973, George drove out from San Francisco to Oberlin College in Ohio. He returned to football as the offensive line coach of a small school in a Tom Sawyer town, quietly and without illusions. By the end of the season he had put in a completely new offense. In the moonlight. The Oberlin practice field didn't have any lights, so the team stayed on the field in the moonlight until they caught on to his new offense, and then the Crimson and Gold Yeomen of Oberlin played John Carroll University in the last game of the season. And lost. In the cold, in the rain and snow. He stood on the sideline and watched. He felt frustrated —because things were happening out there and he was just watching.

In mid-November Sauer borrowed a car and drove down to Pittsburgh to visit John Dockery, his old Jet roommate, who was now a reserve defensive back with the Pittsburgh Steelers. It was nice. At Saturday practice he chatted with the Steeler players and coaches. They remembered him and seemed genuinely glad to see him. He even got to throw the ball around a bit, and that part of the afternoon was especially nice. On Sunday he sat in the stands of Three Rivers Stadium and watched Pittsburgh play the Denver Broncos. That night he and John went out on the town. They toured the bars—Buddie's and Checkers and Monti's—

and listened to high-decibel music and lifted a few beers and laughed a lot, but kept coming back to the old days when they were younger and played football in New York for the Jets. John said he was unhappy sitting on the bench in Pittsburgh. Maybe the new World Football League would give him an opportunity to play more, John remarked. A tingle hit Sauer, a kind of buzzing that made him say above the music that he'd be interested in going over to the new league, too, if it ever became a reality. The next morning he said goodbye to John and Anne Dockery and drove his borrowed car back to Oberlin. In another day or two he was home in San Francisco.

He saw John again on the last weekend of the 1973 NFL season, when the Steelers came out to play the 49ers. After the game they sat in shadowy ease in a pub on Powell Street, drank beer and talked. Then, while most of the city slept, they kept a 3:00 A.M. breakfast date with Babe Parilli in the Mark Hopkins Hotel coffee shop. He liked Babe, who never got to throw many passes to him when they both played for the Jets because Babe was a reserve quarterback behind Joe Namath during that time. Now Parilli was a quarterback coach with Pittsburgh. But he, too, wanted something better than he had at the moment. Parilli said he was seriously thinking about an offer to coach in the World Football League and asked Sauer if he would consider coming out of retirement. Sauer said he would.

The new year started out much like all the others since 1970. He continued to work on his novel, slowly and painstakingly in longhand, stopping often to look out the window, or ride his bike over to the park, or jog. In the evenings he'd read or listen to music on his stereo while his wife Pam talked about the cities she had flown to and the people she had met as a stewardess for American Airlines. And a sadness would come between them, as if they both knew that something was wrong but that they couldn't really talk about it. One day the phone rang. It was Babe. After a while, Sauer hung up with a satisfied smile on his face. He was going to run again, stretch his legs across chalked lines and stick his hands into the wind to catch footballs in the World Football League.

George Sauer's self-imposed exile was over.

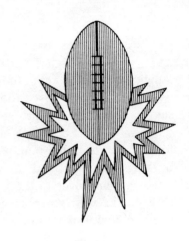

FIVE

Like the natural miracle of organic life, Gary Davidson's WFL crawled from the depths and began the slow process of evolution. In the processional of days in February and March the WFL no longer was the microscopic bacteria of January. Vertebrates had formed; the league stood erect and looked to the future sensing triumph within its grasp.

From his office desk in a modern building on MacArthur Boulevard in Newport Beach, Gary Davidson fed his new creation with elixir:

—He amended one of his rule changes by declaring the two-point conversion null and void. Touchdowns would be worth seven points, and there would be an "action point" attempt from the 2½-yard line for one additional point by running and passing.

—He stated that the World Football League would play its first championship game—the World Bowl—in Jacksonville, Florida.

—He declared that a twenty-two-week diet of WFL games would be televised by TVS.

The WFL schedule had been set for Wednesday evenings, with one game each week held back for television on Thursday nights. "On Thursdays," said TVS president Eddie Einhorn, "people will have stopped talking about last weekend's NFL games and won't have started talking about the games for next weekend."

Einhorn, a short, peripatetic thirty-eight-year-old product of Paterson, New Jersey, confirmed that more than eighty stations had been cleared for the twenty-two weekly WFL telecasts and that eighty-five percent of the nation would be covered by the July 11 opener. Einhorn also announced that veteran sportscaster Merle Harmon, former radio play-by-play announcer of the New York Jets, and Alex Hawkins, an Atlanta garbage hauler and former Baltimore Colts and Detroit Lions receiver, would take over as WFL announcers.

The TVS deal was a real breakthrough for Davidson. The NFL was tied into a multimillion, multiyear package with all three major networks. CBS had TV rights to National Conference games, NBC beamed all American Conference games, and ABC carried both conferences of the NFL on its prime-time Monday Night Football telecasts. Rather than face certain rejection from the major networks, Davidson let two independent syndicators— the Hughes Sports Network and the TVS Sports Network—bid for the rights to carry WFL games. TVS came up with the right numbers. Eddie Einhorn and his crew of thirty, six cameras, and two slow-motion taping machines would televise WFL games in prime time, and the WFL would receive a guarantee of $1.5 million from Einhorn.

"We have the best first-year TV contract any league ever had," beamed Davidson after signing the pact. Undeniably, his ten-percent share of all television revenues for the next ten years helped to sweeten his disposition.

Gary Davidson was born in Missoula, Montana, on August 13, 1934. When he was only a few months old his parents separated, then divorced. His father, Truman Ross Davidson, drifted out of his life to become a farmer in southern Idaho. Gary never saw him again until he started high school. Some evenings he'd lie awake in his bed and wonder about his father and the little things he knew about him that seemed important and worthwhile. He thought about his father's fingers—the fingers on his pitching hand—that had been cut off at the tips in a canning-factory accident. His father was called "Cutty" after that. Gary thought Cutty Davidson could have been a great pitcher for the New York Yankees, because the Yankees had been set to give him a tryout when he had the accident.

His mother, Estella, married again. In time, Gary had several stepfathers. He and his half-brother on his mother's side were moved around a lot, because Estella Davidson could never settle down with one man for any length of time. So he was moved from Missoula, Montana, to Southern California, where his mother lived tenuously with her husbands in towns around the Los Angeles area such as Compton, Corona, Santa Ana and Garden Grove. Gary slept in many bedrooms while he was growing up.

At Garden Grove High School he got mixed up with a rough gang of kids and really began to turn down the wrong road. He was a wild kid. Nobody could control him. His mother tried, but she worked hard in a grocery store and was too full of her own life to do anything but spoil him when she could. So, feeling cheated, he took whatever he could lay his hands on. And he was smart, smart enough never to get caught in all the time that he ripped off stores in Compton and Santa Ana. Then he stopped. More for self-preservation than for any other reason. He knew his luck would run out, that sooner or later he'd get caught.

So he bore down on his studies and graduated Garden Grove High School with a scholarship to Redlands College, only to drop out after one semester. He enrolled at Orange Coast Junior College, tried to make the baseball team, failed, and left the school not knowing what he wanted to do or where he wanted to go. There was so much inside him, but his heart was heavy. The next year he attended Long Beach City College, working after school at all kinds of jobs. He laid pipe, dug ditches, chipped cement, became a plumber's helper for a while. One day he dated a girl who went to UCLA. They walked together across the campus while the sun dipped in the Los Angeles sky. Gary was impressed. He returned to UCLA the next morning and applied for admission. The school accepted him.

UCLA gave him an opportunity to meet the kind of people he had never known before—all-America athletes, social butterflies, undergraduates who drove expensive sports cars to their opulent homes after class—and he felt as though it were the most natural thing in the world to be a part of it all. After years of moving from one dreary town to another, he had gratefully reached a peaceful harbor in the gay, shining festivity of university life—and it became the center of his happiest hours on earth.

He majored in political science, joined the Beta Theta Pi fraternity, and met Barbara Jane Dapper, a lovely and exuberant UCLA cheerleader. Barbie bowled him over.

On dates, he poured out a torrent of words about his earlier life, his loneliness as a child, things he would not reveal to anyone except Barbie. He talked fast. The words stumbled from his mouth like a raging current. Sometimes Barbie found it hard to follow his thoughts. She said, Gary, slow down, talk slower, enunciate. Barbie was an education major and took speech courses. After a while, Gary asked her to help him correct his flaws, improve his diction so that he wouldn't stutter so much or trip over words. She helped him considerably, but with all her patience, with all his concentration, Gary never did lick the problem completely.

He graduated from UCLA in 1958; two years later he and Barbie got married. It wasn't easy. Los Angeles in those days was a vast, infinite receptacle for thousands of young men and women who drove their sun-bleached autos and station wagons out west in a desperate attempt to relieve themselves of isolation, to find a new life and recovered health on Southern California soil. Within the cauldron of movement and change Gary went to work for an insurance company, but he was in no way able to submit himself to its code of conduct. He tired of the discipline, the parrotlike presentations, the dogma of settlement options and death benefits. When he discovered a long-time employee of the firm earned less than $10,000 a year doing exactly what he was doing, he turned in his insurance books and quit. And at the very moment that he felt trapped, suspended between indecision and clairvoyance, a streak of light entered his brain. The law. He would be a lawyer.

Gary matriculated at UCLA School of Law in 1959. In order to support his studies he found an interesting night job in downtown Los Angeles. Most of the time he sat behind a desk and studied. Occasionally the phone would interrupt his reading. Then he'd have to leave his office at the Armstrong Mortuary to pick up a corpse. It was a pretty good job, all things considered. It helped pay his tuition.

The next year he and Barbie were married. She taught grammar school, while Gary clerked in a law office. In 1961 he passed his bar exam and joined an Orange County law firm that specialized in business and tax law. In the time he was there, almost three years, he participated in legal work that launched new businesses and dissolved sick ones. It opened his eyes; there was money to be made—and he wasn't going to get rich working for Schlegel and Friedemann.

Gary formed his own law office with two other attorneys, named Fairbairn and Fenton. The chemistry wasn't right, the dreams unrealized. One day, when it seemed everything was going wrong, Don Regan called him. Regan and he had gone to UCLA together. They had double-dated, gotten married the same year, and moved into the same neighborhood. In their undergraduate days they sweated and grunted together in the love of intramural sport competition. Later, they made enough money in the commodities market to get them through their last year of law school. They were very close. So when Regan asked Gary if he was willing to take a plunge—start up their own law firm —Gary said he was ready. They talked it over some more, brought in a fellow by the name of Pat Nagel to handle labor matters, and formed Nagel, Davidson and Regan in Santa Ana.

Right from the start things began to happen. Good things and bad. But the fellow who really started Gary on his cyclonic journey to Oz was Roland Speth, who was in public relations and had an office across the hall from Nagel, Davidson and Regan. Speth worked for John McShane, and both of them were involved in all sorts of promotions. In the passing of days, Speth and Gary would bump into each other on the street or see each other in the hall and yap about sports. One day Speth came into Gary's office and told him about a big deal he and McShane were working on —with a fellow by the name of Dennis Murphy.

"Now," said Speth, "Murphy has a hell of an imagination. Brilliant guy, really, with a personality that matches his big Irish smile. He's in public relations, like me and McShane. Only his real bag is sports. Crazy about sports. Been into all kinds of ventures. For instance, he tried to put an American Football League franchise in Anaheim. Could've swung the deal, too, if the AFL hadn't merged with the NFL in sixty-six. Well, that didn't stop Murph; next thing you know he's looking into the possibility of putting an Anaheim franchise in the NBA. But he's stymied there, too, because the Lakers own the territorial rights. So Murph figured the only way he was going to lick the problem was to form a basketball league of his own. And that's how me and McShane got involved. Well, Gary, what do you think?"

The door to Oz had opened, and Gary ran inside. He found marvelous beauty there and was very glad, because he had lived so long on the dry, gray prairies. From that moment on, thirty-two-year-old Gary Lynn Davidson—who had slept in clammy diapers near the Bitterroot River during the Great Depression, seeing but not understanding the tears on Estella Davidson's face, feeling a calloused hand on his cheek and not knowing Cutty Davidson would be long gone from his life in another second— pulled the rope taut and began his climb to the summit of Mount Oz. Tanned, dimple-chinned, with sun-washed blond hair and eyes as blue as the Southern California sky above, Gary threw his spike into the wall of the mountain and moved his short muscular body *up up up up up:*

To election as president of the American Basketball Association in 1967; to moving Don Regan in as legal counsel and himself in as a student of franchise wizardry. And the beginning of long trips to big cities in nice clothes, where he would drink rare wine and dine in fine restaurants. Where he would meet fat thin short tall young old people and grab their dry sweaty firm limp hands and learn to say things like *you'll be getting in on the ground floor* and *it's a hell of an opportunity* and *give it some thought*—the rhetoric of franchising.

Gary was handed a $30,000 one-year contract with the ABA, plus an expense account that provided first-class plane trips and assorted fringe benefits. But he didn't get rich. Instead, the league became a monstrous testing of his strength, endurance, and ability to move further upward, even as rocks fell around his head.

In the avalanche, ten franchises were formed: New York-New Jersey, Pittsburgh, Dallas, Houston, New Orleans, Minneapolis-St. Paul, Indianapolis, Kansas City, Los Angeles-Anaheim and San Francisco-Oakland. Only Indianapolis stayed rooted. The others staggered from city to city as though lost in a vast desert. Along the way, Cleveland broke forth like morning sunshine and disappeared in the middle of the night. Seattle, Phoenix and San Diego roared in like tornadoes and faded on the wind. Soon, the path to glory became a maze of thorns, sticking the con artists and dream merchants—driving them into the dust in screaming protest.

Gary ran the gauntlet, too. He invested $4,000 in the Dallas franchise and eventually sold off his interest for one dollar. Don Regan threw $5,000 into his floating franchise, found a group in Louisville and sold it for $30,000. Regan shared the profits with Gary and Mike O'Hara (a Davidson courier in the original Dallas transaction). It was the most money the Santa Ana law partners made in the ABA. Taking heat was one thing. Getting skinned alive was another. Gary resigned under the pressure.

Dennis Murphy fared worse. He was battered in Anaheim, Oakland and Kansas City. So, Murph took off for Denver, but within a year he was back in Anaheim. Recharging his batteries, he lurched forward to Minneapolis, then to Miami in another franchise switch. In the end, Dennis Murphy dropped out of the ABA altogether—disgusted and nearly broke.

Roland Speth was ground up by the pack of ABA wolves who stalked his unchartered outpost. He licked his wounds, then returned to his public relations job—empty-handed and smiling through his sorrow.

John McShane never lived to collect the money he felt the ABA owed him. He died in Hawaii a couple of years later—wondering what had happened to all his dreams and why he never got paid.

Gary kept climbing. Free of the ABA blast furnace, Nagel, Davidson and Regan built up its treasury through less glamorous but more practical ventures. The office developed and ran General Residential Corporation, a retirement home venture. Gary became co-chairman. He took over as president of Mammoth Sports, Incorporated, a leisure-land recreational development company. The California Real Estate Trust named him president and a trustee. He reached into a waiting pool of unemployed workers and found them jobs through his SIS Temporary Services Company. In the process, he built it from $50,000 in sales to $3.5 million.

He had some losers, too—a dune buggy business that dropped $40,000, and a Buffalo Bill Wild West Show that set back the partners $35,000. And he put on a Grand Prix bike race that lost $10,000. Still, he had come a long, long way from Missoula, Montana. He and Barbie were living in a dream house on Emerald Bay in Laguna Beach; their four children felt a security he had never known as a fatherless child, and he began to put a lot of money in the bank.

In January of 1971 Dennis Murphy called to say he was leaving Miami at the end of the ABA season; leaving his thankless job as general manager of the Florida franchise. Murph said he had decided to start a new professional hockey league. He thought Gary might be interested in joining him. Gary laughed, told Murph he was a glutton for punishment, but ended by saying he'd think about it. There was a lot to think about. Gary had never gone to a hockey game in his life.

Investigating further, he discovered that the National Hockey League grossed $50 million a year, had no serious competition and was not represented in many major population centers. He also discovered that NHL players were the lowest paid athletes in professional sports. There was enough interest to lead him to obtain a copy of a standard NHL players' contract. His eyes widened when he got to the option clause. There was a loophole, a glaring legal weakness—the lack of a specific salary arrangement in the players' option year. Gary was lawyer enough to realize a team could theoretically bind a player to perform for next to nothing. He also knew the option clause would more than likely be deemed unfair by every court in the land if put to the test. Don Regan agreed, and so did some outside lawyers who were approached for an opinion. When Dennis Murphy called back in March, Gary said he was all set. Let's get the show on the road, he said. He'd be president of the new league and Murph would be vice-president.

Three months later Don Regan filed incorporation papers in Delaware. Davidson, Regan and Murphy became the corporate operators of the league, and all three insulated themselves in a partnership arrangement to control all intangible league assets, such as team magazines, pennants, shirts and so forth. With the ink dry and the deed done, the search began for franchise operators.

There was a time, in his ABA days, when Gary was in over his head and knew it. Not now. Using his past experience as a brake against any future mistakes, he devised a plan to tap all founding franchise holders for an entry fee of $25,000, and all future owners for $200,000—thereby separating immediate buyers from the shoppers. He also worked up a profit-loss sheet. Player salaries were figured at approximately $750,000, travel at $150,-000, equipment at $50,000. Then there were office expenses, advertising and promotion, insurance, and other incidentals. All told, a typical operating budget would come to between $1.25 million and $1.5 million. Income estimates for the first year ran to around $1 million, with a projected loss for each team set at $500,000. Gary's ledger did show a rainbow at the end of the cloudburst. Second-year losses could be cut to $250,000; some teams might break even by the third year and even show a profit by the fourth year.

Dollar signs and decimal points. Cold, dry statistics one might find in ten thousand prospectus offerings in any given year. If Gary Davidson's prospectus had dealt with another product—orthopedic shoes as opposed to hockey, for instance—his franchise plans probably would have collected dust for perhaps an eternity without arousing so much as a ripple in the financial strongholds of the United States and Canada. But the inherent glitter, the almost erotic appeal of hockey as the product in Gary's prospectus became an unalterable factor of his magical act. And the *macho* designation of THE WORLD HOCKEY ASSOCIATION was the essence that reduced dollar signs and decimal points to agate trivia in the eyes of his prospective buyers. And Gary Lynn Davidson, with a shine on his shoes and a waddle in his can, was going to show the world. Now, at the age of thirty-seven, established as a prosperous California businessman, heralded as a meteoric professional sports promoter, the Missoula Magician opened his suitcase and prepared to dazzle the customers.

The rabbit under his cape was Ben Hatskin, former pro football player in the Canadian Football League, ex-nightclub owner and current operator of a Winnipeg team in the Western Canada Junior League. From the start, Gary understood the only way the WHA could be successful was to build solid franchises in Canada and have Canadian skaters playing in the league. To do that, he needed Canadian owners.

Bill Hunter of Edmonton, Scotty Munro of Calgary, and Ben Hatskin of Winnipeg formed the Canadian mortar which gave the WHA a major league appearance. And it was Hatskin who possessed the foresight to contact NHL superstar Bobby Hull with a proposition that eventually led to his signing a $2.6 million contract as player-coach of the Winnipeg Jets. The final agreement was hammered out by Gary and Hull's agent. The effect was electric—similar to the historic moment when all-America quarterback Joe Namath signed a $427,000 pact with the New

York Jets, a development that saved the life of the American Football League in 1965.

In 1972, however, Gary's WHA was quite dissimilar to Lamar Hunt's AFL. The original ten WHA teams, formalized at a press conference at New York's Hotel Americana on November 1, were: New York, Miami, Chicago, St. Paul, Dayton, Los Angeles, San Francisco, Edmonton, Calgary and Winnipeg. From top to bottom, most of the franchise holders were unlikely candidates to support a $1.5 million budget in the first year of the WHA's operation. Gary, as an example, held the San Francisco territory, while Los Angeles belonged to Dennis Murphy.

During the first two seasons, franchises formed, shifted and disappeared, while NHL players jumped. All the while Gary kept the throttle wide open until the WHA passed from DANGER to SAFE. Along the route, Ontario was admitted, then moved to Ottawa; Bob Schmertz and Howard Baldwin purchased a New England franchise; John Bassett, Jr., picked up a franchise in Toronto; New York crossed over the river to New Jersey; Dayton became Houston; Philadelphia came in when Miami folded; sports promoter Nick Mileti secured a territory in Cleveland when Scotty Munro walked away from his Calgary franchise; Gary unloaded his franchise (for a neat $200,000 profit) on a Quebec City group—and so forth and so on. The pace was almost too rapid to follow.

Meanwhile, a young player-agent named Steve Arnold was appointed director of player personnel. Arnold beat the underbrush to ferret out top-ranked NHL superstars. In less than two years, brilliant skaters such as Gordie Howe, J. C. Tremblay, Derek Sanderson, Gerry Cheevers, Frank Mahovlich, Jacques Plante and Pat Stapleton jumped the NHL to play in the WHA. Defections were so numerous it soon became evident the NHL would have to consider a merger of the two leagues or face a debilitating salary war.

By mid-season of 1973, the WHA situation was almost too good to be true. And Gary's insatiable ambition, his grandiose schemes, his general approach to WHA battle plans created the climate and produced the results which enabled him to reach greater personal triumph. By now he was a *made man,* a celebrity of the American sports scene, and fast entering a plateau of financial security that augured well for his retirement days. And yet at the very peak of his popularity as president of the WHA, Gary changed direction in order to launch the World Football League. He resigned and Dennis Murphy succeeded him to the WHA throne.

Now, as supreme ruler of the WFL, Gary found his greatest love. In his mind he turned over a thousand deals and a million ideas, until the blur of it all became the reason for his living. In the furious spin, Barbie and the children saw him less and less. Now and then there would be ski vacations in the mountains of Colorado, perhaps a strained respite with Barbie at a tennis resort in Palm Springs or Mexico. But after each attempt to rekindle the spark of an earlier exuberance, grave undercurrents of smoldering silence remained. The silence grew and became deeper.

And suddenly the language of a forgotten world sounded in his ears; faint sounds of birth and pain and love—and death. His father's lonely exile entered his throat like a burning coal. It tore into the piece of himself that made him feel young and hot and raw. It slammed him against the cloak of terror. "I wish I had more friends," his father told him one day, when it was too late for friendships. Too many years had passed between them, and now they were strangers to each other and would remain so until death took his father away and separated them forever—on the opening day of the WHA season in 1972.

Cutty comes up high on the mound. A sharp wind kicks dust over the sunbaked diamond. The ball zips toward the plate, but never arrives. His quizzical face is frozen into an orange mask, and the cornfield turns gray near the Bitterroot River. With his hand rigid as stone across his knee, cap tilted, eyes blazing . . . Cutty knows this is as close as he'll ever get to Yankee Stadium in his whole sad sorry life.

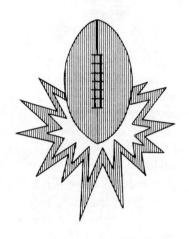

$IX

New York, Feb. 8 (New York Daily News)—*The World Football League yesterday exploded another contractual H-bomb with the announcement that its Chicago Fire franchise has signed National Football League veteran quarterback Virgil Carter to a "multiyear" agreement reportedly worth $100,000 for two seasons.*

Boston, Feb. 16 (AP)—The Boston Bulls of the new World Football League were reported Saturday set to move their entire operation to New York.

Portland, Oreg. Feb. 16 (UPI)—The WFL may switch its Philadelphia franchise to Portland.

On February 19, three days after the *Boston Herald Advertiser* said Howard Baldwin had confirmed the Bulls franchise switch to New York, the official announcement was made in a Manhattan Hotel. Baldwin, Schmertz, Parilli and Commissioner Davidson took turns explaining the reasons for the transfer, but declined to go into the actual circumstances which led to Boston's collapse.

From the moment Baldwin set up his football headquarters in the Whaler offices, a series of real and undefined obstacles brought him to the very edge of disaster. His attempt to secure a playing field at Foxboro's Schaefer Stadium had failed; local columnists theorized that he and Whaler hockey partner Bob Schmertz could create a conflict of interest in a football rivalry relationship; still other sources indicated he was having a difficult time trying to secure financial backers for his WFL franchise. All of it was true, but little of it had been explored for cause and effect.

Baldwin's main contact for backing in Boston was Bob Keating, a promotions director of Schaefer Stadium and general manager of the semipro New England Colonials of the Atlantic Coast Football League. Keating had guided the Colonials to a championship in 1973, which caused his owners—all nine of them—to ask him if he felt happy about winning the title. Keating said yes—but he was just as pleased the league was still there. The ACFL may have produced a lot of exciting football, but it ran mostly on glue and spit.

However, the Colonial owners themselves possessed a combined personal wealth that could easily support Baldwin's financial needs. In a stroke of fate, tracking down every lead, the Bulls president inevitably hit on Keating, who thought he could get his Colonial backers together to consider a fling in the WFL. At its apex the negotiations moved toward a $700,000 commitment. Then came the downdraft. Millionaire Henry Vickers and his fellow Colonial owners bowed out, and Baldwin's options were reduced to speculative meanderings. On a dreary Saturday in mid-February, Baldwin decided to move his carnival south to New York. Once there, he would be wholly renewed and partially financed. Blessed be the Lord—and Bob Schmertz.

Meanwhile, Gary Davidson was hard-pressed to solidify his twelve-team league. Still in possession of the Philadelphia franchise, he had been in deep discussions with a West Coast buddy of his to take over the territory. But fifty-year-old Bruce Gelker—an established Orange County owner of insurance, restaurant and motel businesses—hedged on the investment. Gelker had grown up in Southern California, played tackle on the USC football team, prospered in the state, and wanted to remain as close to home as possible. Philadelphia seemed as remote as Siberia—and just as frigid.

Whatever implausibilities existed in Philly, Portland was another matter. Gelker operated many of his Saddleback Inns in Oregon. He liked the idea of running up there every now and then for rest and recreation. When he expressed an interest in locating a WFL team in Portland, Davidson said it could be accomplished in the following manner: he would fold Philadelphia and sell the franchise to Gelker, who would then take it to Portland.

However, with the Boston switch to New York, Davidson decided to hold on to Philadelphia for a while longer. In doing so, he arranged to have Baldwin transfer territorial rights to Gelker, trade Boston's draft list with New York's—while he concentrated on new backers in Philadelphia. Luckily, he hit paydirt in the Jack Kelly group.

On Saturday morning, February 23, Bob and Donna Keating strolled along the beach of Chappaquiddick Island. The sky was overcast; stuffy clouds rolled out to the Nantucket Sound horizon. Now and then a swoop of seagulls attracted their attention, and the Keatings looked up, almost reverently, until the gulls were small dots in the far-off distance.

"You know," the husband said, "we've never done anything like this before. Jeez, it's like being shipwrecked, or maybe like walking around on the surface of the moon, don't you think?"

Donna Keating smiled. Her husband was telling her he was happy; glad to be with her.

"It was really decent of Mr. Vickers to give us the cottage," he remarked sometime later. They had walked at least two miles, never hearing another human sound; just the wind, the breaking of waves on the beach and an occasional squawk of gulls overhead. The island was a magnificent wonder to them; their walk a simple, ineffable communication with nature.

They needed this time to be alone, away from the kids, removed from the clamor of Boston. The island, stark and mysterious, served as a fundamental, majestic truth, and Bob Keating, together with his wife, could relate to it—and the decisions they had to face before leaving.

Howard Baldwin had called him Tuesday past, starting a chain reaction that moved him from relative tranquility to jangled disorder in the currents of unfolding WFL history.

"How would you like to be general manager of the New York franchise?" Baldwin had asked.

"Is that an offer, Howard?"

"Yes. I've recommended you to Bob Schmertz, and Bob says he'd like to meet you in New York. Can you come down, say, by tomorrow or so?"

"Sure. I can do that."

The next afternoon Keating sat with Schmertz in a room at the Essex House. At first he was somewhat nervous, unsure of himself. But as they talked, he discovered there was something very basic and genuine in the New York owner's mannerisms. In a matter of minutes Keating relaxed.

Allie Sherman's name came up, as did Upton Bell's. Sherman was a former New York Giant head coach and, although fired by owner Wellington Mara at the tail end of a horrendous exhibition season in 1969, still commanded a lot of respect in town. Schmertz had also talked to Bell about the job, but the ex-Boston Patriot general manager professed an inclination to wait for an opening with an NFL team. By default or merit, Keating then became the prime candidate, and the Schaefer Stadium executive guessed his unsuccessful yet earnest effort to overcome Baldwin's financial plight in Boston was reason enough for the sudden trip to New York to discuss his background and qualifications with Schmertz. As the afternoon drifted toward twilight, Keating felt he was *in* as general manager—if he wanted the job badly enough.

"My real strength has always been in finding the right people," Schmertz said at one point, "then leaving them alone to do their thing. I let Red Auerbach run the Celtics. Howard directs the Whalers without my having to look over his shoulder at every

67

turn. And, if you take the job in New York, I won't interfere with you. I'm not the kind of guy to fire people just because they make mistakes. God, who doesn't?"

Their meeting ended soon after that. Keating asked for a couple of days to think it over. Certainly, Schmertz said, but he did want to know one way or another by the following Monday. Keating agreed to it, left the Essex House and caught an early-evening train out of Penn Station. All the way home he thought about where he'd come from and where he might be going.

When snow roared in from the north and cold winds slashed across the lake, the Brattle Street Railroad Station in Arlington was toasty warm all day and night. In the pine-floored sitting room passengers sat on narrow benches and stared with watery eyes at a black fat-bellied stove, until the smell of burning coal sent them spinning off in open-mouthed slumber. Soon, in the near distance, the wail of the Boston train shook them awake. Growling into the station, brakes choking, the train belched to a stop, and the passengers picked up their belongings and shuffled out into the breathless air. In a few moments the train rolled on to Lexington and Concord, whistling and chugging over buried trails of American history.

Edward and Margaret Keating lived in the Brattle Street Station with their five sons and two daughters, in a drab room set aside for them by the railroad company. It was here that Edward shoveled coal by the ton into the greedy stove with his broad Irish hands—while a war was being fought in the frozen mud of Leningrad, over the rooftops of London and on the beaches of Okinawa.

By day Edward drove a truck; in the evenings and on weekends he worked in the station as a maintenance man. With ten mouths to feed, with barely enough income to properly clothe his family, Edward was happy to have a place to live where he didn't have to pay any rent—even if it had to be in a converted storage room of the Brattle Street Railroad Station.

Bob Keating, the fifth son of Edward and Margaret, would lie awake on his bunk bed when he was only nine or so and listen to the sound of the Boston train going through—so close to the station the walls shuddered from the force of its mighty charge. Later, when he attended Arlington High School, the sound of boat whistles and airplane engines played in his ears. He yearned to get out of Arlington and see the rest of the world. At the age of seventeen he joined the Marine Corps, saw seventeen countries in Europe, then came home two years later as a sergeant. A month after his discharge he fell in love with a dark-haired colleen who lived in the neighboring town of Winthrop.

Bob and Donna Keating had two children before they were twenty-one years old. So Bob labored, like his father before him, to feed his family and leave something of himself behind. But there was a different light in his eyes. He saw what his father only imagined—a better life for himself, his wife and his kids. While working at the Raytheon Electronics assembly line in Waltham, Bob Keating enrolled at Boston University. He took night courses for nine long years. When he graduated, with a degree in business, he quit Raytheon and its nine-to-five drudgery; there had to be something better out there.

Ironically, like his father before him, he wound up in the trucking business, starting out as an accountant for a small beer distributing firm in Framingham. In time, he found himself working nineteen hours a day, while his company expanded to a fleet of thirty-seven trucks with 172 employed drivers. For five years he checked the books while the beer trucks sped along to distributing centers from Worcester to Cape Cod.

If only he could find something that would free his hours, get him away from the desk he was chained to. What? He knew a lot of people in the beer business, liked going to their annual parties and Roaring Twenties Nights. He thought he could handle a public relations job somewhere in the industry. One day, in the dying winter of 1968, the Schaefer Brewing Company ran an ad in the *Boston Globe*. The Brooklyn-based firm had expanded into the area. They needed a PR man for the New England territory. Keating was the last one interviewed out of seventy-two applicants, but he got the job. It was a step up—a way of life that would broaden his contacts and make things easier for his family.

69

After Keating was hired, he stopped at a florist shop and bought two dozen roses for his wife.

There was a change. Donna and the kids saw more of him; they took vacations and talked more and laughed more and made plans for the next vacation. He was making $18,000 a year; his American dream seemed fulfilled.

The Schaefer Company had partially financed a new stadium that was going up in Foxboro in the spring of 1970. Phil Fine, a wealthy Boston attorney, had masterminded the planning and building of Schaefer Stadium. In doing so, he came to know many of the Schaefer executives. One day, shortly before the stadium opened, Fine called Keating and asked him if he wanted to run the place. "I'll double your salary," he said. Keating swallowed hard, almost not believing his ears. But he told Fine he'd have to speak to Mr. Schaefer first, talk things over and see what happened. He felt loyal. It was part of his nature. "Sure," said Fine. "Go right ahead and do that." Keating phoned Mr. Schaefer that night.

"Take the job," said Mr. Schaefer. "It's a wonderful salary, more than we can pay you. If you're not happy there, you can come back and work for us again."

Keating became director of operations for Schaefer Stadium. He put on Boston Pops concerts, rock shows and other extravaganzas. And he got to meet people such as Billy Sullivan, owner of the Patriots, Upton Bell, the team's general manager, head coach John Mazur, a nice young gal with the unlikely name of Dusty Rhodes who worked in the Patriot office, and most of the Patriot players.

In the summer of 1973 Bert Alessi, part-owner of the ACFL Colonials, came down with a serious illness. Alessi asked Keating to take over the club—run it for him. Keating jumped at the opportunity. As vice-president and general manager, he brought the Colonials to a 13–1 record by season's end—and a league championship.

It was nice; everything was nice. He was making $34,000 a year at the stadium, was proud of his position with the Colonials, and still came home almost every evening to sit around the fireplace with his family and enjoy a good laugh or watch television or hold Donna's hand. And then, one day, a phone call came in from Howard Baldwin, who owned a Boston franchise in the new WFL.

Bob Keating looked out the window of the speeding train, watched the telephone poles whip by, saw the reflection of his face and remembered his discussion with Bob Schmertz earlier in the day. In a short while he would be home. He'd tell Donna about their discussion. What would she say? How would she feel about moving to New York? They'd have to sell their house, leave their friends, start anew. He tried to shut his mind from it all. Soon he'd be home. Soon there'd be some answers.

As the train left Back Bay, Keating stirred in his seat, rubbed his eyes and remembered the good times in his life. Suddenly, he thought of a fat-bellied coal stove in the Brattle Street Railroad Station. Maybe, he thought, when he was just a kid, when the weather got real cold—when he could come out of his room and stand near the red-hot coal stove in his father's railroad station—maybe those were the best times of all.

A weird twilight fell beneath the rise of a brilliant moon. Ahead of them the ocean lay flat and silvery; the gulls flapped their wings in giant rhythms and disappeared into the orange-red sky over Nantucket Sound. And in their silent walk along Chappaquiddick's gray beach, the Keatings felt a gentle breeze at their back, as if some shadowy spectre were pushing them toward an uncertain future—where fabulous forbidden treasures were yet to be discovered.

They had gone down to the beach again from Henry Vickers's cottage, the cottage he had graciously opened so that Bob Keating and his wife could spend as many hours as they wished on the almost deserted island to think out their lonely decision. They had gone down to the beach, and they walked until the moon turned white in the pitch-black sky.

Finally, Bob Keating said: "I don't want to leave all this. I wish I could stay. But I feel that not leaving would be wrong."

"Then let's do it."

"Are you sure?"

"If you are."

"Well, it's all so awesome. There's no guarantee the WFL will go, or that I'll have a job beyond this year. But it's a great opportunity. I may never get a chance like this again."

"Then there's nothing else to think about. If that's what you want, go to New York. And we'll go with you."

The ocean waves rolled up on the beach and then slipped back again, following a process that began long before man and woman walked the earth.

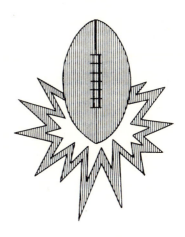

SEVEN

While Bob Keating pondered his WFL future at Chappaquid-dick Island, E. Joseph Wheeler, Jr., president and owner of the Washington Ambassadors, signed NFL New Orleans Saints reserve quarterback Bob Davis to a future contract. Davis, a seven-year NFL veteran, said that he hoped to play for the Ambassadors in 1974—if he could obtain a release from the Saints.

"The WFL gave me an opportunity to play," he said. "I just want to play. Hell, I could have made a career out of sitting on NFL benches."

A week earlier, New York Giants defensive back Richmond Flowers had inked a future pact with the WFL Hawaiians. Flowers had also expressed a desire to escape from his NFL option year so that he could perform in the WFL in 1974.

In conjunction with the Davis signing, Joe Wheeler announced he was ready to operate in 1974 "even if we have to be the travel-ing Ambassadors and play our games at different sites in the Maryland, Virginia, Delaware and Washington, D.C., area."

Wheeler's statement was based on his continuing frustration in trying to rent RFK Stadium, home of the NFL Redskins.

Meanwhile, in Miami Beach, the twenty-six owners of NFL teams opened their winter meeting by reaffirming New Orleans as the site for Super Bowl IX, by cutting the twenty-four-city list of possible expansion cities to five—Honolulu, Memphis, Phoenix, Seattle and Tampa—and by informally briefing each other on the ominous signs of an impending NFL players' strike before the start of the exhibition season.

Dan Rooney, vice-president of the Pittsburgh Steelers and head of the NFL's expansion committee, was asked by an AP reporter if Honolulu and Memphis were on the expansion list in order to deal with the threat of two WFL franchises already in those two cities.

"We haven't taken the WFL into consideration," said Rooney. "We're considering expansion only on what it will do for the NFL."

On Tuesday morning, March 5, sports photographer Bill Crespinel strolled from his 57th Street apartment in New York City to a Schrafft's Restaurant one block away. Under his arm he carried a copy of the *Daily News.* Once seated at the restaurant counter, he began his solemn ritual of sipping coffee while reading the sports pages. Every now and then he would see something that might add up to an assignment: a famous athlete in town for television commitments, a sports dinner honoring most valuable players, a press conference that might have national implications —any number of news items that might lead him to a free-lance paycheck. On this particular morning there didn't seem to be anything worthwhile to follow up—until a second glance brought his eyes close to the printed page. It was a two-paragraph boxed story that read:

N. Y. STARS

The New York entry in the fledgling World Football League came up with a name, team colors, a vice-president and several players Monday.

The team will be called the Stars and will wear black and gold.

Bob Keating, former G.M. of the ACFL's New England Colonels, was named vice-president. Players signed were Darryl Bishop, a defensive back from Kentucky, former Steelers' wide receiver Tom Spinks, and Ted DeMars, a running back from the Colonels.

If Crespinel had been a proofreader instead of a sports photographer, he might have caught the error which gave the New England Colonials a military nickname. But he wasn't in the least interested or even knowledgeable about such trivia. The important thing was that the New York Stars had set up shop, hired a front office and signed players. Perhaps, Crespinel thought, he should contact them now, while they were still putting together a staff. They needed a team photographer, didn't they? Of course. Finishing his coffee, he paid the cashier, stepped jauntily out on the street and walked back to his apartment. In a matter of minutes he would call the Stars office. Maybe the job was still open. Maybe, he thought, he could arrange to travel with the club. Crespinel loved to travel—perhaps as much as he enjoyed taking pictures.

Once it was a plush, expansive office occupied by a brokerage firm. But when the company dissolved, the New York Stars moved in. A sublease agreement was negotiated with the landlord—$5,000 a month, which included the use of all the furniture and a sophisticated phone system. Located on the twenty-second floor of a modern building at 415 Madison Avenue, the office had distinct advantages. For one thing, one of the rooms was set aside for Gary Davidson, whenever the commissioner decided to come into town for official business. Also, in a city that thrives on action, it was well within walking distance of Rockefeller Center, St. Patrick's Cathedral and Times Square.

With the Boston Bulls now dead and in its football grave, Bob Keating, Babe Parilli, Tom Beer and Dusty Rhodes flew down to open the New York office. By then the team nickname had been selected. It was Babe Parilli's idea, with an assist from Dusty

Rhodes. On their flight in to LaGuardia Airport he told Dusty, "I finally feel like a star . . ." and she said, "Yeah, a New York star . . ." and he said, "That's it!" And that's how the New York Stars got their name—some 35,000 feet in the air, somewhere between Boston and New York.

In the middle of March, Parilli brought Stew Barber, former offensive tackle of the Buffalo Bills, into the fold as his first assistant coach. Barber was a serious, tight-lipped individual; tall, dark-haired and large-boned. For nine years he inflicted heavy pain on opposing NFL tackles and linebackers; for five years ('62–'66) he was an all-pro at his position. Now, after four years of retirement, Barber was coming back as an offensive line coach of the New York Stars.

"I remember Stew when I played against him with the Patriots," Parilli said after the signing. "He really knows how to diagnose a defensive line, and I wanted an offensive line coach to be my first choice in building a staff."

A few days later, on March 18, the WFL held a draft of negotiation rights to pro players in the NFL and the Canadian Football League. Before the first-round selections got underway in New York's Marriott Essex House, the Stars announced the signing of New York Jet defensive tackle John Elliott to a multi-year contract.

It was a solid victory for the WFL, because Elliott had been a Super Bowl star for the Jets in 1969 and was the first major NFL player to defect to the fledgling league. And now he was at Essex House, slipping on a black jersey with the white Number 80. At his side was Star owner Bob Schmertz, who had just inked the good-looking, Texas-drawling Elliott to a whopping $51,000-per-year contract.

On Monday, March 25, Hank Stram, head coach of the Kansas City Chiefs, learned that he had lost his fourth-round draft choice to the WFL. A chubby moon-faced assistant named Frank Ross relayed the information to Stram. Matt Herkenhoff, the six-foot-five-inch, 265-pound offensive tackle from the University of Minnesota, was now a New York Star. Ross said he heard that

the massive lineman had signed a contract worth around $150,-
000. Stram whistled and said it was a hell of a lot of money to be
paying for an offensive lineman, but he still hated to see a prospect like Matt Herkenhoff get away.

Actually, Ross was close to the figure. At the Stars office in
New York, Herkenhoff, accompanied by his agent, signed a
three-year WFL pact which called for a $40,000 bonus, plus a
$35,000-per-year salary—for a total of $145,000.

"I weighed all the pros and cons," said the sandy-haired lineman after the inking. "I feel the WFL is definitely going to make
it, and this is a chance to get in on the ground floor."

With the press conference concluded, Herkenhoff and his
agent took the elevator down to the ground floor and celebrated
the signing over juicy steaks in the nearby Dallas Cowboy restaurant. The Stars, meanwhile, pumped out further news which indicated the team was meeting its commitment to open the season on
schedule. A ticket office (under the direction of newly appointed
ticket manager Dave Sullivan) was established, and a season
package of ten games was offered to the public for ninety dollars.
End-zone seats sold for fifty dollars. There was one fly in the
ointment. As of the date of the Herkenhoff signing, the Stars
were still without a home field to play in.

Still, the team did secure a training camp. For well over a
week, Bob Schmertz had picked up Bob Keating, Babe Parilli
and Dusty Rhodes in his chauffeur-driven limousine to scour the
metropolitan area for a training site. The foursome looked at
various locations such as Hofstra University (used by the Jets)
and C. W. Post College on Long Island; Monmouth College in
New Jersey; and Columbia's Baker Field in upper Manhattan.
For one reason or another, all proved to be unsatisfactory.

They were finally rescued by their new equipment manager.
Mike "Tiger" Ferraro, a forty-eight-year-old Long Islander with
ten years' experience behind him as assistant equipment manager
for the New York Jets, ended the search for training facilities with
his discovery of the La Salle Military Academy in Oakdale,
Long Island.

Tiger had fallen in love with the place long before he ever

thought of working for the Stars. When he was with the Jets, he occasionally went out to La Salle before summer camp opened to visit John Schmitt, who ran an instructional football clinic for youngsters on the Academy grounds. Schmitt was the Jets center —the player who wore No. 52 on his back and who always saw Joe Namath from an upside-down position every time Namath barked out an offensive signal.

One chilly clear day in late March, Tiger drove Keating and Parilli out to La Salle in his car. "You gotta see it to believe it," he said. They crossed the city line into Nassau County, sped along the Southern Parkway, turned onto the Montauk Highway in Suffolk County, passed gas stations and liquor stores and Bronco Charlie's Restaurant and a large shopping center, and went through the stone pillars which led them down a long narrow road to the entrance of La Salle Military Academy—exactly fifty-one miles from Madison Avenue in New York City. Parilli and Keating stood there for a while with their mouths open. A few minutes later they were deeply involved in negotiating a lease to use La Salle as the training site for the WFL New York Stars.

April ripened on the calendar as March withered. In the mid-day sun, a soft drowsiness fell across the La Salle campus; gentle gusts of wind swept through budding trees; greenery sprouted on the still, cool ground; the ring of hammers and buzzing of saws split the air, and Tiger Ferraro began work in the musty basement of La Salle's St. Joseph Hall dormitory. Old lockers were thrown out and replaced by new ones. Cluttered rooms containing desks, chairs, and other forgotten relics of long-ago school years were emptied so that New York Star coaches, players, doctors, dentists, public relations personnel, administrative staff and visitors could function in a professional manner. Only two months were left before the singing, laughing, shouting sounds of 107 athletes would be raised in the pursuit of glory. There was much to do, and Tiger Ferraro had made a good start.

Fifty-one miles away, in the tangle of metal and glass that is the city's stark heritage, the Stars accelerated the signing of players. Brian Oldfield, a member of the 1972 U.S. Olympic team, created a flash by holding up a football in one hand while fingering the shot in the other at his signing in the Stars office. Oldfield, who had played defensive end at Middle Tennessee State University in 1969, was better known for his prowess as a world indoor shot put record holder. At six feet five inches and 270 pounds, he was brought in as a fullback prospect for the Stars offensive lineup.

On the day of Oldfield's pact, thirteen players came to terms with the New York franchise, almost all completely unknown. Among them were free agents Rick Sharp, a defensive tackle who had been released by the Denver Broncos, Bill Janssen, who had played briefly with the Pittsburgh Steelers, and Larry Shears, a cup-of-coffee defensive back with the Los Angeles Rams. These were the biggies. Quietly slipping into the group was a muscular, craggy-faced, towheaded offensive guard from the University of Minnesota. His name was Darrel Bunge, pronounced with a hard g.

And two others had signed their contracts at an earlier date.

Back home in Youngstown, Ohio, Lou Angelo covered his eyes and tried to blot out the memory of a showdown he'd had with his foreman on the platform of that lousy warehouse he'd worked in before his foreman fired him from his job, the fifth one he had lost within a year. Nothing but a lousy redneck, he thought in the dark of his mind. Jealous, that's what he is, Angelo muttered over and over. The sonofabitch never had a college education, and he did, and that's why he was fired, Angelo reckoned. But it didn't matter much. Not now. Angelo didn't give a shit about the job, anyway. All he wanted to do was play football. And there was no way it was going to happen; not with his lying on a bed in his apartment dreaming about it. So he kept his hands over his eyes and hoped everything—the job, football, the thought of many terrible disappointments—would just go away for a little while so he could get some sleep until it was time to get up and see what was happening on the street.

Sometime later, while he tossed about in a stormy nightmare, the phone rang. Angelo heard the operator say it was a long distance call from Coach Babe Parilli. At first he couldn't believe his ears. He was still asleep, he thought, and the nightmare had become a wonderful dream. But he was awake, and Parilli's voice was real. The coach wanted him to play, wanted him to come down to New York and play football in the WFL. They would be back together again, said Parilli, who had been quarterback coach of the Pittsburgh Steelers the previous year, when Angelo had hung around uneasily in their camp.

"Well, Coach," said Angelo, "I busted my ass. I gave it everything I had and I thought I made the team, but I didn't. I'm not going through that again—and get cut."

"I think you can make my team," said Parilli.

"Coach, I trust you. You're a sincere man and a good person. If you mean that, I'll play ball for you."

"I mean it, Lou. I want you to start getting in shape. I'll send out, you know, papers during that time period before you have to leave, and I'll let you know what's going on."

"Yes, sir."

Angelo was all hopped up; electric. His mind spun into a million corners and came back to one thing. He'd have to start a schedule, work off some of the sludge around his rib cage. Man, he blurted out in his dimly lit room, the coach really wanted him, all right. It meant he'd have to stay off the streets, stay out of the bars. Jesus, all he'd have to do is walk into a bar in Youngstown and some guy would look at him wrong and shoot him. Well, he wasn't going to be knocked off by some asshole. Shit, no. Lou Angelo was going to play pro ball.

Back home in North Arlington, New Jersey, Moses Lajterman sat at the kitchen table with his two brothers, Abe and Tito. For a while they talked about Marcel, whom they would never see again, because Marcel was dead. And Moses said, "I wish Marcel were here to share this with us." In his hand he held a $20,000 contract to play for the New York Stars of the World Football League. Moses was a sidewinding soccer-style kicker who had played his college ball at Montclair State. Very few people had ever heard of Montclair State, but Moses didn't care very much about that. He had kicked eleven out of fifteen field goals for the school in his senior year, including five for over forty yards.

"That's pretty good, right, Abe?" said Moses, who innately believed in himself but somehow always got around to asking questions like that, as if he really didn't know the answer.

"Are you kidding?" said Abe. "That's good enough to make any team in the NFL. Are you kidding?"

"Yeah, I guess you're right. How much more can you do?"

The WFL pageantry of March ended on a spectacular note, at once beautiful and simple, like a clarion call. It resounded all over the land, in every bar from Flatbush to Hollywood; at every office, in every factory, wherever men gathered to talk football and root for "the new kid on the block"—the WFL.

Until the explosion in Toronto on the last weekend in March, the WFL's most important player acquisition was John Elliott of the Jets. Then came Csonka, Kiick and Warfield of the Miami Dolphins.

Here were three of the most dynamic personalities in the NFL. Larry Csonka, most famous of the trio, was a bull-driving fullback who had rushed for 5,151 yards in six seasons with the Dolphins. Jim Kiick, his backfield partner, blasted his way to 3,370 yards during the same period, while Paul Warfield, with the Cleveland Browns for six years before joining Miami in 1970, was poetry in motion as he snared 344 passes for a career total of 7,165 yards and seventy-five touchdowns.

Now, even as federal legislation was being drafted to exclude the Toronto Northmen from playing in Canada, the three stars of Miami's Super Bowl VIII championship team rocked the pro football universe by signing three-year contracts with the Northmen, beginning in 1975. The total package came to $3.5 million!

"We notified the Dolphins what was going on about eighteen hours before the contracts were finalized," said Csonka, "but didn't get any specific counteroffer. Joe Robbie [Dolphin owner] finally told Ed Keating he needed two days to think it over. Keating said he had two hours, but Robbie told him he didn't want to negotiate over the telephone."

Ed Keating (no relation to Bob Keating of the Stars) was business agent for Csonka, Kiick and Warfield. He had taken his charges to Toronto on Friday, March 29, as guests of John Bassett. During the weekend the players were driven around in limousines, ate in the best restaurants and slept in satin-quilted beds at the fashionable Sutton Place Hotel.

On Saturday morning negotiations began. Keating told his clients he'd try to get a three-player package deal of $3.5 million. Why don't they go over to Hy's Restaurant? Keating suggested. He'd work on the deal with Bassett and his staff, and they'd all meet later for lunch. The players agreed and went to Hy's at noon to keep their appointment.

To their surprise, Keating, Bassett, Northmen general manager Leo Cahill and team lawyer Herb Solway were already seated; they were laughing and joking as though they hadn't a care in the world. After a while, when the group ordered their third round of beer, Csonka started to get worried. There wasn't one mention of the contracts. Keating just kept eating his shrimp and drinking his beer and smiling through Zonk until the big fullback felt like throwing a shoulder into his agent's belly.

Finally, Keating rolled his eyes at Csonka, put down his beer and said, "Excuse me, gentlemen. Duty calls." A few seconds later Csonka got up and went to the men's room after Keating.

"Well?"

"We got everything. Everything and more."

"All of it?"

"All of it. The works, Zonk!"

Csonka looped his arms around Keating and the two men let out loud whoops as though they had just made a million dollars.

The deal was truly amazing. Csonka received a $500,000 bonus for signing his part of the $3.5 million offer. He also received a $1 million salary over the next three years. Thrown into the package was a luxury automobile plus a rent-free three-bedroom apartment in Toronto. An ironbound clause in the contract insured his money against a contingency the franchise might fold before Csonka's playing obligations were due in 1975.

When word of the incredible pact got back to Miami, the Dolphin front office went into a deep swoon. Coach Don Shula said he was "disappointed, shocked, sick" over the defections. Owner Joe Robbie claimed, "We were torpedoed." And at Lake Havasu, California, vacationing Miami defensive back Dick Anderson said, "There isn't a player in professional football who wouldn't jump to the new league for that kind of money."

Complacency had been shattered. The NFL suddenly lost its sense of perspective, as though all reason had become a jumbled madness. Was it possible that Gary Davidson's league possessed unlimited wealth? Was the Toronto caper a prelude to an even greater thirst for NFL blood? When and where would the WFL body snatchers strike next?

These were just a few of the many morbid questions NFL owners asked themselves after Csonka, Kiick and Warfield defected to the WFL. Almost immediately, the answers were provided in a chilling sequence of fast-breaking events.

On April 2 Ken Stabler, conference-leading quarterback of the NFL Oakland Raiders, signed a multiyear contract to play with the WFL Birmingham Americans, starting in 1975. When pressed by reporters, Stabler's agent said the contract "makes Kenny the highest-paid player in professional football history." However, a smiling Stabler and Birmingham board chairman Bill Putnam refused to comment on the terms of the agreement.

Exactly one week after the Stabler signing, Randy Johnson, number two quarterback of the New York Giants, and Calvin Hill, the Dallas Cowboys' two-time 1,000-yard rusher, signed multiyear contracts in Honolulu to play for the WFL Hawaiians after playing out their NFL options in 1974.

No figures were announced, but Hill's agreement called for a three-year $500,000 salary and bonus, Johnson's for the same number of years at a $375,000 figure.

For both players, the jump in earnings was dramatic proof of the WFL's ability to mesmerize "underpaid" NFL players with a wave of green treasury paper under their noses. In 1973 Hill and Johnson earned basic salaries in the neighborhood of $50,000, with additional bonus arrangements totaling about $20,000 each.

By now it was clear that the WFL raids were just getting started. On the very same day that Hill and Johnson basked under a Hawaiian sun with *nouveau riche* grins on their handsome faces, Dallas Cowboy quarterback Craig Morton met with Steve Arnold in Houston to put the finishing touches on his six-figure contract to play for the WFL Texans in 1975. Among the batch of other NFL stars rumored to be in line for a league change were: Claude Humphrey, Atlanta Falcon defensive end; Tom Mack, Los Angeles Ram guard; and John Brockington, Green Bay Packer running back.

NFL nerves were rubbed raw by the stealth and daring of the WFL foragers. With every new signing, a deep frustration grew within the established league. In a concerted effort to head off the incursions, NFL owners resorted to the courts with a flurry of restraining orders. The Cowboys, for example, started the ball rolling with a trip to the courthouse less than twenty-four hours after they learned of Morton's defection.

Not to be outdone, Dolphin owner Joe Robbie had his lawyers burn the midnight oil in preparation for a projected $4 million lawsuit that would name Larry Csonka, Jim Kiick, Paul Warfield, the WFL, the Toronto Northmen, John Bassett and Ed Keating as defendants in the action. Robbie's argument was that his naive, innocent players were led astray by Bassett and Keating, who, with malice aforethought, induced them to break their Miami contracts.

Nevertheless, all the restraining orders, temporary injunctions, and damage suits did little to halt the spreading epidemic. On April 15 veteran quarterback Daryle Lamonica, playing out his option year with the Oakland Raiders, signed a high six-figure multiyear pact with Larry Hatfield's Southern California Sun. With Oakland teammate Kenny Stabler already captured in the

Bill DeFlavio relaxes.

Gerry Gluck

Gerry Gluck

George Sauer and Al Barnes watch the action from the sidelines.

Gerry Gluck

Babe Parilli and Upton Bell at Charlotte press conference.

Bill Crespinel

Don Maynard stops by to say hello to former teammates George Sauer, John Elliott and Gerry Philbin.

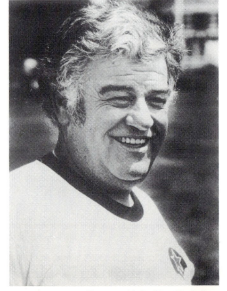

Mike Ferraro, equipment manager.

Courtesy of the New York Stars

Bill Crespinel

orge Sauer on a long gainer.

Bill DeFlavio nurses injured knee, with sympathy from author.

Gerry Gluck

Greg Lens joins the wounded list.

Gerry Gluck

A Chicago "C" on a New York "Star" equals a Charlotte Hornets helmet.

Gerry Gluck

Gerry Gluck

Gary Davidson and Bob Keating.

Ex-NFL star Leroy Kelly does his thing for the WFL.

Gerry Gluck

George Sauer studies on the plane.

Gerry Gluck

Ike Thomas in the Florida rain.

Gerry Glu

Moses Lajterman.

Gerry Philbin.

Sometimes you win and sometimes . . .

Gerry Gluck

Dusty Rhodes watches her boys from the sidelines.

Gerry Gluck

Birmingham net, it appeared certain that Raider quarterback strength would be crippled at the start of the 1975 season.

Around this period of time, another jump took place—in the WFL. Joe Wheeler officially removed his franchise from Washington and placed it in Norfolk, where it became the Virginia Ambassadors. At his new Scope Plaza office, Wheeler produced a contract from his desk, a pen from his pocket, and handed them to a powerful young man who happened to play professional football for a living.

On that day, April 17, Cincinnati Bengal middle linebacker Bill Bergey signed a personal-service contract to play for the Ambassadors, starting in 1976. He was still under contract to play for the Bengals through 1975.

At Bergey's press conference, Ambassador head coach Jack Pardee introduced him as "the premier defensive player in football." When Bergey was asked why he was jumping to the WFL, he said, "I want to help promote and develop the new league, but the big thing is financial security for my wife and family."

How much was Wheeler paying him? Terms of the contract were kept under wraps at the press conference, but the Bengal linebacker disclosed to a Cincinnati writer that his three-year Ambassador pact was worth $250,000.

Bergey's defection might have been written off as nothing more than a disagreeable fact of life by the Bengal front office. However, his ill-advised admission that he planned to help promote the WFL caused Bengal assistant general manager Mike Brown (a graduate of the Harvard School of Law) to diligently assess the implications of the remark. In short order, Brown located a protective clause in the NFL players contract. It started a litigation which eventually led to an historic decision laid down by U.S. District Judge David S. Porter. The judge's ruling, on May 14, damaged the NFL claim that its monopolistic practices were justified by the unusual nature of team competition in pro football.

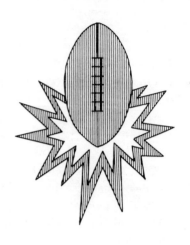

EIGHT

The New York Star boundaries pushed to a last clearing in the pre-season wilderness. In March a few straggling players made up the team roster. Now it was May. More than eighty-five free agents, draft choices and NFL veterans had signed contracts. Fifteen more would be added to the list before the end of the month.

For the older ones, it was another chance; one more try to find order in their lives after a winter of confusion. In their winter homes and apartments, east and west, north and south, they felt naked and alone, no longer able to communicate with their bodies or utter their most passionate thoughts about the game they still wished to be part of.

In the winter, Homer Jones spent his days lifting heavy steel equipment and tools and entering the weights in a book that was the property of the Lone Star Steel Company. In the winter, Homer Jones worked in Lone Star, Texas, and ached with the thought of returning to New York, where he had once played in Yankee Stadium. He wanted to play again, but he was like rust in the midst of all the gleaming steel that he had to lift and weigh. He was thirty-three years old. His feet didn't fly like they used to. When he had left the NFL, it was 1970 and his legs were slowing down; slowing down like a tired machine with most of its pistons blown. There was an unhappy season in Cleveland. Then he was through.

On summer afternoons he'd sit on the bank of a murky Texas river and wait for the catfish to bite. In the long winter evenings he saw visions of himself sprinting down the sideline, all alone, on his way to another Tarkenton-to-Jones touchdown, hearing the Yankee Stadium crowd erupt in a rising flood of ecstasy. Those were his thoughts, and they went spilling out into the long Texas nights during the endless winters.

Now it was May. The better life awaited him at the summer camp of La Salle. He was sure of it. He could feel it in his hands and in his tired old legs.

In the winter, Greg Lens worked for the Tyson Trucking Company in Minneapolis. He made $6.50 an hour loading cartons of candy into Mr. Tyson's trucks. Sometimes, when he clocked out at midnight, he'd go down to the gin mill with his buddy, Bill Lindren, and have a few beers. Bill was his foreman and loved to listen to his stories and hear him sing funny songs while they drank their beer. Sometimes, Greg told Bill inside stories about Joe Namath and all the guys he'd played with that summer. Bill's eyes would light up. Then he'd ask Greg if he was going to look for a football job again, and Greg would say darn right he was, and then he'd start singing his head off until they were the only two left in the bar.

On a cold Saturday morning in the Minneapolis winter, Lens had jogged two miles in the snow when he felt a sharp pain in his side, as if a knife had pierced his lung. He reached his apartment in a lifeless, rubbery state, wondering why he was punishing himself, why he was kidding himself into believing he could make it back. He felt like the oldest twenty-nine-year-old in the world just then.

The winter snow in Minneapolis melted under a spring sun.

Then Parilli called and offered him $23,500 to play for the Stars in New York. Lens was excited. He was wanted again; he was remembered. He said yes, because only Washington and Chicago had answered his letters, and nobody had called him, as Parilli had, to say that he was remembered and truly wanted.

He waited for the contract to arrive, and all the while he never told Bill or his mother, who taught grade school in Marshall, or his girl, who worked as a desk clerk at the Ramada Inn—or anyone—until he got his contract in the mail three days later. Then he called his mother and his girl. In the afternoon he drove his car to Mr. Tyson's place. When he saw Bill he started to sing one of his funny songs:

> The Stars at night
> Are big and bright
> Deep in the heart
> of Minn-eee-apolis . . .

In the winter, Lloyd Voss reported to work every morning for the Allegheny Parks and Recreation Commission in Pittsburgh. He had security and enough time to count up his years and be satisfied that his life was filled with mostly good memories. In the winter Lloyd Voss thought about Lombardi and the freezing cold in Green Bay, which reminded him of how it was in Magnolia, Minnesota, when he was a kid fullback in high school and the snow followed his footsteps to the goal line.

Now it was the winter of his discontent. Most of the laughs had died away in the snow. He was going on thirty-three. He was secure, but he didn't laugh quite so hard as he used to. Maybe because there were a few extra tackles to be made, he thought; people to hit, games to win, cheers to be heard. Ten years of pro ball had done that to him, conditioned him to think it would never never never really be all over. But after ten years of pro ball, he had retired to develop a beer belly and go to bed almost every night with an acid taste in his mouth.

In the winter, Lloyd Voss clutched his wife in his sleep and dreamed about the games—all 137 of them—seeing smoky visions of all the players he had laughed with and yelled with and cried with in the locker rooms of Green Bay, Pittsburgh, Denver and Foxboro. In the winter of his retirement there would be some mornings when he would get up with a scowl on his face, and his wife would fix his coffee knowing that he had slept through another terrible night.

One evening in April, Babe called. Lloyd Voss listened quietly, then told Babe he'd be happy to get back into harness again. Retirement was okay for the old guys but not for this young stud, he laughed. He was in good shape, working out every day and all that, he told Parilli. When he hung up he clapped his hands together, grabbed his wife around the waist and lifted her above his head. They were going to the Big Apple, he shouted. Lloyd Voss was going to give it one more try.

In the winter, thirty-two-year-old Dick Hart operated his Carvel ice cream franchise in Morrisville, which sat like a pinpoint on the map of Pennsylvania, ten miles from the Jersey capital of Trenton. Business was not so good as the year before, and his left knee still ached from the two operations that had forced him to quit the game of football. He stayed out a year, spent his days mixing ice cream in the big machines and thinking, every so often, about his four seasons with the Eagles and his two years in Buffalo. Man, how he wanted to hit someone again, he would ruefully daydream sometimes, perhaps when his wife Jeanne was handing out a cone to some bull-necked kid who reminded him of himself—when he was only twenty or so and could hit a baseball just as hard as he could pop a defensive lineman.

Well, it was all over now, he thought. But not quite. At home there were his weights, which he had worked on all summer to strengthen his knee. And he kept hoping that maybe all those letters he had sent out to the NFL and WFL would mean something, that somebody "out there" would call him and ask him about his knee. He'd tell them it was strong again, maybe stronger than the other one, and that he could move just as fast as ever.

In the spring, he talked to Bob Keating, who put Parilli on

the phone, who told him he was wanted. And Dick Hart, who never went to college, started to prepare for his postgraduate studies in New York . . . for a career in the WFL.

In the winter, Gerry Philbin drove his Cadillac from Pawtucket, Rhode Island, to Boston, Massachusetts. He picked up his two small sons from Trudy, who was living with her mother, and drove them back to Pawtucket for the weekend.

Damn it, he cursed inwardly on the ride back to Pawtucket, it could have been different. But it wasn't. In Boston, Trudy just gave him the kids and told him to take care of himself. Then he was gone—angry that it had come down to a few empty words.

Gerry Philbin's Cadillac crossed the state line into Rhode Island. In the cold winter afternoon, he noticed the darkening skies. Soon the snow would fall. He let out a long sigh. In his isolation he was not alone. At least he had the kids for a while. At least he had *them*.

By May, Babe Parilli had a coaching staff, a team doctor, team dentists, team trainer, team equipment manager and most of his team players signed for the season.

Tom Moore became the second assistant coach after Stew Barber, and was followed by Lamar Leachman, George Boutselis and training camp coach Dick Connors. Except for Barber, none of the others had ever played or coached professional football, though Connors had had brief trials with the Giants, Patriots and Dolphins.

Maurice Cowen, an adjunct orthopedic surgeon at New York's Lenox Hill Hospital, was named the team physician; Stanley Datlow and Fred Cornell were appointed team dentists; and Lew Cohen, former assistant trainer of the New York Jets, became the Stars head trainer. Within a month an infinite amount of their understanding, intelligence and talent would be tested by the 107 players and would-be players due to report for first practice on June 3.

But the basic structure of administrative personnel, coaches and players meant nothing unless the team secured a decent playing field. Yankee Stadium, in the Bronx, was out of the question. The House That Ruth Built was in the beginning stages of a rebuilding program, still two years away from completion. Besides, the city shied away from making a guarantee that the facility would be available to the Stars at that time.

The New York Giants, former tenants of the stadium, were now playing at Yale Bowl in New Haven and were scheduled to occupy a new complex in the New Jersey Meadowlands in 1976. That left Yankee Stadium open for a football bid from both the NFL and the WFL. With two metropolitan teams already part of the NFL lineup, it seemed to Bob Schmertz that chances of obtaining an eventual lease on the historical ball park were better than even. But for now, a temporary home had to be located— and with utmost speed.

In March, Star officials toured Roosevelt Stadium in Jersey City. The place was a horrible blight by any standards. With the exception of the interior facilities—locker and training rooms— which the Giants had rehabilitated a few years back for summer practice use, Roosevelt Stadium was less than bush league. It was hopeless.

In mid-April, Keating announced that three thousand season tickets had been sold, "and we expect to sell between fifteen thousand and seventeen thousand by July 17."

There could be no further delay. A home field *had* to be found for the opening game of the season. Shunting aside all practical considerations in favor of an emotional need, the Stars secured a two-year lease from the city to play at Downing Stadium on Randall's Island. Unfortunately, Downing was only a slightly improved version of Roosevelt Stadium. Its turf was scarred, press box facilities were strictly high school level, the old stands were a splintered eyesore, the lighting system was totally inadequate for Wednesday-night football, and the locker rooms were built long before the age of present-day professional football squads. Nevertheless, Bob Schmertz signed the papers. The New York Stars had a home—be it ever so humble.

"By the time we're finished with repairs and all that," said a worried Bob Keating to his boss after the papers were signed, "the place is going to cost us around $600,000."

"That's life, I guess," returned Schmertz, who had thrown more than a few bucks down the drain in his time.

Two further WFL developments in May cast a settled "look" on the form and shape of Gary Davidson's Frankenstein creation.

Hounded by seen and unseen enemies in the Canadian Football League and the Canadian government itself, John Bassett packed up his Toronto Northmen franchise and moved to Memphis, Tennessee, where he renamed his team the Memphis Southmen. Bassett was furious over the treatment he had received in his own country. He castigated Health and Welfare Minister Marc Lalonde as the motivating force behind his ouster from Canadian territory.

"If an election is called," Bassett said on the eve of his team's departure, "I hope the people of Toronto will remember that Lalonde denied them football of a superior quality."

The next day General Manager Leo Cahill and Head Coach John McVay flew out to Memphis, where rights to Memorial Stadium were secured with a $75,000 cash deposit.

The last pre-season shifting of WFL clubs occurred on May 19. Rommie Loudd returned to Orlando, Florida, from a visit to Gary Davidson in Newport Beach with a brand new franchise for the Disney World city. Loudd had swung the deal because Joe Wheeler was unable to meet his rising costs while operating the Washington-Baltimore-Virginia entry. In essence, Wheeler dropped the franchise as soon as he realized he might wind up as a pro football pauper.

Loudd was a former UCLA football player who became the first full-time black assistant coach in pro football. A year later, in 1967, he was promoted from linebacker coach to director of player personnel for the Patriots—the first front-office black *ever* in pro football. Then, with the emergence of Upton Bell as Patriot general manager, Loudd was again promoted, this time to the newly created post of director of pro personnel. He held the position for two years, supervising Dusty Rhodes and others in the signing of free agents, players in trade, waiver-list rejects and college stars.

Predictably, Loudd's nature was such that his ambitions soon reached beyond the mere buying and selling of football flesh. Rommie Loudd needed a black success story in his life—his own. In early 1974 he induced real estate interests in Orlando to back him in an expansion franchise venture that was being kicked around by NFL brass for the area. But $16 million was just a little too steep for his benefactors, so Loudd turned his hunger toward the neophyte WFL. The price for a Gary Davidson franchise was considerably less—almost nothing when compared to the NFL asking price. Loudd convinced his people he could bring home the bacon. He called Davidson, was told of Wheeler's fiscal weakness, and promptly moved in for the kill. Although the official announcement of the transaction claimed that about $5 million changed hands, only the least sophisticated could have believed the figure. In May of 1974 millions of fans were ready to believe anything that Gary Davidson was involved in.

The New York Stars hadn't kicked a ball or thrown a pass or scored a touchdown, yet the team was theoretically ready as one of the WFL twelve starting blocks, with players signed for every offensive and defensive department. Reduced to cold statistics, the New York Stars had signed five quarterbacks, fifteen running backs, twelve wide receivers, four tight ends, seven offensive guards, six offensive tackles, five centers, six defensive ends, six defensive tackles, thirteen linebackers, twelve cornerbacks, thirteen safeties and three kickers—for a grand total of 107 players. It meant that seventy of the 107 would be dropped—because a WFL ruling stated that each club was allowed to carry only thirty-seven players on its roster during the season. Using the Star signings as an average for all twelve WFL teams, it meant that approximately 1,300 football players would compete for 450 jobs in the WFL.

Gerry Philbin was one of them.

In his ten-year NFL career, Gerry had never had one easy day on the field. Not one. Even when it was easy, he *made* it hard.

That's the way he played the game—as if the sum total of his whole life rode on everything he did . . . because people were out there . . . lots of them . . . and they were trying to look into his life to see what he was made of.

Pawtucket is the second largest city in Rhode Island. Nearly 100,000 people live there, and most of them work in the cotton thread, bleaching and dyeing, silk and rayon, insulated wire, rolled steel, and chemical plants. Pawtucket gets its name from an Indian word meaning *falls at the mouth of a river*. That's where it is—at the head of Narragansett Bay, about five miles from Providence and forty miles southwest of Boston.

Gerry was born in Pawtucket on a summer day in 1941. He was one of seven children. When he was ten years old his father died. John Philbin was his name, and he fixed television sets. Twenty-three years after his father's death, Gerry remembers him as a good man, a fun-loving man who inspired him to cultivate a love for sports.

Hermine Philbin worked in a cotton-threading mill, threading cotton through the machines at night so that she could be at home during the day to feed her children in the morning and get them off to school. She slept part of the day, and then went back to work again. Sometimes Gerry would look down from his tenement window, see his mother walk along Arch Street to the bus that carried her off to the mill and wonder what it was like behind the high gray walls. Sometimes he'd think about the people who worked there. He wondered if they treated his mother with as much respect as he did.

As a grade school kid, he delivered newspapers to the doorsteps of the old tenement apartments.

He delivered the *Pawtucket Times* and the *Providence Journal* every morning . . . every afternoon . . . and on Sunday. When he was old enough he went to work for the cement people. He worked his way through the best and worst of it while he studied hard and played football in the autumn for Tolman High School.

One day he told his mother he had received a football scholarship to the University of Buffalo, and his mother said go to school, Gerry, and get an education. So he went off to the university—the only one in his family ever to go beyond high school. But Gerry felt he was going for all of them.

In 1963 his name began to appear in the *Pawtucket Times* sports section. His sister Pat, whose husband owned the apartment house he and his mother lived in, would show the whole family his picture and say: there he is, look at that, can you imagine? And everyone in the family would make a big thing over it because Gerry gave them something very precious.

He graduated from the University of Buffalo as an all-East and second-team all-America; playing tough, hard football for the Blue and White Buffalo Bulls. At the age of twenty-three, Gerry Philbin graduated from the University of Buffalo with a Bachelor of Arts and Sociology degree—and as an academic all-America.

Ten years had passed since he came up as a third-round AFL draft choice. All those games—109 of them in regular-season competition—had taken some of the brashness out of his style, the cutting edge from his tongue. He was no longer the blazing-mad Philadelphia Eagle—no longer the ebullient New York Jet. Gerry Philbin was more subdued now. But in his suede jacket and brown turtleneck sweater, he appeared mellow-handsome and charming to those who said hello.

Philbin was in the New York Stars Madison Avenue office on May 14 while a press conference was going on. He had some time to kill, so he stopped by. Later in the afternoon he'd meet Tiger Ferraro in Oakdale and go over to his house for a big Italian dinner. Time was like an empty arena. Without Trudy, he could run and shout and play all over the place; do as he wanted. But he dreaded the ghosts of good times past. At the end of a lot of great evenings lately, Philbin felt the same sadness come back.

While he leafed through one of the Stars press guides in the outer office, sports reporters and radio, television and promotion guys moved into the East Coast "White House" office set up for Gary Davidson. The conference was opened by Vince Casey, newly appointed public relations director of the Stars. Youthful, red-haired and ingratiating, Casey had been an advertising copywriter for the William Esty Company when he applied for a job with the Stars. In January he'd dashed off a letter to Bob Schmertz that began, "I gotta work for the New York Whatchyamacallits." It was the best copy he ever wrote. Schmertz hired him as an assistant to George Bernard, a rah-rah type who spent his brief career in the WFL trying to figure how he could get into another business. Casey replaced Bernard in early April.

Now, with reporters surrounding Gary Davidson at his desk, while WFL aides, Star officials, TV personalities and assorted hustlers jammed the room, Casey brought on Bob Keating, who introduced Sal Marchiano, a baby-faced, dark-haired TV sports commentator hired to call the play-by-play of eight Star road games over WOR-TV.

"Sal is one of the top sportscasters in New York," said Keating. "We're lucky he's going to be the voice of the Stars."

A thick-set fellow with thinning red hair and a goldfish face squeezed his way forward to make a few self-serving remarks about the WFL. He was D. Max Muhleman, WFL vice-president of marketing/public relations, a onetime sportswriter in Charlotte, North Carolina, and a former general manager of Dan Gurney's All-American Racers. Smooth and ice-watered, Muhleman announced that ". . . a legal decision in Cincinnati provides a significant breakthrough for the WFL, so let me turn this over to Gary, who will fill you in on the details."

Media pressed in to hear every word.

"Judge Porter has ruled againt a request on the part of the Cincinnati Bengals for a preliminary injunction on Bill Bergey," intoned the commissioner. "Bergey, as you may know, signed a contract with the Virginia Ambassadors last April 17. We feel that Judge Porter's decision has helped the WFL position considerably. We are also very pleased that Judge Porter declined to issue the injunction because *'it would cause harm to the concept of establishing free competition in the market place for the sports dollar,'* and those are his quotes."

Sitting quietly in the room, taking down notes, *New York Times* sportswriter Bill Wallace waited until the preliminaries were over. In a few more minutes, when the room cleared of the television crews, when the hangers-on and fringe crowd departed, he'd be able to ask a few questions that had puzzled him for weeks. Finally, his turn came.

"Gary," asked Wallace, "maybe you can enlighten me as to how the original WFL franchises were granted?"

"In accordance with the bylaws of the original board of governors," answered the commissioner.

"Well . . ." said the still puzzled reporter, "okay. Now, maybe we can get into something closer to home. Can you tell me who paid what to whom for the right to own franchises in the WFL?"

Davidson narrowed his eyes. The other reporters sensed the immediacy of the tension. Gene Roswell of the *Post,* and a regular on the New York Giant beat, released a chuckle.

"I don't have to answer questions about money," Davidson shot back.

"I don't know, Gary, it seems to me that, with conflicting estimates of WFL franchises selling for anywhere from $250,000 to $500,000 apiece, you'd be in a position to reveal if you personally benefited from the sale of those franchises."

"Fortunately, Bill, this is still a free country and I don't have to answer that."

"That's what Nixon has been saying about the Watergate questions."

"I don't think that's funny." Davidson heard the snickers.

"Well, one more time, then. Have you personally benefited from the sale of WFL franchises?"

"Yes, of course."

There was a deep, fiery glare in Davidson's eyes. He sat in his swivel chair, hands folded, lower lip caught between his teeth— seethingly silent. Gene Roswell perked up with a question about the upcoming schedule. Wallace got up and left. The press conference ended within minutes after his departure.

Six days later, an NFL player spokesman conducted an entirely different kind of press conference.

"There has been no response of a meaningful nature from the owners since we last sat down with them on April 4. In the meantime, I remember reading quotes from the owners after our demands were published. They were characterized as anarchistic, ludicrous, destructive, ridiculous, and so on—and those were the nicer remarks."

The words came from Bill Curry, veteran Houston Oiler center, ex-Green Bay, ex-Baltimore lineman, and current president of the National Football League Players Association. Curry was referring, of course, to the twenty-six NFL owners—who faced fifty-seven player demands for "better treatment" before the opening of the established league's training camps in July. His remarks were made shortly before the annual Pro Football Writers Dinner at the Hotel Americana on May 20. The New York chapter sponsored the affair, and the guest list was a veritable Who's Who of the most powerful and influential owners in the NFL, plus the entire league office.

In the Imperial Ballroom that night, conversations centered mainly on the clear danger of a catastrophic player strike, one that could knock out the entire NFL exhibition schedule and possibly erase the NFL season. Even Commissioner Pete Rozelle seemed affected by the gathering holocaust. He was, to be sure, not his effervescent self while seated on the dais, listening to a carping reference by Giant owner Wellington Mara that he hadn't seen or heard from Curry since April 4. Five hundred guests also picked up Mara's remarks on the microphone.

At Table 16, Bob Schmertz, Howard Baldwin, Bob Keating, Dusty Rhodes, Vince Casey, and Babe Parilli and his entire coaching staff sat in veritable quarantine under the massive NFL guns. They had every right to be there, as it was a New York writers' dinner. Magnanimously, the NFL chose the better part of valor in not placing the PFWA in a defensive position over their decision to invite WFL representatives to the affair. And yet, aside from the Stars, no other WFL club had appeared. Admittedly, the Philadelphia Bell public relations director did inform PFWA ticket manager Herb Gluck he would try to convince owner Jack Kelly the dinner was worth attending. And Tom Origer of Chicago sent in a response. He couldn't make it, but wished everyone luck. The tickets were thirty dollars apiece.

Bill Lyons, well-known roastmaster of the Lambs Club, provided the Halftime Show, a welcome break after all the speeches, awards and special citations. Running down a prepared list, Lyons laced humorous barbs at everyone from Howard Cosell to Weeb Ewbank, who was the recipient of the evening's Arthur Daley (*New York Times* sports columnist) Memorial Award for long and meritorious service to pro football. One of the heartiest laughs of the night, in an evening of precious little humor, occurred when Lyons directed his attention to Table 16.

". . . I also see that Babe Parilli of the WFL New York Stars is here," said Lyons, pushing his horn-rimmed glasses to the bridge of his nose while cornballing a glimpse into the smoke-filled ballroom. "The reason why Babe may look a little dazed is because he's been spending the last few weeks trying to find Randall's Island."

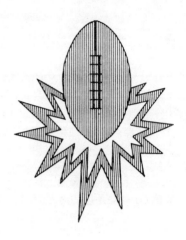

NINE

Named after a seventeenth-century priest, La Salle Military Academy is a forty-six-year-old institution governed by the Christian Brother order. At one time it was an opulent paradise for Isaac Singer, who brought the sewing machine into universal use.

Located in Oakdale, Long Island, La Salle blankets 202 acres of swamp maple, giant oak, and willow trees; of toyland bridges with sleepy ponds that run silently along soft earth beds. During the school term, boys of high school age receive academic, religious and military training there. They are fed in a cafeteria-styled dining hall, bedded down in high-ceilinged dormitories, go to class, march, play games, ride horses, pray, and graduate to seminaries, universities, and military colleges.

This is the school, cloistered, stately and old. It ultimately became the training-camp home of the New York Stars.

The players appeared on an early Sunday morning in June. They arrived from the way stations of Minnesota and Vermont, from the port cities of Louisiana and Pennsylvania, from the cotton centers of Texas and Georgia, from the tobacco kingdoms of North and South Carolina, from the ghetto towns of New York and California—from the hills and valleys and mountains and concrete canyons of their American experience.

Dozens of them; flopped or sprawled or standing against the walls, in two lines of jumbled corduroy and denim. They faced each other in the basement of St. Joseph's dormitory and read Sunday comics, filled in player questionnaires, studied training schedules, and occasionally just stared at one another. In time, familiarity, and new friendships, would be born. But for now, the players waited for the doctors, dentists and trainers in distrustful silence.

Jimmy Sims sat hunched over against the wall, with his knees jacked up under his chin, eyes focused on the WFL player questionnaire. The University of Southern California six-foot, 190-pound defensive back filled in the upper portion of the form. Near the bottom, at the line that asked him to list his professional experience, he wrote *none*.

Sims was a twelfth-round pick of the New York Giants in the January NFL draft. On April 20 he showed up at the Giant rookie workout session at Fordham University. There he met General Manager Andy Robustelli, who offered him a minimal salary and a small bonus. Sims thought he deserved more.

"I played in two Rose Bowls. I was good enough to win four major awards in my junior year," he told Robustelli.

"Well," said the pro football Hall of Famer, "we've got a lot of good young fellows coming to camp this year. As it is, we'll be taking a chance on you."

"In that case," said Sims coldly, "I don't think I want to play for the Giants."

Tom Sherman unpeeled his shirt for Dr. Cowan. Staring straight ahead, he felt the stethoscope against his hairless chest. He was in good shape. He always was. Four years of quarterbacking the Hartford Knights had conditioned him to all kinds of pain, both mental and physical.

"You're fine," said Dr. Cowan after the rubber wrapping came

101

off Sherman's arm. "You can go in now to see Dr. Datlow. He'll check your teeth."

Sherman wanted above all to get through this day. If he could get to tomorrow he'd be okay, he thought to himself as he put on his shirt. There were four other quarterbacks in camp: Gault, Danielson, Longmire, and Mackey. There'd be plenty of time to say hello, to see what they were made of.

That was his nature. He never went out of his way to seek the affection and esteem of his fellow players. The thing that counted in Tom Sherman's heart and mind was daily perform- ance. Fulsome praise was not essential to his life—not after all those bone-crunching bus rides down the back alleys of pro ball. By holding fast to that principle, he had been rewarded. He was getting another shot in the major leagues. Thinking about it all as he went in to see Dr. Datlow, Sherman allowed a big grin to spread across his face. The dentist smiled back, impressed. His patient had just unveiled a substantial upper row of spaced teeth.

Don Gault had played for Hofstra University and had been a campus hero. He broke almost every passing record in that Long Island school's history. Hofstra wasn't a football power by na- tional standards, but it did turn out a number of fine players who made it into the pros in the mid-sixties. John Schmitt and Mike D'Amato played for the New York Jets; Jim Thorpe did well in Canada; Fran Lynch and Wandy Williams went on to the Denver Broncos; and Don Gault made it to the Cleveland Browns—where his NFL career went down the drain on a rainy, windy night against the Pittsburgh Steelers in 1971. After the game, Gault sat in front of his locker and swallowed hard to keep from throwing up. All those dropped balls! He hit them in the *breadbasket,* and they were dropped!

He was shuttled over to the San Diego Chargers, was waived, and lingered for a year in Canadian ball. The Jets signed him as a free agent in the summer of 1973, then released him before regular-season play. That was the sum total of Don Gault's pro career; five incredibly long seasons, only two regular-season games—and recurring nightmares of a rainy night in Cleveland.

He was twenty-eight now and had a good job with A-Drive Auto Leasing in Hicksville, Long Island. He liked to lounge around in his large, attractive home in Dix Hills. His wife and baby daughter lifted his gloom and made him realize he had had enough football. He became a normal human being again, right up to the moment he signed his New York Stars contract.

Now he was thinking football again. Right now, standing in the locker room, getting his equipment from Tiger Ferraro. It was a sunny June morning. His arm felt good. His mind was clear. He was happy.

Em Burnam, Jim Kinsley, Riley Moore and Jan Nelson flunked their physicals. Brian Oldfield passed up the season because of a bad leg. John Kondrk and Bill McKoy never reported. John Carlos and Sam Walton were delayed in transit. As the Monday-morning haze lifted above Great South Bay, the players started their first practice as so many ciphers—ninety-seven in all.

They ran out on the field, breaking through the wind like cattle charging out of a pen. Some were lean and well-conditioned, others moved with the lard of winter showing through their white polo shirts. They poured from the dormitory as one big mass, kicking earth beneath their feet with an authority unduplicated by those who have never played the game.

Greg Lens ran with his shoulders back, with his mouth flopping in rhythm to his heavy, squashy steps. George Sauer ran with his hands clenched, elbows close to his sides, letting his shoulders and legs carry the rest of him along the grass. Jimmy Sims purred over the ground, moving his black marble legs like a quarter-miler approaching the tape. Manny Brown's wide shoulders were borne on toothpick legs. Bill DeFlavio rolled across the turf like a small cabbage. Earl Christy's bald head gleamed under the tracking rays of Long Island sun. Ray Parsons's monumental biceps pumped fiercely, and Moses Lajterman ran on thick, heavily matted stumps. In their own fashion, the ninety-seven ran and would continue to run until their season ended—either by a tap on the shoulder or after one last effort on a football field six months later.

"Gitta-gitta-gitta. . . . Let's get it right this time. . . . All right . . . set . . . hike . . . hut. . . . Hey, Philburn, get your nose out of that dust. C'mon you're not moving. . . . You're not making that lateral cut. . . ."

Gerry Philbin shook sweat from his eyes and got down into his stance again. The sonofabitch better stop calling me Philburn, he muttered under his helmet.

"Gitta-gitta-gitta. . . . One more time, darlin's. We're gonna do it ovah until it comes out exactly like I want it. All right . . . set . . . hike . . . hut. . . . Now, that was considerably better. Way to go, little man. . . ."

Lamar Leachman bestowed his begrudging accolade on Bill DeFlavio, a short, heavily muscled 230-pound defensive tackle who had played for Bob Keating's New England Colonials the previous season. Leachman was just the last in a long procession of coaches who appreciated his skills. Ever since DeFlavio was a junior in high school he was called "little man" or "shorty" or "plug." At five-nine, counting his cotton-candy hair style, De-Flavio was an incongruity beside the behemoths in his unit. Larry Estes towered over him at six-six, while Greg Lens stood six-five. Lloyd Voss and John Elliott were six-four, Jerry Ellison reached six-three, and even Gerry Philbin, considered small for the tackle position, did pretty well as an all-pro Jet at six-two. But DeFlavio had a couple of things going for him that the others couldn't match. There wasn't a pro tackle who could get any lower to the ground, and *nobody* moved any quicker. Now those assets needed recognition by his defensive line coach. If Leachman knows anything about football, thought DeFlavio, there is nothing to worry about. But then again, the stubby tackle wondered as the second day of practice ended, maybe Leachman doesn't know anything about *anything!*

Some years back, Rod Serling presented a classic television drama. It dealt with the life and dreams of an ulcer-ridden New York advertising executive who fled from his insurmountable business pressures by entering "the twilight zone"—a Currier and Ives-type town named Willoughby. "Willoughby" exists in real life, some forty-five miles north of Atlanta, Georgia.

About nine thousand people reside in Cartersville, perhaps somewhat more than in 1947, when Lamar Leachman was thirteen years old. In 1947 Cartersville townfolk strolled in their Sunday best along clean sidewalks, or rested on freshly painted benches in a small park next to the train station, or glanced up at a big clock above the city hall portico, or gossiped near the town square fountain, or went to the white-columned First Methodist Church or, if not of that denomination, to the First Baptist Church to pray for salvation and Harry S Truman.

Walton Leachman was not a religious man. He didn't have that much time for the Lord. Not with bringing up a family through the Depression and working long hours in Leachman's Garage for his brother Carl. But each Sunday he'd go to the First Baptist Church as a concession to his wife. Eula Leachman took her God very seriously. When Reverend Atkinson spoke before the congregation, breathing fire into his sermons to smoke out the sinners in his midst, Eula Leachman would nod her head and glance at Walton and her four children, as if to say, "Don't you feel better now?"

Thirteen-year-old Lamar felt better when he could run and jump on some field with his friends. Most of all, in a town where baseball was the most popular game, Lamar felt *best* when he could frolic with a football under his arm, or roll on the grass with someone to get the ball away, or simply toss it around until it was time to go home for supper. For some reason it was football that "made him feel better now."

105

The first cuts came on June 5. DeFlavio was not one of them. Parilli and his assistant coaches gathered in their room after the morning scrimmage and then called the players in to tell them the bad news. Earl Christy, former New York Jet kick-return specialist, was one of them. It wasn't easy for him to say goodbye. He hung around for a while, watched afternoon practice, kibitzed with his former Jet teammates, and walked to his car with Randy Beverly. Then, bald-headed Earl Christy sadly left the grounds.

The survivors slammed their shoulders into blocking dummies, strained against blocking sleds, gasped under a broiling sun while they ran forty-yard sprints, grunted during pushups and knee-bends. From every direction footballs spun into the air and receivers chased after them and defenders screamed, "BINGO! BINGO! BINGO!" meaning an interception was unfolding in the pattern.

It was a time for sweat. The hibernation period for veterans such as Voss, Philbin, Elliott and Lens was over. The fat had to come off. After every practice, morning and afternoon, Leachman would run his crew at half-speed across the length of the field, back and forth, until they covered their six hundred yards. Lens was remarkable. Although he moved like a wounded bear, he nevertheless managed to stay within a few yards of the pack, clearing his esophagus with a "hnn . . . hnn . . . hnn . . ." as he struggled valiantly to keep his legs moving. For him, it was unthinkable to quit. He was running for his life. It meant that much to him. Then, as he neared the end of his run, always beaten by the others but never defeated, Lens would throw his shoulders back, snort "hnnnn . . . hnnnn . . . hnnnn" in mating call response to Leachman's foghorn "gitta-gitta-gitta" and burst onto the concrete path that led to the locker room, shaking his head as if he had been slugged by an invisible punch.

In the first week, a pervasive tension gripped the locker room. The majority of players stayed mostly to themselves, dressed quickly and departed as silently as they had arrived. Almost every rookie worried about his performance, or fretted about his mistakes. But there were a few who turned their thoughts elsewhere. Word got around that a nearby bar held intriguing possibilities. Those who followed up on the rumor were greeted by a blast of concussive rock music—fanning images of wild freak scenes with gorgeous sex-starved nymphomaniacs. Within a day or two even the most naive knew better. Disappointing contacts with a sad collection of teenage witches and unscrubbed uglies sent them reeling into the night to hunt for other spots.

The most popular was Vanderbilt's Wharf, a pleasant, dimly lit establishment that perched on the edge of a small dock facing Great South Bay. Getting there required a five-minute ride, but once inside, the players generally stayed until close to curfew. A juke box spun Top 40 tunes, smiling bartenders served up large pitchers of cold beer for only two dollars a round, and smooth-skinned, long-legged college girls laughed and mixed easily with the males. Romances kindled, blossomed and died there almost every evening.

The coaches chose more sedate places to throw off their tensions. Bronco Charlie's was a wood-paneled restaurant bar that provided a restful watering hole for Parilli and his staff. Generally, their conversations ranged from small talk about the day's practice to tall tales of past adventures. Parilli, in particular, told many Bear Bryant stories, waxing nostalgic for long stretches about Bear's legendary coaching exploits at the University of Kentucky. Another regular hangout was the Red Snapper Inn, a rather expensive seafood restaurant not far from Vanderbilt's Wharf. When his coaches had a satisfying day on the practice field, Parilli shepherded them to the Red Snapper and bought everyone rounds of drinks. It was, for the coaches, a time for congeniality and warm friendship, a time for kinships to be formed in wordless toasts to faith and courage. For them, duty followed a stoic, inviolate course; their paean to dogma and tradition remained absolute. On the practice field, the reality of speed and muscle ruled above holy writ, above the hopes and fears of every coach and player.

All morning, beneath a cloudless sky, red-jacketed quarterbacks fired footballs at white-jerseyed receivers. Don Gault ran a series, then Tom Sherman and Gary Danielson; pumping balls long and short to speeding pass catchers. In the defensive back-field, cornerbacks and safeties bounced up and down on their toes, arms outstretched, heads stuck forward, waiting for offensive patterns to develop. Soon, running backs, flankers and ends would pour into their territory. In an instant, a slip or a missed assignment or a dropped interception could bring a sudden halt to a promising career.

So it was that on this breezy, beautiful morning at La Salle, a celebration of exalted competition caused defensive backfield coach George Boutselis to march forward with his face turned backward.

He arrived at camp like a young god, with an easy smile, smoldering eyes, and a shock of prematurely gray wavy hair. During his first embattled days in camp, Boutselis rigidly upheld a Platonian principle that warriors should be carefully educated but not allowed to have minds and lives of their own. His main concern was not the rights or the happiness of individuals but the stability of the majority. Inexorably, it led him to a bitter confrontation with John Carlos and Manny Brown.

In 1968 track stars John Carlos and Tommie Smith stood on an Olympic victory stand and thrust black-gloved fists into the Mexico City sky. Their symbolic act of black protest caused thousands of tourists in the stands to shake their own fists and hurl abusive threats at the American sprinters. One Olympic official called them "jungle bunnies." But six years later, with the controversy still trailing his footsteps, haunting his long-distance run for dignity, Carlos could somehow maintain, "We reached millions of black people and we didn't get anybody shot. We can still be proud of what we did."

Standing quietly now, with his black fists riding on top of his football pants, Carlos waited for Tom Sherman to call signals. It was a passing drill. On this play he'd be going out for a long one. It was his third day in camp, a gloomy three days of running a lot and talking very little to anyone. Concentrating almost entirely on his assignments, absorbing a few pass-catching tips from George Sauer, paying strict attention to his playbook during classroom instruction, Carlos wanted this pro camp, his third in four years, to be a complete success. He wished to culminate his life-time search for dignity here and now at La Salle. And he knew that part of the price he had to pay was to shrink from contro-versy, keep cool, with his eyes wide open and his private thoughts kept to himself. It would be hard, but he knew he could do it. At the age of twenty-nine, he could no longer afford to think other-wise.

A short distance from Carlos, Manny Brown of Hofstra min-gled with his teammates in the defensive backfield unit. Every so often he'd cup his hands to his mouth and yell, "I'm gonna beat you, Carlos. I can beat your ass and your hands to the ball, my man."

Carlos grinned. There was something about the nervy kid that relaxed him for the first time in days. The funny-looking dude kept bobbing up and down like a cork on reed-thin legs, merry-eyed and full of funky humor in a sea of vapid sanctimony. Yeah, Manny Brown was a brother, all right. Carlos could accept the kid's good-natured challenge without feeling guarded or uptight about it. Shit, he thought, he'd give Brown a run for his money, and he'd leave his skinny legs in the dust, for sure.

"First unit in," barked George Boutselis. Without hesitation, Brown jumped forward, clearly aware he was in the second unit, but not caring because he wanted a go at Carlos.

"Watch my speed, old man. I'm gonna whup you good."

Brown palmed the former track star with a loud slapping sound, then hustled back to his cornerback position. Boutselis glowered at his second-stringer. Sonofabitch, he muttered under his breath, the kid crashed the first unit without any regard for procedure. Well, he'd straighten the little wise-ass out. But not now, not in front of the others.

The play was a standard fly pattern, straight out toward the bay. Sherman took seven mincing steps backward, saw Carlos snake down the sideline, and let a long spiral go. The ball disap-peared in a mass of arms and legs, then bounched along the grass to a clump of bushes.

"Tie, my man! I win!" chortled Manny Brown between rapid gulps for air.

"I was just playin' with you, rook," exploded Carlos in a spasm of mirth. "But stick around. I'm gettin' used to your shit!" It was the first time Carlos had laughed out loud since he showed up at camp.

During lunch, Manny Brown of Hofstra University talked slowly and eloquently with a local writer about his football dreams. He was going to make it big, become a star like O. J. and Mercury Morris and John Brockington. Only he was going to do it in the defensive backfield, where he'd starred for two years under head coach Howdy Myers. When he came up from Statesboro, Georgia, he said, he couldn't talk right, could hardly be understood. So he made up his mind to get an education. At Hofstra he majored in management and communications, and wound up in the top third of his graduating class. But football was his life, his reason for being. Skinny legs and all, he pushed himself to make the all-ECAC Team of the Week five times during his college career. And one day, he said solemnly, he was going to make a lot of money in the pros, and give half of it away to his family and to all the black kids who would look up to him for inspiration. When he said that, Manny Brown seemed far removed from all the jive talk he had used on the playing field.

In the locker room, after practice, Boutselis heatedly told Brown he didn't appreciate the way he was carrying on in the field, jumping assignments and shooting his mouth off so much. Brown looked absolutely flabbergasted. For a minute or two a thick silence separated them. It triggered an involuntary clearing of the room. Eventually, only Stew Barber remained on the scene, a melancholy witness to Manny Brown's impending decline and fall from grace. But like most civilized men, Brown didn't give up without a struggle. He lashed back at Boutselis, protested vehemently that he was being harassed for no logical reason, that he was as good as any cornerback in camp, and that Boutselis should not judge him by his personality, only by his performance on the field. Then the rage within Brown simmered and died. He sank down on a stool and looked helplessly up at Boutselis.

"Coach, I want you to level with me. Do you think I have a chance to stick?"

Boutselis pulled at the sleeve of his windbreaker. "I think you're going to be cut," he said. Then he walked out of the room. Brown lowered his head, staring sightlessly into a bottomless well. A few moments later, Barber stirred from his seat and approached the dejected player. He felt he had to say something, provide some kind of explanation on behalf of his fellow coach.

"Manny," he said, "if you believed in yourself, you never would've asked the question."

That night, at bed check, Coach Tom Moore looked into Brown's room. His bed was empty, his clothing removed from the locker. Only a faded newspaper clipping was left behind. It lay on the rookie's bed, like a suicide note. Moore picked it up. Later, in his own room, he read about a relatively unimportant college football game between two small eastern schools:

Manny Brown, Hofstra defensive back, who electrified the crowd with an interception return for a touchdown. . . .

The next morning at breakfast, John Carlos received word of Manny Brown's sudden departure from camp. Sipping his tea, saying very little to his table companions, he thought of the previous day's practice and remembered Manny's palm-slapping, jive-talking ways; so cool and natural it was, and now Manny was gone because The Man didn't dig it. Yeah, the little sucker was so cool, and now he was gone.

He felt a tightening of the knot, as though he were in Mexico City with Tommie Smith all over again. He sat brooding over tea, adrift on a bobbing raft in a noisy New York Stars dining room that throbbed with excitement.

He remembered the 1970 Philadelphia Eagle camp, and the smell of dew-wet mornings, the pungent kitchen smells of hot buns, bacon and buttery eggs; and, yes, the smell of The Man, odorous and heavy, bearing down on him oppressively. He was told to stand up and sing his school song. What kind of shit was that? he wondered then, as he wondered now. He had passed through East Texas State and San Jose State and Seamanship Institute to lay down some glory for his people on cinder track, not to learn some dumb-ass school songs. He didn't have any time to learn them, anyway. So he stood up tall and sang out a chorus of "Jingle Bells" until they told him to shut up and sit down.

Boutselis moved Carlos into the kickoff-return unit one morning. The sun was out and a light breeze wafted through the wide plain.

"C'mon, you guys. Stop dawdling around. Let's get back here for the kickoff," Boutselis shouted to Carlos and a couple of others in the unit. The defensive backs were tossing a ball around to one another at the time, waiting for the offensive unit to make some last-minute adjustments.

"C'mon, damn it, let's go!"

"Hey," Carlos cried out to his teammates, "listen to the coach. Let's cut out all the chickenshit."

Boutselis wheeled around, livid. "What did you say, Carlos?"

"Hey, Coach, I wasn't talking to you . . . "

"I heard you. You called me *chickenshit!*"

"Coach, you got it all wrong. I was just talking to my man here . . ." Carlos pointed in the general direction of safeties Lou Angelo, Steve Dennis and Randy Beverly. "I wasn't saying anything about you being chickenshit. I'm just doing my job."

"That's your opinion."

"Oh, man . . . "

In another minute an advancing forward wall came thundering down the field, converging in one solid mass of humanity as a football dropped from the sky. John Carlos stuck it under his ribs and took off like a shot. He never stopped until he got past the goal line. Then he spiked the ball with all his might.

Morning drill. Lamar Leachman, face twisted, doughlike, into puffy lava, rattled off a string of orders so rapidly he sounded like a tobacco auctioneer gone mad.

"C'mon, c'mon, c'mon, move it, move it, move it! Engage, goddamn it, penetrate! Stick it to 'em, y'all! Aw-raht, now, Gitta-gitta-gitta, c'mon, c'mon, c'mon . . . "

Gerry Philbin came out of the defensive huddle, breathing heavily next to his line partner, John Elliott.

"That sonofabitch'll kill us yet," he croaked, sweat pouring from almost every gland.

"He sure is a rough cob," agreed the Texan.

A moment later they pushed their weight against the opposing line. Philbin missed a swipe at running back Bob Gladieux, who busted through the left side.

"You gotta watch that, Philburn!" fumed Leachman as the defensive huddle formed again. "You gotta move to the outside faster'n that or the man's gonna beat you every time. Aw-raht, c'mon, c'mon, c'mon . . . "

At the end of the drill, Philbin yanked off his helmet and walked over to Leachman. "Coach, I've been hearing you loud and clear all morning. Now, just to set the record straight, the name is Phil-*bin,* not Phil-*burn!* If you don't like to call me Phil-bin, my first name is Gerry. And if that doesn't suit you, call me by my number. But from now on, don't call me Phil-*burn!"*

Leachman seemed genuinely astonished by the outburst. For a second, his eyes hardened, then he broke off a watery grin.

"Shit, Gerry, you just ain't used to my Jawja accent, tha's all."

"Well, practice a little so you can get it right," Philbin said unsmilingly before walking off the field.

Morning drill. The passes stuck to John Carlos; short bullets that he caught cutting across the field, and one long over-the-shoulder catch in full stride past his defender—reading admiration in the man's eyes as he gleefully swept by. He thought he had turned it around, after a week of cement-fingered failure.

Coming off the field, he decided to call his girl friend in Los Angeles. He'd tell her he expected to be in camp awhile longer, that he was doing well. The thought pleased him, because he'd had enough problems in his lifetime. He had navigated through garbage-strewn streets in Harlem as a youth. His mind still ached with the memory of Mexico City and, later, the barbed-wire resistance of NFL and Canadian League training camps. He had fled from the straight world to enter an underworld of chain-locked apartments in New York and Los Angeles, only to come out again to face more humiliation. He desperately wanted to forget his final pro track race at Madison Square Garden, where he tossed away a chance for a record in the 300-yard run because he thought he wasn't being paid enough. And, just a week ago, he tried to erase the image of a Los Angeles divorce court, where a honky judge refused to try his case, admitting to prejudice because of the Mexico City incident. Yeah, he had his problems, all right. But things were beginning to look up.

Before lunch, Parilli called him into the coaches' room. A short time later, John Carlos, wearing green shades and bell-bottom slacks with nailhead designs on the outside seams, sat on the front steps of St. Joseph's Hall with Ray Parson. The big tight end felt there was something going on inside the brother's head, so he remained mute, figuring it would come out when Carlos was ready to speak his piece. Finally, it did.

"Coach just cut me."

Parson blinked his eyes, then looked straight ahead. After a while he got up.

"You be hangin' around here today?"

"No. As soon as I pick up The Man's bread, I'll be heading for LA."

"Where can I reach you," said Parson, "in case I want to check you out?"

Carlos dug into an old wallet containing pictures of smiling children. He removed a card. There was an address: Athletic Department, Pepperdine University, Malibu, California. There was also an inscription:

JOHN CARLOS
New York
"Los" is my name
track is my game

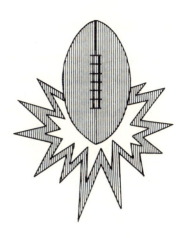

TEN

June pushed forward with little ticking sounds of a football training camp on Long Island waking up and going to sleep. With each passing day, the sound of barking dogs, of muffled voices whispering in alien rooms, of purring motors flying into a singing wind, of trees rustling in the dead of night, of crickets and birds at dawn, of water hissing from a dozen shower heads, of chalk squeaking across blackboard, of bandages ripping, of crunching plastic on the playing field, of football players and coaches shouting, laughing and groaning in their limited hours of youthful passion: all the sounds of pulsating life rushed up to join a universal hum of life.

For the borderline players, time was measured in joyless hours and minutes of excruciating punishment. Under the hot sun, ankles wobbled and tongues thickened. The coaches never seemed to tire of barking out commands, pushing rookies and veterans alike to the ultimate, without once letting up their pressure. Through this process the coaches made their evaluations. The weak were separated from the strong, and pro football careers went on or ended. In this manner, Homer Jones saw his football odyssey of good and bad times come to an end at La Salle. He was out of shape, bloated to a cartoon facsimile of the athlete he used to be. The salty gray in his hair turned his face old, and the kick in his legs had vanished. Now he would be going home to Pittsburg, Texas, perhaps to sit on a riverbank once in a while, pole stuck over the water, waiting for the catfish to bite and for dreams of far-off Sundays at Yankee Stadium to tell him his days had been more good than bad.

A week after Jones's departure, the Stars held their first intra-squad scrimmage: three sections of offensive plays, twenty plays per unit. Don Gault was handed the honor of quarterbacking the initial series. His five years of sitting on NFL benches had trained him well for this moment. He caught his receivers with sizzling bullets and short lobs, and got off one bomb to Terry Swarn in the end zone, some fifty yards from the line of scrimmage. Swarn folded his arms around the ball, then dropped it. Parilli's eyebrows knotted.

Next up was Tom Sherman. Unlike Gault, who liked to throw from the pocket, Sherman rolled out, steaming left and right to find an open man.

On one play, he threw deep into a crowd. In the scramble, Beverly came away with an interception. Rich Pelletier, who had performed for Bob Keating's Colonials the year before as a safety, wide receiver and team punter, was cracked hard by an offensive lineman. Pelletier fell back, spread-eagled and unconscious, to the ground. Trainer Lew Cohen rushed over to revive him with smelling salts.

"Are you okay?" Cohen asked. Pelletier wagged his head like a punch-drunk fighter.

"Who do you play for?"

"Uh . . . uh . . . wait . . . I'll get it in a minute."

Cohen lifted the stunned player to his feet and slowly walked him back to the training room. The scrimmage continued on a down note after that, although young Danielson showed everyone he had the best stance and strongest arm of the contending quarterbacks.

After the last series, Parilli called the team together at mid-field. In a packed circle, the exhausted players removed their helmets to listen to his words.

"You're all working hard out there," he said, "and you're going to get better. We'll have a good team out there on July 11, the day all of us are pointing to. So we're going to show a lot of dedication from now on. Oh yes, one last thing. As you know, the johns in the dormitory aren't working too well, but I understand the sinks have been fixed. That's about it. See you tomorrow."

Pelletier had suffered a mild concussion. He was rested for a few days, then rejoined the club. But his lethal toe, which had once caused mouths to open because of the distance and height he normally put into a ball, suddenly went awry. Puny squibblers and sinking line drives became an embarrassment to him and the team. Parilli decided to bring another punter to camp. Lamar Leachman thought of someone, a dependable if not spectacular punter from the University of South Carolina—where Leachman had served as defensive coordinator before joining the Stars. Robbie Reynolds was a red-headed, fuzzy-cheeked youngster with a handsomely shy smile. He possessed a forty-one-yard punting average at the school. His first punt in the Empire State was a beauty. Rich Pelletier watched it rise majestically in the air, counted off a five-second hang time, and knew he would be cut from the roster within a matter of days. He was.

As June waned, a period of momentary pause embraced the camp. At night, under a splendorous moon, Vanderbilt's Wharf pulsed with the sweet-sad songs of The Carpenters and Carole King, the raunchy ballads of Tony Bennett and Ray Charles, and the western blues of Charlie Pride and Lynn Anderson. At the Wharf, everything seemed good and warm and new. Nothing was old. Life was a vast experiment, full of undiscovered formulas, charged with ideas and dreams yet to be born. In groups of twos and threes and fours, the players sat languidly at their tables, vibrating with the music, exchanging stories of cheap loves and great romances, believing everything, doubting nothing. And in

117

the crowded, noisy hubbub, there also existed an enormous silence, where hope and kind thoughts met, and every human being had measurable worth.

From their place by the window, George Sauer and Gary
Danielson saw Gerry Philbin, in white ducks and captain's hat,
on the deck of his 25-foot Donzi cabin cruiser. A group of players
gathered around him.

"Hey," said Danielson, "there's Lou Angelo and Lens . . . and
there's Elliott. I guess they're going to Fire Island."

Sauer took another swig of beer from his frosty glass, brushed
foam from his mustache, and stared at the cruiser. Slowly, silently, it left the dock. Moments later it was lost in the velvet
darkness of Great South Bay.

"I wish I owned a boat like that," said Danielson.

"They're very expensive," said Sauer, now looking toward the
bar, about to get up to order another pitcher of beer. Danielson grinned. "Right now I couldn't manage a down payment on
the motor."

"Everything is subject to change. That's axiomatic. And, I
might add, also very true."

"Way to go, George, but I figure my chances of breaking into
the lineup are pretty thin."

"Oh, maybe not. Don and Tommy are ahead of you in experience, but that doesn't mean Babe has made up his mind."

"I guess you're right," said Danielson, as if Sauer had given
him a gift. "Anyway, things will be a lot better when Kristy gets
here. Boy, that'll sure take a load off."

"I imagine it would," said Sauer with a far-off expression in
his eyes. He had never met Danielson's wife, but he had seen
snapshots of her. Beautiful girl. Maybe as pretty as Pam, whom
he hadn't seen for nearly a month. He wondered about her, where
she was at the moment, what city she might be staying in, or
what city she was flying to, or when he'd see her next. Their lives
had been regulated by flight schedules ever since they got
married. Not that he was paranoid about it. He enjoyed, to a

large degree, the random freedom of his married life. There were his books—Dickens, Blake, Camus, Sartre, Fielding, Spinoza—hundreds of books that he had read, fulfilled by their company and bolstered by their promise of unfettered wisdom. He could wait, in solitude, until hours girded the days and became weeks, without an awareness of time or people. He could do that, gladly, exultantly, and not miss a moment of Pam's absence. But now he missed her, needed her, and wished at that instant she would walk through the door with her cheery smile.

"How about another beer?" he suddenly said to Gary Danielson.

In the early mist before breakfast, Bob "Harpo" Gladieux came out on the practice field and threw a rubber ball into the air, like an outfielder flipping an easy putout to his second baseman. Mr. Brown, his shaggy pomeranian-corgi-pekingese mutt, scampered after it. Yelping over the grass, more tail than body, Mr. Brown caught up with the ball, then triumphantly trotted back to his master.

They were inseparable. For five years they had traveled together, man and dog, through the camps of New England, Buffalo, Kansas City and Calgary—five years, and seven cuts by four pro teams. And now Harpo was out in the Long Island air, enjoying the view and thinking about some of the good days he and Mr. Brown had shared in Boston. Harpo thought the highlight of his pro career was when his brother found Mr. Brown in a box. That was in 1969, when he was just a rookie—an eighth-round draft choice of the New England Patriots out of Notre Dame. He had a comfortable pad in the Back Bay section of town, where he raised Mr. Brown, learned how to cook gourmet meals, and went to bed every night feeling it was great to live without a rope around his neck. Maybe that's why he almost never put a leash on Mr. Brown.

Now he was running in wide circles on the La Salle practice field, jumping up and down like Harpo Marx, every fiber of his soul bursting in paroxysms of gleeful merriment. Mr. Brown shot between his legs, then scooted along the grass toward the dormitory. It was almost time to eat. By now they had developed ravenous appetites.

On a quiet Sunday evening, Darrell Bunge called his fiancée from a pay phone on the second floor of St. Joseph's Hall.

Marsha Simon lived in Moorhead, Minnesota, where her father owned a big furniture store. Bunge's home town was Caledonia, some three hundred miles southeast of Moorhead. As undergraduates, they had attended the University of Minnesota, where he starred as an all-Big Ten football lineman and she majored in education. They met there, fell in love, and planned to get married. But Marsha was Jewish, with an orthodox mother who could never imagine her daughter running off with a football player—and a *goy*, no less!

Darrel's father, Reinhard Bunge, was a Houston County road contractor and soil conservationist. Mr. Bunge couldn't quite understand why Mrs. Simon felt as she did. As far as he and the missus were concerned, if the kids loved each other, then God would love them, too.

In time, Mrs. Simon softened, and when Darrel and Marsha became engaged, she breathed a big sigh of relief, as though she had been blind for a long time and an operation had restored her sight. She told Darrel he could pick out anything he wanted in her husband's store as a wedding present. Marsha's almond eyes filled with tears of happiness.

Now they were separated, longing to be with each other, counting their days apart as loving stepping stones to the moment they would be married, in a Unity ceremony. They were talking to each other, tense, tingling with excitement, but sounding almost matter-of-fact on the phone. There was so much to say, but few words came out. Things were going well, Darryl said. Tom Chandler had looked good in practice, and so had Matt Herkenhoff, and Tom Moore was real enthusiastic about coaching in the pros. The WFL wasn't going to keep these Minnesota boys down, that's for sure. Ha ha. How was her mother? Well, he was glad to hear that. And how were her studies coming along? Uh-huh,

great, great. Well, his three minutes were up. Time to say goodbye. Take care. Love ya.

Darrel Bunge walked down the hall in his beach sandals and
cut-off jeans and heard music playing from behind the closed
doors. Inside, players were reading, or writing letters, or shooting
the bull. He had his own plans. He'd look in on Tom and Matt.
Maybe, if they could get Kreg Kapitan to join in, they'd sing in
four-part harmony for an hour or so. He thought of a song they
had never tried before, a Carpenters tune called "For All We
Know." Maybe they could do that one at his wedding. Well, they
had plenty of time to learn. It would be a long season.

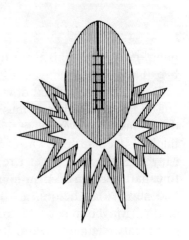

ELEVEN

A new dawning brought an end to the pause. In a deep-throated roar of movement, players thundered across the practice field as if they had come out of the ground, smashing into each other in a release of raw power.

At one morning practice, Lamar Leachman, all excoriation and anger, whipped his defensive unit with galvanized savagery, goading them into each assignment as though it were a pivotal moment of a championship game. John Elliott viewed Leachman's coaching tactics with casual distaste, but Gerry Philbin's attitude bordered on downright revulsion. In earlier times, Philbin had led an almost monkish existence as a Jet in Weeb Ewbank's summer camps. Through the dog days of July and August, he rounded into shape with limited prodding from his defensive line coach, who deferred to his all-pro status. But now things were entirely different. At every turn, Leachman seemed to be scant inches away from his helmet, hollering for him to show more hustle, badgering him about alleged miscues, taunting him with deprecating asides—turning each practice session into a painful crucible. At times Philbin felt like having it out with Leachman right on the field, but with Herculean will power he managed to keep his temper in check. Elliott, though, found other ways to cope with Leachman's provocative nature.

The La Salle Academy stabled a number of fine riding horses. Occasionally they were exercised on the spacious grounds alongside the playing field. On this particular morning, Elliott gazed upon a beautiful chestnut being led down toward Great South Bay, and he was suddenly struck with a brilliant idea. He told it to Philbin. They fell into each other's arms, splitting the air with loud guffaws. Immediately, like prisoners passing along the word of an impending escape, Philbin and Elliott relayed the idea to Lloyd Voss, Bill DeFlavio, Greg Lens, Jerry Ellison and Larry Estes. Everyone was in on the secret, and all were in favor of the plan.

That afternoon, with the sun burning into his neck, Leachman removed his windbreaker, containing a bag of his favorite chewing tobacco, and placed it on the sideline grass. Later, during a break in the action, he held a short conference with Boutselis on defensive strategy.

"We're doing a lousy job," he grumbled. "These guys of mine are gonna do better or they're not gonna play for me."

Stomping back to his unit, he swept up his windbreaker and removed the bag of tobacco. Into his mouth went a juicy pinch.

"Awraht, gitta-gitta-gitta . . . what are you guys waitin' on? Let's get movin' out there!" he chanted while working the wad around in his jaw. But this time nobody jumped. The linemen moved their arms and legs in slow motion until Leachman, cold and choking, spat the wad out.

"This goddamn tobacco tastes like shit!" he gagged.

"That's what it is, Lamar," said Elliott. A moment later Philbin wriggled out of his helmet. Leachman looked into the face of a laughing hyena. And down by the edge of Great South Bay, a horse whinnied.

On Saturday, June 22, at 2:30 P.M., the New York Stars and the Philadelphia Bell football squads played a scrimmage game before approximately one thousand fans at nearby Central Islip

High School. For Babe Parilli it was like launching a ship, not knowing whether his team—or, for that matter, the WFL itself—would stay on top of the water. His coaches and players had worked hard for three weeks. He had looked at and evaluated 107 players, and was down to seventy-three. Still, there was just so much he could learn from the inside. He'd have to go outside to tell what his club was really made of, what they could or couldn't do against real competition. If his sweeps and trap plays and power plays would work, if his quarterbacks were leaders, if his defense could operate against the pass and run, if there were surprises, good and bad—that would all be revealed in the course of the game.

He was pleased with the progress of some, discouraged with others. Running back Dave Richards and offensive guard Larry Butler were pleasant surprises, but quarterback Don Gault had him worried, and a decision had to be made between kickers Pete Rajecki and Moses Lajterman. The surface was hardly scratched, but the Bell scrimmage would give Parilli some answers.

Dave Richards was a find. His face played a brooding dark symphony, full of subtle progressions and ominous overtones, and his sinewy-black, compact body contained a storage house of pure, unadulterated energy. He had attended Miami of Ohio University, where he had built a 40.8-yard receiving average and a sixteen-touchdown record into an all-conference rating. In 1973 Richards signed on as a free agent with the Cleveland Browns but was cut in summer camp. One day he wrote Parilli a letter, boasting that he could run the ball as well as Leroy Kelly. Parilli almost tossed the letter into a wastebasket—the mere idea of it sounded so hilarious—but then decided to sign Richards and see what he could do. In three weeks the Cleveland Brown reject became the best New York Star running back in camp.

Larry Butler had walked into camp an unheralded, unusually quiet youngster from Appalachian State. Sunflower-topped and apple-cheeked, Butler went to work in the offensive line almost anonymously, yet nobody struggled harder or seemed more dedicated or complained less than he. One day a reporter asked him if he thought he could make the team, and he said only God could answer that question. Then he ran back to his unit, pulled his helmet tight over his bull-like neck and took out two linemen on an inside trap play. In three weeks Parilli hardly spoke a word to him but could tell that Larry Butler was one heckuva football player.

Don Gault was undoubtedly the smartest quarterback in camp, but more phlegmatic than either Tom Sherman or Gary Danielson. Although he carried off his assignments with precision, there was a touch of the matador in Gault: slow, mincing, deliberate, but quick when thunder approached. Well, Parilli thought, football was no bullfight. Gault would have to move a lot better than he had shown during his three weeks in camp, or Sherman would be his starting quarterback.

Parilli liked Pete Rajecki, a German-born, Georgia-educated kicker who spoke with a peculiar accent, a blend of Bavarian and hillbilly-American. Stubby-short, straw-blond, with small green-blue eyes and the look of impending disaster in his face, Rajecki came to the United States in 1967 as an orphan. "My parents were killed in a way nobody ever wanted to talk about," he'd whisper when asked. In this country, he found a new way of life—football. At the University of Georgia he was known as the "Bootin' Teuton" and was voted Georgia's Outstanding Player in 1969. Rajecki joined the Pittsburgh Steeler camp in 1972 as a born-again Christian, carrying a Bible with him and seeing visions of earthly glory in the NFL. He was beaten out during the exhibition season by Roy Gerela, who later became an all-pro. Returning to his adopted parents' home in Marietta, Georgia, Rajecki sold insurance, some real estate, studied the Bible and prayed for a call. He got it from Parilli, who remembered him from the Steeler camp and thought he could do a job for the Stars. So far, Rajecki had—displaying long-range ability if not altogether satisfying consistency.

Moses Lajterman had shown very little of anything. Parilli was impressed by the youth's willingness on the field, his puppy-dog attention to everything asked of him, even his brief flashes of kicking power. There *was* something about the way the ball lifted off the ground once Lajterman hit it right. It would go up

125

like a rocket, and leave a sonic boom behind as it crossed high above the goalpost. Still, Lajterman was off more than he was on. After three weeks, Parilli all but gave up on the good-looking kid with the mau-mau hair which sprung out like a ball of black tumbleweed every time he removed his helmet. In order to make a final decision, Parilli arranged to hold a toe-to-toe kicking contest at the end of the Philadelphia scrimmage. Rajecki would take six shots at the ball, then Lajterman would follow with six more, with the better man kept aboard as field goal specialist for the New York Stars. In his mind, if not in his heart, Parilli wrote off Lajterman.

The curious event starts in eighty-two-degree heat with Philadelphia marching to the mouth of New York's goal line in its first series of fifteen plays. Parilli shuttles in player after player, frowning, pacing, saying little. The Stars take over, unscored on but slightly bloodied, then shock Philadelphia through the air on their fifth play from scrimmage, a perfectly thrown pass from Don Gault to Dave Richards, covering fifty-two yards. Richards runs it in for the first Star touchdown ever, and Gault lets out a whoop, rushes up to his receiver and grabs him in a bear hug. But lightning suddenly deserts Gault. Philadelphia scales the outer wall, traps him in the backfield, chases him into throwing errors, limits him to harmless screen passes that go nowhere. His glorious scoring thrust, so beautiful to watch only minutes before, has been tarnished by the howling winds of change.

In its grasp, Tom Sherman reels under the impact. He is less than effective, operates on the edge of grievous fault, falling on two of his own fumbles, rushing into the arms of grinning tackles, passing often yet completing a pathetic few for short yardage. One is to George Sauer, whose only catch of the day nets him six yards and a slight hematoma of the left ankle.

The Bell are on offense, and the Star defense holds. Rookie linebacker Art Reynolds shows Parilli he can do the job. Philbin at end and Elliott at tackle don't let down for a moment, Lamar Leachman spits in the sideline dirt, wondering why in hell they can't do that in camp, and Greg Lens, Lloyd Voss, Jerry Ellison and Larry Estes do their part, while Bill DeFlavio brings the crowd up with two unassisted tackles of Bell quarterback Mike Yancheff. It's close to five o'clock; the players are tired, sweating through the grime.

A fresh Star quarterback trots in for the last series. Gary Danielson throws an interception to Bell cornerback Ron Mabra, who takes it in for a score. Danielson bounces back with an eighteen-yarder to little Bob Hermanni, then hits big Ray Parson for fourteen more yards. Pete Rajecki places his kicking tee down and boots a thirty-seven-yard field goal. New York wins the scrimmage.

Dragging their tired bodies off the field, the players were delayed by autograph collectors. They smiled drearily, chatted mindlessly, then moved on, feeling the need to remove heavy equipment from their aching limbs. As the field emptied, the Pete Rajecki-Moses Lajterman post-scrimmage kicking duel began. Rajecki lifted five out of six balls over the crossbar. Lajterman connected only twice, the other four trailing off like dying quails in a crossfire. It was no contest. Lajterman, in defeat, lowered his head and delivered one final kick at the ground, spraying dust off to the sideline. Rajecki noticed it all from the corner of his eye.

Lajterman was cut the next week, as were Don Abbey, Lynn Crawn, Frank Smith, Mark Kaczmareck, Rod Plummer, Gordon Taylor, Frank Brohm, Pete Bush, Dave Laputka, Gene Schaefer and Judge Mattocks; sixty of the original 107 New York Stars remained.

On June 29 two chartered buses departed from La Salle, carting off the players for a last pre-season scrimmage against the Bell at Glassboro State College in New Jersey. Seven years before, almost to the day, Lyndon Baines Johnson and Aleksei N. Kosygin had met at Glassboro to confer on a Middle East crisis, the war in Vietnam and the danger of an atomic Armageddon. When their historic meeting ended, the globe still shivered in an atomic Ice Age. Now, on a hazy Saturday morning in Oakdale, Long Island—with President Johnson seventeen months dead and President Richard Milhous Nixon on his way to Moscow to confer with Premier Kosygin on the same basic international problems—Star buses drove out onto the narrow pathway leading to Montauk Highway. Isolated from international intrigue, like drifting twigs in a stream, the players rode through sleepy towns of Suffolk and Nassau counties, past Deer Park and Farmingdale, cutting over from Route 27 West to the Long Island Expressway, past Glen Cove, Roslyn and Great Neck, and then to the city line, where the first signs of high-rise apartments appeared under a late-morning sky. Bypassing Manhattan, crossing the Verrazano Bridge from Brooklyn, rumbling into New Jersey, the buses edged closer to Glassboro.

The players sat stiff-legged, finding surreptitious comfort in socio-ethnic seating arrangements. By choice, a majority of the blacks moved to rear seats while the whites found positions up front. As the miles lengthened, some players chatted nervously; others tried to sleep or stared blankly out of their windows. Thrown together in the promise of adventure, each of them, coaches and players, heard the ticking of a doomsday clock over the constant din of their mechanical bug: time and distance reduced to an infinite second in their improbable lives.

ONE O'CLOCK. Pete Rajecki looks up at the student center bulletin board in Glassboro College:

"Read and subscribe to New Solidarity . . . National Caucus of Labor Committees . . . News Bulletin No. 126 . . . CIA's Methadone Zombies Attack U.S. Labor Party."

Rajecki sits down on a bright red drum chair and turns a page in his Bible to the ninth chapter of John: *Since the world began, there has never been anyone who could open the eyes of someone born blind.* And Rajecki wonders if those sacred words are meant for the CIA or the U.S. Labor Party.

TWO O'CLOCK: Lamar Leachman sits in the Glassboro dining room and tells George Boutselis he thinks his wife can get a job as a school teacher in Long Island. They pay a helluva lot more up here than back in South Carolina, he says. And now that he has bought a house in Sayville for $42,000, every little bit helps.

THREE O'CLOCK. Don Gault, Tom Sherman and Gary Danielson are playing a famous-initials game. It's Sherman's turn to guess the personalities. He's right on baseball's EK (Eddie Kranepool), misses on record shop owner SG (Sam Goody), names Hollywood's ZP (ZaSu Pitts), but throws up his hands on history's XS. Are you putting me on? he asks. Schmuck, laughs Gault, that's Xantippi, Socrates's old lady. You're full of shit, says Sherman. Gault flexes his arm. It hurts in the bone, not in the muscle. It's sore as hell, he says to the other quarterbacks, no longer smiling.

GAME TIME. A smattering of applause greets the Stars, a loud cheer for the Philadelphia Bell. About four thousand people are in the stands.

FOURTH PERIOD: Boutselis is up in the press box, on the phone, spotting plays for Leachman:
"Cover one . . . you should have gone on one so we could get more help . . . four-three red . . . flood R . . . it's third down and very close . . . no . . . they gave 'em a first down . . . they went with the fullback to one side . . . double wing L . . . we're not hitting . . . what's your front? . . . go . . . cover two Lamar . . . slant cover two . . . L formation . . . fifty slant . . . power . . . power . . . POWER!!!"

NIGHT: A United Press International reporter calls in his lead:
"Glassboro . . . The Philadelphia Bell of the World Football League held off a fourth-period rally by the Stars to take a 24–22 scrimmage. The Stars had a chance to win the game, but a forty-two-yard field goal effort by Pete Rajecki with 1:20 left was blocked by Ron Mabra."

Through the long, tired night, players slumped in their seats or, propped up on their elbows, stared as if bewitched upon the dark Jersey countryside. All that had gone on before was done with. On the field they lived in a ghostly world, filled with mad-

129

dened warriors who, like themselves, were trained in the devotion to fanatic idealism and unyielding strength. On the field, as always, they loyally gave their minds, muscles and blood for the cause. It could be no other way, for football was rooted in the marrow of their bones.

And yet, as the chartered buses gunned along the Jersey highway toward New York, a mellow glow, like warm wind blowing through frigid wasteland, eased the sense of battle and restored the players' spirit of self. They no longer were imprisoned by plastic equipment, no longer shackled by benevolent oppressors, but were now free to sit numbly in their seats to ponder or dream, or drink the night away on cold beer and sparkling champagne. For those who chose the latter, the ride was a joyous release from pain, a glorious regurgitation of frustration and disgust. And for Greg Lens it was a time for a funny song or two.

"Here's one you might like," he said to Gerry Philbin, who stood in the aisle with a can of Carling Black Label in his hand.

> "Nothing could be finer
> than to be in her vagina
> in the morning . . ."

Philbin loved it. Lamar Leachman, the ex-University of South Carolina line coach, heard the bellowing from three seats down and rubbed his forehead in a sudden flash of annoyance.

Meanwhile, Don Gault and Tom Sherman, sitting up front, talked about the Glassboro scrimmage and about other games and other times. A mist swam across Gault's eyes when Sherman asked him about the Pittsburgh game in 1970.

"I can remember every play," said Gault, "every friggin' play like it just happened."

"What happened?"

"Okay, Bill Nelsen's legs were in bad shape and Nick Skorich gave me the nod over Mike Phipps, figuring I deserved it off my showing in the 49er game the week before. That's when I came in

130

late in the fourth period and completed two out of three for forty yards, so Skorich let me open against Pittsburgh. Well, it turns out to be a real murderous night, raining like a sonofabitch, with the wind blowing right through our jocks. I mean, it was terrible. Anyway, my first pass is a quick out to Gary Collins, but they roll to his side. I throw the ball away. There's a running play, and then I hit Milt Morin in the chest and he drops it. Okay, we punt, and by the time we take over again, Pittsburgh has us backed up against our goal line. I call for a screen, but they have it covered so I throw another one away. Now I come back with a perfect pass to Collins, about fifteen yards out, and it hits him on the forearm. Shit. So I call for a draw and the quarter ends."

Sherman groaned in sympathy.

"Okay, the second period begins and I'm calling audibles, get a good drive going, and it's third down and seven. I set up a screen again, spot Leroy Kelly . . . but Pittsburgh closes in so I pitch the ball to the bench. Fuck it, right?"

"Right."

"Next series. I run a bootleg, but everything gets jammed up in the rain, and Andy Russell picks up the ball for the Steelers. By now it's raining so hard and the wind is so strong it's almost impossible to concentrate. All right, on the next series my first pass is a fifteen-yard out to Fair Hooker. Guess what?"

"He drops it."

"Give the man a cigar. Now dig this. Next play the whole front line comes in on me. I'm in no condition to find a receiver, so I throw another one away. Only, Chip Glass makes a one-handed catch out of it. We make forty-five yards on the play."

"Whee."

"That's what I thought. I figure if they can catch it, I'm going to throw them all bad. Anyway, we're around the thirty-two-yard line on third down. I pop one to Collins down by the goal. He's wide open. I mean *this* wide, and the ball hits him right in the *gut!* And he drops it. So we go for the field goal and the half ends."

"I guess that did it."

"No, not quite. Skorich let me open the second half after telling me in the locker room that I did the right thing, called the right audibles and so forth. Hold your head up, he says, you'll be all right. So, I go out in the rain again, start the first series with a screen that's covered, and throw my first honest-to-goodness incomplete pass. Do you know what happens after that?"

"Sure. Skorich yanked you."

"Yeah, and to this day I still have a lump in my stomach that won't go away. Shit, Tom, that was my NFL *career!*"

Meanwhile, George Sauer sat in the bus and read the poetry of Blake and chuckled every so often when Lens got off a good verse.

Meanwhile, Pete Rajecki slept with his head against the window, mouth clamped shut, making little squeaking sounds in his sleep.

Meanwhile, John Elliott, Gerry Philbin and Greg Lens were wide awake, singing at the tops of their lungs:

> "He's a fucking wreck
> from Georgia Tech
> and a hell of an engineer . . ."

For over an hour their off-key voices scraped against Leachman's spine, sending him farther down in his seat, intimidating him into choked silence, or goading him, on occasion, into surly retorts.

"Keep it up, you guys. I'll get you out on the practice field Monday."

"Fuck you, Lamar." Philbin laughed. "You college coaches from Alabamey or Caroliney think you can come up to the pros and run us to death, but it ain't going to work *Lay*-mar!"

Philbin had been drinking beer and champagne by the quart. His eyes drained fire, his pulse thickened in the full release of pent-up emotions.

"Philbin," growled Leachman, "if you could play with your mouth, you'd make All-Pro."

"I was an All-Pro, *Lay-mar,* while you were still farting in a Georgia shithouse. Hawr-hawr-hawr . . ."

Meanwhile, the buses carried the football cargo past Newark, into the Lincoln tunnel, and clattered through the empty streets of Manhattan toward the Delancy Street Bridge leading to Queens. It was after three o'clock in the morning, and there were still miles to go.

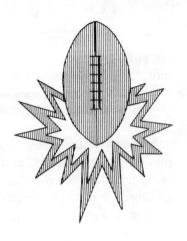

TWELVE

Somewhere, in the long hot summer, between the months of July and September, between Jacksonville and Hawaii, between joy and sorrow, there was once a professional football team named the New York Stars. And when the leaves of September turned to rust, the Stars shivered and fell to the ground.

On July 10, at exactly 10:30 A.M., a chartered Southern Airways DC-9 wheeled out of its roosting position at Kennedy International Airport. At 10:54 a stabilizer problem was corrected, and the jet lifted off the ground, nose pointed toward Jacksonville. On board were the New York Stars and their guests: thirty-seven active players; head coach Babe Parilli; five assistant coaches; team doctor; one team dentist; two trainers; four equipment men (including Tiger Ferraro's son Mike, who had been hired as a full-time assistant before the Islip scrimmage); assistant general manager Dusty Rhodes; a contingent of local reporters, and Bill Crespinel—who didn't get the team photographer job but was happily going along on a *Pro Quarterback*

134

magazine assignment that promised to keep him busy through the entire WFL schedule.

In the storage compartment of the jet, forty-five bags, three trunks, two laundry carts, one dozen freshly dyed footballs, and miscellaneous cartons—over five hundred pounds of equipment—waited to be lifted out on arrival at Jacksonville Airport, then checked and placed into a waiting truck that would speed it all off to the Gator Bowl.

The total cost, human and otherwise, based on Southern Airways rates (approximately $2.80 per ferry mile, 1,720 nautical miles round-trip with deluxe service), came to $9,000.

While breakfast was served, Parilli talked to *New York Times* columnist Dave Anderson.

"How's George Sauer?" Anderson asked as Parilli sliced into his eggs.

"Sauer looks terrific. I really don't see any difference in him, even though he's been out three seasons."

Toward the rear of the jet, George Sauer worked on a *Times* crossword puzzle; Gerry Philbin and John Elliott played poker with Greg Lens, Lloyd Voss and Tom Sherman; others read, or daydreamed, or curled up as best they could and dozed. At 12:35 P.M. the DC-9 rolled to a stop at Jacksonville Airport. Public Relations Director Vince Casey, waiting at the bottom of the ramp and grinning from ear to ear, escorted Parilli, his assistant coaches and Doc Cowan to a waiting limousine. The players piled into two buses. Within minutes a pair of police motorcycles and a patrol car, sirens wailing, sped the New York Stars along the expressway to their lodgings at the Jacksonville Hilton.

From his terraced suite, hours later, while looking out at the St. John's River toward downtown Jacksonville, Parilli saw the sky turn pink, saw boats glide lazily under the Alsop Bridge, saw the far shore, where the Timucua Indians had made their homes and raised crops of beans and corn long before the first French settlers arrived there in 1564—and wondered if his team would be able to beat the Sharks in the Gator Bowl the next evening. Then he went to a party.

It was held in a flower-scented courtyard of the Baymeadows

135

apartment complex, approximately five miles from the Hilton. Hors d'oeuvre were served, a rock band performed, suntanned men and women chatted gaily, and Shark owner Fran Monaco introduced Parilli to the mayor. The New York Star coach even got around to wearing a *GO SHARKS* button on his lapel before the night was over. It was an interlude filled with the aroma of pine and maple and magnolia, of perfumed skin, of good food and liquor—and it contained a few laughs.

Tall and handsome George Plimpton, author of the best-selling *Paper Lion,* in town to join Merle Harmon and Alex Hawkins as guest commentator on the TVS broadcast of the game, patiently waited out a sugar-coated compliment paid him by one of the female guests.

". . . Marvelous, simply marvelous," she went on and on. "I can't begin to tell you how much I've enjoyed meeting you. I've read all your books and I'm not even a sports fan . . . not really."

"The point is, did you enjoy them?"

"Well . . . I'm not sure."

"Why is that?"

"I . . . uh . . . can't quite remember what you *wrote.*"

Game day broke with a few scattered clouds hanging over the Jacksonville skyline. At 10:30 A.M. Lew Fishman of the *Long Island Press* strolled out to the Hilton pool deck with a newspaper under his arm.

"Hey." He signaled to Norm MacLean, a reporter for *Pro Football Weekly* and other sports periodicals. "Have you heard the latest?"

"Latest what?" MacLean looked up from his lounge, showing signs of much-needed sleep. "I just got in. Missed connections. The whole bit. What's up?"

Fishman sat down at an adjoining lounge and began reading an AP story in the *Jacksonville Journal:*

The World Football League was a box office success in its debut last night, with over 200,000 fans in attendance in five cities. Philadelphia announced 55,534 fans paid their way into John F. Kennedy Stadium, tops

*in the league, and only the Florida Blazers played before an announced
crowd of fewer than 30,000.*

*The Birmingham Americans played before 53,231 fans, the Chicago
Fire estimated their attendance at 42,000, the Memphis Southmen announced 30,122, and the Florida Blazers announced 18,625 in Orlando.*

"Unbelievable," said MacLean.

"Yeah, but you know what, Norm? I think those figures may
have been padded."

"Really? I don't know about that. Something tells me the
Whiffle is for real."

"Well, this is only the first test. Let's see what happens next
week, and the week after that. One swallow does not make a
season, as the saying goes."

"It depends on who's swallowing, Lew. Anyway, I'm going in
for a dip."

Ten hours before the game, Norm MacLean belly-whopped
into the Jacksonville Hilton pool, winced, then let the cold, in-
toxicating water wash over his tired bones.

At 8:00 P.M. the players clattered out of their Gator Bowl
locker room to the runway beneath the stands, gathered strength,
then sprinted over the manicured natural grass surface to the
north side of the field. The waiting throng cheered them, actually
loved them at that moment—for they were new and professional
and belonged to the World Football League. The Sharks followed
them out. Thunder rolled down from the highest seats, and the
players—all of them—responded with a sharp workout; dash-
ing, cutting, prancing, throwing and catching footballs in a
magnificent ballet of choreographed improvisation.

Bob Keating (who had arrived the previous evening) and
Dusty Rhodes watched it all from the sidelines, feeling ecstatic,
filled with an unbearable joy. The intense pressure of four
months' work, the personality conflicts that had put an edge on
their relationship (she being impulsive and exacting, Keating
more deliberate and easygoing), and the sheer volume of un-
counted sleepless hours had all but vanished. For now, they were

137

two of the happiest people in the Gator Bowl—not counting Gary Davidson.

The commissioner walked along the sidelines with Keating an hour before game time, supremely confident, rattling off the previous night's WFL attendance figures as though he were a political candidate reviewing election returns.

"Gosh," he said, "every report kept getting better and better. And it looks like tonight will top them all. I think we'll do around sixty thousand here."

"Fantastic. It seems almost too good to be true."

"Yeah . . . I'm awestruck."

At 8:20 P.M., in a small booth above the press box, TVS producer Eddie Einhorn time-checked the opening segment of the New York-Jacksonville telecast with Merle Harmon and Alex Hawkins. The withering heat melted Harmon's face into a river of sweat.

". . . and before we turn the mike over to Alex Hawkins and some important matchups you are likely to see in tonight's contest," said Harmon in the run-through, "let's take a look at the defensive line of the New York Sharks . . . uh . . . Stars . . . and a few of the familiar faces . . ."

"Hold it, Merle, we're running over," advised a TVS technical director.

"Who gives a shit?" said the chubby, baby-faced producer. "This is our first shot on national TV, and we're going to get it off like winners. If we run over, so what? So they'll start the fucking game at nine-twelve instead of nine-eleven!"

It was a rousing evening. A Navy band struck up "Hey, Look Me Over" as fifty high-stepping Sharkettes moved across the field. Banners were unfurled, plaques given, speeches made. A three-hundred-voice choir sang "God Bless America," a symphony orchestra saluted Duke Ellington, fireworks exploded, a power failure delayed the game for seven minutes at halftime while 59,110 WFL fans lit matches and cheered . . . and the Jacksonville Sharks beat the New York Stars on a blocked Robbie Reynolds punt late in the fourth quarter.

"Wyatt's picked it up . . . there he goes . . . straight up the sideline . . . he's cutting inside . . . into Star territory . . . the fifteen . . . the five . . . he's over!!"

On a chartered DC-9 Southern Airways jet winging its way to New York, Babe Parilli closed his eyes and sensed his own detachment, as though he were a sprig of seaweed washed from a rock. In his mind he saw that life was a continuum of growing disappointment. In his heart he could not understand defeat, even though he had learned how to accept it.

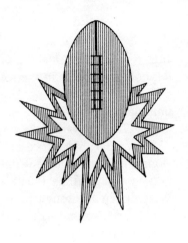

THIRTEEN

What then remains, but that we still should cry
For being born, or, being born, to die?

LORD BACON

Downing Stadium is a 21,000-seat concrete horseshoe that squats in shadowy repose alongside the Triborough Bridge; a forlorn artifact stuck into a rock called Randall's Island. Built by WPA money during the Great Depression, the stadium slowly crumbled before whiplash winds of winter and under the blinding rays of summer sun. In time, its concrete pitted and cracked; its once-proud turf withered to yellow-crowned seediness.

But beyond the ghostly echoes, beyond the neglect, vandalism and rape, the stadium lived. It still contained vivid memories of high school football games that were fought out as bitterly as any between the New York Giants and the Brooklyn Dodgers. While those two NFL rivals attracted vast crowds to their slugfests at the Polo Grounds and Ebbets Field, Downing Stadium played host to a more intimate audience. In the glad season of life, they came to witness the football exploits of Commerce and Evander Childs, Boys High and Erasmus Hall, Stuyvesant and DeWitt Clinton, and all the other schools caught up in the annual race to a city championship.

It was here, at Downing Stadium, that the illusion of professionalism overcame the realities of amateurism. It happened at a time when the schoolboy names of McCullough, Glickman, Wizbicki, Yablonski and Luckman resounded around the field like cannon shot, growing louder and louder until it seemed as if the stadium itself would burst under the shattering noise. Then the sounds faded, vaporized into the chilly Saturday sky, and the games drifted into a timeless void.

The player had a lot of cowboy in him. It was easy to tell by the rolling walk and the way his eyes swept around the stadium, as if they were checking out a possible ambush. Then he relaxed. Butch Brezina may have been a long way from his hometown of Louise, Texas, but any field where he could hang his football helmet was home enough for him. Downing was no exception.

Brezina was a square-jawed, dark-browed defensive tackle of the Birmingham Americans. He was named the defensive player of the year for the University of Houston in 1971 and, when the Cougar season ended, continued to crack a lot of heads in the Bluebonnet Bowl, winning the most valuable lineman award in that post-season classic. But he never made it to the NFL, even though he was an honorable mention all-America and his older brother Greg was a starting linebacker for the Atlanta Falcons.

In June, Brezina sauntered into the Birmingham American training camp at Marion, Alabama, as a free agent, a muscular six-foot-two-inch 250-pounder with a special quality about him that soon caught everyone's attention.

One tough afternoon in the second week of practice, a few of the defensive linemen began to wilt under the sticky June heat. It soaked their sweatshirts and baked every blade of grass on the field. Suddenly, Brezina's voice rose above the crunching of helmets and shoulder pads.

"I'm prayin' for you, men! So let's dig in and do it for the Lord!"

Coach Jack Gotta chuckled as the defense tore into their next assignment. Then he tugged at his craggy beak and said to Marvin Bass, his defensive coordinator, "Shit, Marv, I thought *I* was God around here."

Brezina made the team and played in the first professional game of his life when Birmingham scored a win over the Southern California Sun in its WFL debut. Now it was a week later and Brezina was in Downing Stadium, around six o'clock in the early evening of July 17.

He saw Tom Beer out on the playing field, standing tall and comfortable in his New York Stars tee shirt. Beer had played college ball with Brezina's brother.

"How're you doing, buddy?"

From some invisible center, in a kind of nostalgia for the fairest days of their youth, they began to talk pleasantly about places they had been to and mutual acquaintances. They were attached through a common interest—football—and that was enough to bring them together, as if they were long lost brothers reunited after a long separation.

"You should have won that game against Jacksonville," said Brezina. "I'm tellin' you, Tom, you were the better team that night."

"Yeah, but we lost."

"Well, you'll be doin' okay, pardnah, that's for sure."

Tom Beer smiled. He knew Brezina didn't *really* mean it. How could he? In two hours the Americans would be clawing at the Stars with fire in their eyes and hatred in their hearts. The thought prompted him to ask the big lineman about his organization.

"It's a real nice place to be. We've got Christians on this club. I mean, *real* Christians. I tell you, Tom, this mornin' the whole team had a prayer meetin'. That's somethin' we do regular. It gave us the chills, just thinkin' about how the Lord looks after us."

"Gee, that's terrific, Butch."

They shook hands and returned to their separate worlds.

As Brezina threaded his way to the Birmingham dressing room, he brushed against Bob Keating, as if a wave had passed under the bow of a ship, touching once and never again. And Keating came out of the darkness into the bright sunlight. Shading his eyes, he squinted up at the canary-yellow press box that jutted out from the top seats of Downing Stadium. He could see the writers, mostly the upper portions of their heads, which formed little quarter moons in each of the window sills. A few were standing in full view, talking to each other, looking down on the field, perhaps looking at him. He had checked the press box minutes ago. The mimeograph machine was in good working order, team statistician John Hagrogian and his three helpers had a bird's-eye view of the field, the phones were properly hooked up, sandwiches, beer and soda were available for over ninety correspondents and guests; everything seemed a lot better than it had the day before.

The day before, Keating had been down on his knees, painting white stripes on the parched stadium grass, sweating in the sun with two dozen college kids who were hired to paint numbers on seats and clear away the dirt and garbage at $2.50 per hour. He watched the workers scamper up the derelict light towers, watched them wipe off layers of filth that caked the bulbs, watched them untangle rotting wires and grapple with unyielding sockets. In the end, the workers turned their palms upward and shook their heads in defeat. Their struggle against time and reason availed them nothing. The towers couldn't accommodate the high-intensity circuitry needed for television. In fact, there wasn't enough candlepower available to send the pictures back to Birmingham in black and white.

The towers belonged to another age. Purchased from Ebbets Field in 1939, they had once cast a yellow-orange glow on the white-flanneled uniforms of the Brooklyn Dodgers baseball team. Now the Leo Durocher-led Dodgers were gone, but not the light towers. On a hot July evening in 1974 they sat high above Downing Stadium on Randall's Island—with only eighty-five percent of the bulbs working.

It was a little after seven o'clock. Bob Keating's attention turned elsewhere: to the stands, to the bright red uniforms of the

Vikings and Vikettes Marching Band, to the photographers, television crews, stadium officials—and Charlie Grossberger, a thin-faced man with small eyes who wore dark suits and spoke in a gravelly Bronx accent, and who was the team's director of special projects.

"Hey, Charlie," Keating hailed, "how're we doing?"

Grossberger crossed the cinder track that circled the playing field.

"The scoreboard is working okay, but look at those lights. Jeez, we've got only ten candlepower, and the joint needs at least fifty . . ."

"Do you think we'll be able to see the ball?"

"Sure . . . if we spray it with luminous paint."

The bulbs above Downing Stadium weep in the fast-closing night. The Birmingham Americans run through the tunnel to un-caring silence. One by one, the Stars separate the curtain of Starlets and line up between the forty-yard stripes, facing the press box. Pete Rajecki is first, then Bob Hermanni, Gary Danielson . . . George Sauer . . . masked and padded . . . with his little boy's face, sad gray eyes and whimsical smile in wayward flight, seeing beyond the light, beyond the moment, facing the press box and knowing the nearness of truth. An enormous cheer greets George Sauer and echoes again and again for John Elliott and Gerry Philbin.

At midfield, Julie Budd caresses the National Anthem before 17,943 fans as though she is working to a Blue Angel crowd . . . which has long since dissolved in a city of fallen angels.

"The ball is up, Davey Richards takes it on the six, heads up-field, oops, he's brought down around the twenty . . . let's make that the nineteen . . ."

Babe Parilli paces with his players at the bench, craving only the football victory, seeing nothing but *that* as a way out of his deep forest. Sauer floats to a Sherman pass, and then Sherman goes in for a touchdown. Parilli rubs his palms and walks into the shadows near the goal line to relish the moment alone. *"The snap,*

144

Rajecki's kick . . . it's good! And the Stars go off the field at the half leading 29–3 . . ."

And Pete Rajecki goes into the locker room with his ribs cracked while an unknowing Moses Lajterman listens to the game on his radio back home in New Jersey, thinking about Rajecki's field goal and dreading the morrow, when he will have to visit a dozen or more grocery stores as a detail man for Dannon Yogurt.

"Kill the motherfuckers . . . rip out their assholes . . . get those cocksuckers!" The Birmingham bench was holding its usual prayer meeting.

Vince Casey was the last Star to leave Downing Stadium. He saw his team lose, heard Parilli's whispered replies to postgame questions, helped assistant PR director Tom Hogan carry the mimeograph machine down from the press box, and laughed in sorrow as ink ran all over Hogan's shirt.

It was close to three in the morning when he opened the door to his car in the deserted parking lot. Emptied of all feeling, too tired to sleep, Casey figured he'd wake his wife when he got home, and then they'd sit and talk in the kitchen while he finished off two or three quarts of milk. He turned his key to the ignition.

Nothing.

The chartered buses burst out of the sticky heat of Manhattan, finding clearer air on the Jersey Turnpike. Shaken by the second-half Birmingham surge, the players rode on to Philadelphia showing perceptible signs of strain. For some, like running back Andy Huff, quarterback Gary Danielson, and defensive back Jimmy Sims, tension dug much deeper than the mere winning or losing of a football game.

Andy Huff's father had had a stroke while driving his car in Toledo on a blistering afternoon. By the time they got him to a hospital his left side was paralyzed. "He's doing better now," said Huff to Danielson during the ride to Philly, "but I'll go home if there's a change for the worse."

Gary Danielson's father worked for a Dearborn printing firm.

145

For more years than he could remember, Danielson had seen his father come home from the shop with ink-stained hands, and now the stuff was in his system, sticking like corrosive rust to his lungs. "It's a hell of a thing," said Danielson to Huff. "My father gave so much, and now there's so little I can give him in return."

About a half-mile back, a second bus carried Jimmy Sims on to Philadelphia. A week before, he was in Koontze, Texas, where his mother lay quietly in her bed recovering from a stroke. Parilli let him off for a couple of days so he could be with her, and when Sims came back he was no longer a strong safety because Parilli, after seeing the Birmingham game films, had decided he'd be better as a weak-side linebacker. Well, that was all right with Sims. Anything would be cool, as long as his momma got well.

He looked out the window as Camden slid by, and remembered how it was and always would be for his mother and himself:

"Koontze? Oh, it's a bitty town about thirty miles north of Beaumont. I guess two or three thousand live there, something like that. It has a couple of stores, a gas station where they sell Dr. Pepper, dogs running around and barking. That's about it, if you really want to know. Well, there were nine of us, not counting my mother and father. I guess I was closest to my brother Charles and my sister Virginia. We didn't have much. We had clothes on our backs and shoes on our feet and food to eat, but nothing more than that. Anyway, I went to an all-black grade school. When I was ready for high school us blacks had a freedom of choice. The white high school let three of us in on some kind of quota system. That was in my junior year. There were just two of us in the history class, one girl and myself, and we had this lady teacher who kept putting us down. Like, she'd talk about the Civil War and look right at me or the girl and say things like, 'The niggers started the war by killing the whites,' and, 'Thank God for the KKK.' This got me real mad. I went to the principal and told him what she was saying. The next day she went right back to the same bullshit history, only this time she changed the word to nigra, and after class she said I was nothing

146

but a troublemaker. Man, that old bird had prejudice sticking right out of the bottom of her feet. One day she gave me a bad mark, saying that I did the wrong lesson. I knew she was just getting back at me because I went to the principal. So I walked up to her and laid her out right in front of the class. Whooey! I knew I was in bad trouble, so I ran home and told my mother and father. My father said they'd probably come out to the house to do me. I told him that whites could die as well as blacks. That's when my brother Charles went out and bought shells for the shotgun. My momma cried and told me I'd better leave. There was no use arguing about it because I always listened to her, always went to her when I was in trouble. My father was hard, stubborn, you know. Anyway, momma called my sister Mary, who lived in Los Angeles, and told her what happened. That night we drove to Houston, where I caught a plane to stay with Mary. Wouldn't you know, when I called home the next day my brother Charles told me, 'Jim, I'm sure glad you left because they were out to the house to do you.' Later, I found out they came around for a whole month to check me out, but they finally gave up. I never went back again until after my second Rose Bowl game. That was six years later. By that time the white folk got word that I was a big-time football star and could put the town on the map. Next thing that happened was they arranged a big celebration for me. When I came back home the white folk shook my hand and said, 'Hey, make sure you tell everybody you're from Koontze.' Anyway, we had this thing going at the high school I went to, and the place was filled up. There was my old history teacher sitting in the audience, smiling away, and most of my family were there. My brother Clarence, who was stationed at the Fort Polk Army base in Louisiana, he was there, too. Well, my old principal got up and said the whole town was pulling for James Sims, the son of Mr. and Mrs. W. J. Sims. He said everybody hoped I would get bigger and better, and that I was a credit to the school, an outstanding student and a good citizen. I was glad for my family but I got out of town a few days later, because Koontze wasn't for me. Now I only go back to visit, because the family is close. And I miss my momma a lot. You know, she showed me the way. She always told me, 'Jimmy, just be yourself and you'll always be straight with Jesus.' I believe that. As far as I'm concerned, Jesus Christ is the only straight thing we've got in this world."

The buses slowed in heavy traffic after they left the turnpike. Moses Lajterman of New Jersey had a window seat in the lead bus. Beside him was Robbie Reynolds of South Carolina. Lajterman had been lifted to an heroic world again. On the night of the home opener he slept in an interior space. He saw himself as a withered old man checking shelves in strange stores that smelled of cheese, and he dreamed of being swallowed up in a huge vat of yogurt. Parilli's call stayed the nightmare. But for how long?

A blue truck with LONARDI BROTHERS lettered across the cab door pulled abreast at a stop light. "Hey, Robbie, see that?" Reynolds looked out the window. "I bet that truck belongs to an Argentinian," said Lajterman.

"How can you tell?"

"By the name. Lonardi. That's an Argentinian name."

"It sounds Italian to me, Moe."

"Well, maybe. But when I was small, this general . . . Eduardo Lonardi . . . took over when Perón resigned. I guess I was around four or so when it happened. My father used to talk about him a lot when we lived in Buenos Aires."

"I didn't know you were from there. Golly."

"Oh, sure. I thought you knew."

"No. Honest, I didn't. I thought you were an American."

"I am. I'm a South American Jew. What do you think of that?"

"I'll be darned."

"I hope this doesn't affect our friendship."

"Heck, no."

A few minutes later Reynolds mused, "Hey, Moe, when did you leave Argentina? I mean, you have a New York accent, so I guess you've been here for a while, right?"

"I came here when I was twelve."

"Are there a lot of Jews in Argentina?"

Leroy Richardson signs an autograph.

The twelve-minute run.

Gerry Gluck

Bob Hermanni pulls one in during a practice session.

Gerry Gluck

Defense Coach Lamar Leachman

The soccer style of Moses Lajterman.

Gerry Glu

Tom Beer and TVS announcer Alex Hawkins discussing *Sunday's Fools*.

ere the boys are.

Stew Barber conducts a clinic.

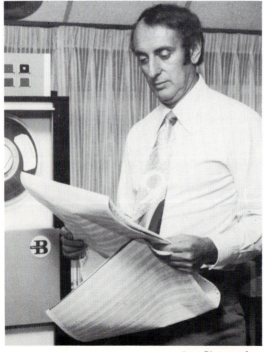

Bob Schmertz.

Tom Baldwin and Dusty Rhodes.

Four yards and a cloud of dust.

Larry Butler and Billie Jean King.

George Boutselis lets off steam.

Action in the WFL.

Bill Crespinel

Gerry Gluck

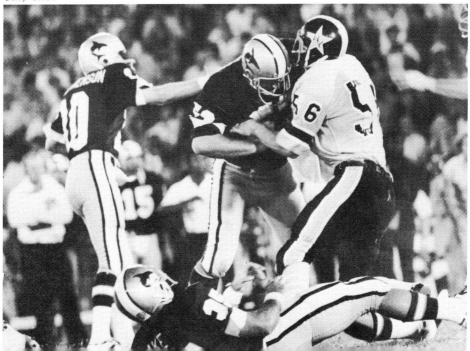

"Plenty. But we didn't live in a Jewish community. My father owned a furniture factory, and we had a big house in a nice Gentile section of the city. It was a beautiful house. You know, big kitchen, patio, a living room like a hundred yards long, and four bedrooms. It was some house. We even had a sleep-in maid. Her name was Cuca. She slept with me."

"You're pulling my leg."

Lajterman giggled. "I was only a baby, Robbie. What's the matter with you? Anyway, Cuca was like a second mother to me. She was maybe twenty-three or so when my mother took her in. She came from a poor family. In Argentina lots of girls become maids because they know they'll have a good home with plenty to eat. So Cuca came to live with us. I went everywhere with her. To tell you the truth, I regretted leaving her when I came to this country."

"Was she pretty?"

"She was very good looking. She had long black hair and big brown eyes, and her skin was very smooth. Yeah . . . Cuca was very good looking. She must be around forty by now. We hear from her once in a while."

"Is she married?"

"Naw, she's still trying to catch a nice Jewish boy."

The buses moved on past the airport toward the Hilton Inn, only a short distance from John F. Kennedy Stadium. A circling jet skimmed along gray cloud cover without making a sound. Lajterman followed it for a while, then closed his eyes.

He remembered the big house, with the mezuzah on the front door, and how happy he was when his mother came home with bags of matzos for the Passover holiday. And he thought of the Herzlia Temple, the biggest synagogue in all of Buenos Aires, where Abe and Marcel were bar mitzvahed. He remembered that like it was right in front of him: the food, the big table with the blue linen, the swirling lights, and his family and friends—so many—dancing the hora while two bands played. He could see it all. God, it was so real, now. He wanted the powerful images to go on. But the bus swung into the Hilton driveway, so he got up from his seat and followed Robbie Reynolds into the lobby. Scared.

Before the largest crowd in the three-week history of the World Football League, Moses Lajterman was still scared. Not of the unruly kids who kept spilling out on the field all through the game, and not because TVS cameras were sending his picture into millions of homes throughout the country. On the sidelines, engulfed in sound and fury, Lajterman paced the bench, flexed his kicking leg, and withdrew into a narrow channel where fear became the haunting stream, where faith moved him toward a dim light. In the great light he saw Marcel:

"What can I say about my brother? Marcel was like a god to me. I worshiped him, ever since I could remember. He was fourteen when we came to this country, and the next year he began kicking for Passaic High School. I was just a skinny little kid at the time. I kept asking him, 'Marcel, when can I put a helmet on and play football?' and he'd laugh and say, 'When you grow up, Moe.' At first he didn't accept me. He wanted to be with kids his own age, but I kept following him around. He didn't like it very much, and he'd say to my mother, 'Ma, take him off my back. I think Moe has gone queer.' He was so cool. I loved him so much."

A King Corcoran pass, intended for Linzy Cole, is picked off by Lou Angelo, who runs it back to the Stars nineteen-yard line.

"I made the varsity team at Lynhurst in my sophomore year. Marcel was a senior at Passaic, and our schools were scheduled to play each other. Man, you should've seen me then. I looked like a clown in my Knute Rockne boots. Well, I didn't care much about that. All I could think about was that I'd have a chance to kick against Marcel. I told Coach Joe Cipoli about it and he said, 'Does your brother live in Lynhurst?' I said, 'Sure. He lives with me.' He said, 'Well, then he can't kick for Passaic. He has to kick

for Lynhurst.' So, Marcel came over and I became second string. That year he kicked thirty points for Lynhurst and I got to kick three extra points."

Bob Gladieux goes over the left side for a three-yard gain and is stopped by middle linebacker Wally Dempsey one yard short of the Bell goal.

"Marcel went to Marshall College on a full scholarship. In his freshman year he kicked a fifty-two-yarder. I was a senior at Lynhurst then, and when he came home for Christmas vacation I said, 'Hey, Marcel, I want you to be my kicking coach,' and he just laughed and said someday I'd be better than him. So I kissed him, and he said, 'Hey, Ma, Moe's at it again.' "

Corcoran hits LeVell Hill with a nine-yard Bell touchdown pass.

"Two days before Marshall went down to play East Carolina, Marcel called home. He was in his sophomore year then, and I was a freshman at Montclair State. There are three phones in my house, and all of us were on, talking to him at the same time. I kept asking him a lot of questions, and I guess I was the most excited of all. I said, 'Hey, Marcel, I'm having trouble with my right angle,' and he said, 'I'll call you after the game. I'll help you.' I was so happy I nearly cried."

Tom Sherman passes to his left and completes it to Al Young for a seventeen-yard gain to the Stars forty-four-yard line.

"I'll never forget the day because it was a black Friday in November 1970. I was going with this nice girl, Lou Anne Latella, nothing serious of course, and on that day we took a ride with her grandparents down to the shore. We had a nice time. You know, walking on the beach and watching the waves, things like that. Then we headed back. Well, we had a flat tire and pulled into a gas station. The radio was on, and we heard an

151

announcement that a plane went down over the mountains of West Virginia. Right away I thought of Marcel, and I said to Mr. Latella, 'I hope it's not my brother.' He said I shouldn't worry. He could see I was afraid."

Sherman hands off to Gladieux for no gain at the Bell twenty-three.

"A couple of minutes later the announcer said that a plane carrying the Marshall football team had crashed. My world fell out. I ran out of the car and fell down in the station rest room. Mr. Latella came in to get me and said maybe it was a mistake, maybe Marcel didn't make the flight, maybe he was hurt and stayed behind to get treatment. But all I could say to Mr. Latella was, 'I gotta get home. Please take me home.' "

Sherman throws an incomplete pass, intended for Young. It's the fourth quarter, fourth down and eight, Bell leading, 15–14.

"All the way home I kept saying to myself, 'He's all right, he's like a god, nothing can destroy him.' But when we got to the house my Uncle George was outside, and there was a look on his face that I'll never forget. I didn't say anything, and neither did he. I just went inside. My father came up to me. He kissed me and said, 'Moe, your friend has died.' "

"Hey . . . Moe . . . ," yelled Parilli. "Field goal . . . Field goal!"

From his window seat on the bus going home. Lajterman dissected for Robbie Reynolds each stage of his winning forty-yard kick, breaking down the play from snap to follow-through, from point of impact to the ball's flight over the crossbar. And he told Reynolds about his brother.

". . . Marcel kicked two extra points against East Carolina. And he could've tied the game, but there was an interception in the last minute of play, so he never got to kick again."

"Golly. No wonder you were yelling like you were out there. I mean, with everyone jumping on you, there you were, right in the middle of the field, yelling, 'Marcel! Marcel!' "

"Yeah, it was like my brother knew I made it for him. You know what I mean?"

Reynolds looked at his new roomie. His eyes were closed. He was smiling peacefully.

Moses had reached the promised land.

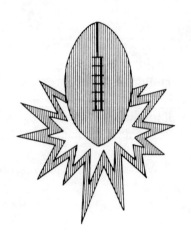

FOURTEEN

The World Football League season pushed on. In August the Philadelphia Bell and Jacksonville Sharks admitted that paid attendance figures for their first two home games had been greatly exaggerated. Philadelphia initially reported the sale of 121,000 tickets, when actually only 20,000 were sold. Jacksonville gave away 44,000 of their 106,000 tickets. Nailed by an IRS investigation, Bell Executive Vice-President Barry Lieb insisted he released the phony figures because "if the truth got out we would've been a joke." Shortly after Lieb's confession, Jack Kelly found a back door and resigned as president of the Bell.

"I was aghast at the way the Philadelphia situation was

handled," piously declared Southern California Sun owner Larry Hatfield. "It's atrocious. It's bush. Now we're all suspect."

In the face of dwindling gate receipts and an inability to launch a public sale of stock, one of the thirty-three Detroit owners suggested to General Manager Sonny Grandelius that it would be a fine idea to abandon the Wheels training headquarters at Ypsilanti, Michigan, and camp out in a city-owned tract on Belle Island. The players could be put up in tents, said the obdurate owner. Grandelius advised him they'd be the laughing stock of the league if the plan was carried out.

While an unsuspecting Babe Parilli led his players to battle against the Sun at Anaheim Stadium, New York Star Owner Bob Schmertz informed General Manager Bob Keating that he was being plagued by financial problems. Schmertz had just lost a lawsuit involving his ownership in the Boston Celtics. The plaintiffs were Harold Lipton and Irving Levine, who had sold the Celtics to him in 1972. The two former owners claimed that Schmertz reneged on an oral agreement that would have allowed them to buy back half of the Celtics stock. They were eventually awarded $4.2 million in damages.

Another factor contributing to Schmertz's financial malaise was a national recession that snapped at the heels of runaway inflation. Schmertz's major asset, stock in Leisure Technology, dropped from a high of $34.75 in 1970 to a low of $2.25 in August 1974. In order to keep his head above water and his sanity intact, the Stars owner sold off a large amount of stock in his New England Whaler hockey team. Staggered by financial setbacks that diluted his net worth from a reported $25 million to approximately $5 million, Schmertz instructed Keating to do the best he could to hold off a growing list of creditors.

"You know," he ruefully confided to his general manager, "when I was just starting out in business, I thought if I could make $20,000 a year I'd be the happiest guy in the world. Maybe I would've been better off it had stopped right there."

Robert J. Schmertz was born in Hackensack, New Jersey, a small industrialized town of about 30,000 people in Bergen

County. As a child of the Roosevelt Thirties, he went to summer camp in the Catskills, spent winter vacations in Lakewood, played high school basketball games, and had lots of good times across the Hudson River—where his first heroes of sport ran in Millrose Track and Field meets at Madison Square Garden. His father had been a Millrose sprinter before the Great War, and his uncle Fred had promoted the event through five exciting decades of competition. In time, Bob got to meet all the outstanding runners—Gene Fenske, Chuck Venske, Hal McCluskey, Glenn Cunningham, Les MacMitchell, and little Greg Rice, who had a barrel chest and ran on blazing legs. And, one night, before a capacity Garden crowd, he stared in disbelief as Greg Rice flashed by—jock strap split, balls bouncing—on his way to a new Millrose record in the two-mile run.

Boyhood ended. There followed a short period of stateside duty during World War II as an Air Force cadet, then a college education at NYU under the GI Bill of Rights. When Schmertz graduated in 1950, a flood of visionary hopes unlocked hidden secrets. It opened each dawn, finding him one step closer to abundant favor, fame, and decent means.

On a raw February morning in 1952, he stood on brittle, frozen Lakewood ground and listened to a chorus of metal implements ring out on fresh-cut pinewood. In the spring, birds chirped, a million buds filled the branches of nearby trees, and his first house was built. Then, while leaves tumbled, while the damp New Jersey earth recycled and yawned itself into long winter sleep, he stepped back to observe the fruit of his labors. At the age of twenty-five, Schmertz had constructed thirteen modest one-family homes. He had cleared over $20,000 in profit. He was rich beyond his wildest dreams.

Then he built twenty more, fifty more, one hundred more. In 1963 Schmertz put up seven hundred and fifty retirement homes in the Lakewood area. Two years later he founded Leisure Technology, and four years later it went public and was listed on the American Stock Exchange. By then he was truly wealthy.

Still, there was more pain and fewer dreams as he approached fifty. His marriage was on the rocks, his corporate stock had tumbled, the Celtics damage suit had drained his fortune, the New York Stars were collapsing before his eyes, and he was under grand jury investigation for allegedly bribing an Ocean County freeholder in order to win approval of a $200 million project for senior citizens.

It is August. And hot. Emerging from dark shadows into sunlight, a long line of white-and-yellow-shirted players walk the distance from St. Joseph's Hall to the old varsity field, some with helmets dangling from tape-stiffened fingers. The air is swollen with mosquitoes, the field steams with ancient odors, and a breeze fans through the tall pine sentinels and cracked wooden stands that guard the gridiron from goalpost to goalpost. Beyond the field, a dappled stream slides under a red-bricked crossbridge, appearing black and polluted to the naked eye. But it is clear and cold, and wriggly-tailed fish cavort in small circles beneath the surface. Mr. Brown trots up to the stream. Sniffing his way down to the edge of the bank, Harpo Gladieux's dog selects a thin branch that has speared itself in the mud. He pulls it up with his teeth, shaking himself to remove the water from his butterscotch coat, then works on the bark, delighted with his find. A part of the branch breaks off, and Mr. Brown triumphantly holds it between his jaws. He turns, bounds onto a gravel road, past fir and maple and willow, toward his master, who is doing knee bends and pushups with the other players at the old varsity field.

In early August the team flew to Southern California and talked about Nixon. During the flight, offensive coach Tom Moore told a writer that his kids asked him why the president had lied about Watergate. Moore said he didn't have any answers but he did tell his son Daniel that America was the greatest country in the world.

Gary Danielson, still worried about his ailing father, said he heard the news of Nixon's confession to Watergate "omissions" on the radio that morning. He didn't think anybody could have been so stupid, but he felt that back in Lafayette, Indiana, where he and his wife lived in the off-season, most of the people still thought Nixon was a great man.

Matt Snell, a TVS game analyst and former New York Jet fullback, remembered a brief audience he had with the president.

"I met him once, while a few of us were in Washington on an anti-drug-abuse program. When I shook his hand, he said, 'Oh yes, Matt Snell, how are you? How's the knee?' Shit, there wasn't anything at all wrong with my knee. He just tried to jive me. Personally, I think he's crazy."

The plane was late getting in, circling Los Angeles International Airport for more than twenty minutes while a bomb squad cleared away debris from an explosion that had ripped down a ceiling at the Pan-Am World Airways terminal. The bomb killed two people and injured thirty-six others. There were no suspects.

The players flew back to JFK in New York with a victory over the Sun. Coach Parilli singled out Jimmy Sims for special credit. "He was all over the field. Jimmy likes to hit, and I think he made eight unassisted tackles, including two quarterback sacks." Parilli was almost right. Sims made nine tackles.

On the day the Stars left Southern California, Richard M. Nixon, thirty-seventh president of the United States, calling for a "process of healing that is so desperately needed in America," announced his resignation from that revered office.

In mid-August the team beat Portland at Randall's Island. George Sauer caught seven passes for ninety-two yards and one touchdown, Gary Danielson played in his first WFL game, Bill DeFlavio, rolling like a cabbage down the field on the opening kickoff, ripped his right knee ligaments and was carried off the field—and only one of the eight light stanchions atop Downing Stadium operated at full strength.

In late August 12,000 fans came out to Randall's Island to see the Stars maul the Houston Texans. The game was highlighted by a four-touchdown performance by Harpo Gladieux, the WFL debut of all-time NFL pass-catching leader Don Maynard, who caught one for the Texans that night, the installation of a second bank of powerful lights above Downing Stadium—and a halftime press-box conference in which Bob Schmertz told a cluster of sweating reporters he was not actively trying to sell the club. If someone made the right offer, he added, he'd naturally listen. How much would he take? someone wanted to know. "About $6 million sounds right," said the owner.

At the end of August a United Airlines charter flight, #5109, carried the Stars to Houston for a rematch. The team bedded down at the Astroworld Hotel on Interstate 610, across the way from the Astrodome.

On the night before the game, George Sauer's mother and father stopped by to see their son.

George Sauer, Sr., had a fabled college and pro player-coach career. At the University of Nebraska, playing fullback for the immortal Dana X. Bible, he made Grantland Rice's all-America team in 1933, then went on to play pro ball with the Green Bay Packers for three years. He began his college football coaching career in 1937 with a four-year stint at the University of New Hampshire. After Pearl Harbor, the elder Sauer joined the Navy and served eighteen months aboard the aircraft carrier *Enterprise.* Returning to football after the war, he shared the Big Eight Conference title twice as Kansas head coach, then moved to Annapolis to guide the Middies to a 1948 tie with favored Army. Next he went to Baylor University, where he coached for six years before settling down as athletic director for five years. In 1961 he became the New York Titans' general manager and assistant head coach. When new owners took over the AFL franchise in 1963 and renamed it the Jets, George Sauer, Sr., stayed on as director of player personnel, signing most of the talent that won Super Bowl III. Among them was his own son— George H. Sauer, Jr.

It was a reunion of sorts, since George and his parents hadn't been together for almost a year. Now they were standing in the Astroworld lobby with a small circle of writers, photographer

Bill Crespinel and team trainer Lew Cohen, enjoying a joke or two and reminiscing before going into the dining room.

"Did George always like football?" Cohen asked the elder Sauer.

"Oh, yes. Didn't you, son?"

"Yes, sir."

"I can tell you a fine story about George that you might like to hear. Remember when you wanted to get into the Baylor game, son?"

"Uh-huh."

"Well, I guess George was about ten years old at the time, and he loved football so much I had a special Baylor uniform tailored for him to wear. We were playing an important conference game on this particular afternoon, and I allowed George to sit on the bench in his new uniform. He even wore a regular pair of football shoes, and, I must say, they were a trifle large. Anyway, during a very crucial point in the game, I heard this clop-clop-clop sound getting nearer and nearer. I slowly turned around. It was George, pulling at my sleeve and saying, 'Can I talk to you?' I said, 'Well, son, I'm a little busy, but what is it?' He said, 'If you put me in the game, I can win it for you.' "

Everybody laughed, including George Sauer's son.

"The thing is," said the father, "George really meant it. Isn't it so, son?"

"Oh, I don't know about that. It's all ancient history now."

A few minutes later the Sauers went in to dinner.

Lamar Leachman and Gerry Philbin had a reunion, too—in the Astro Bar of the hotel about fifteen minutes before curfew. Leachman was bantering lightheartedly with a barmaid when Philbin and Lou Angelo walked in. Philbin, in particular, carried a warm glow to his cheeks.

As soon as he saw Leachman with the barmaid, the veteran defensive end walked over and planted a big kiss on the astonished girl's lips. "Darling." He chuckled while winking at Leachman roguishly. "I'm so glad you waited for me. I hope I haven't kept you long." With a flourish Philbin led her off to the other end of the bar. Leachman grabbed his shot glass and gulped down the contents. It didn't stop there. The two of them began to exchange bitter insults, until Philbin, in a white rage, challenged Leachman to a fight.

"Gerry," said the defensive line coach, "maybe I can whip your ass, and maybe I can't. But I'm the coach and you're the player. If we fight and I win, I'll lose in the end. Meanwhile, it's curfew." Without another word, while every customer in the place sat in stunned silence, Leachman walked out of the bar. A few minutes later, Philbin and Angelo called it a night.

The Stars and Texans fought it out in the domed palace of the Astrodome the following evening. John Matuszak, a six-foot-eight-inch, 285-pound defensive tackle who had announced on the previous day that he had broken his NFL contract with the Houston Oilers to sign an "expensive" multiyear contract with the Texans, played for one series in the first quarter. Then a sheriff handed him a temporary restraining order on the sidelines. Matuszak left the field, waving to a crowd of not more than 7,000 cheering fans.

The Stars suffered two casualties. Wide receiver Al Young sustained a dislocated right elbow and Greg Lens saw his right ankle balloon to the size of a grapefruit after a pileup in the second half. It was a miserable trip for most. The team lost a close game, and the sight of so many empty seats left a queasy feeling in the pit of the players' stomachs. Still, there was one saving grace. During the return flight to New York, Gerry Philbin stuck out his hand to Leachman and apologized for the barroom blowup. Leachman was genuinely surprised. He patted Philbin on the back. "Forget it," he said. "Let's just go out there and do our jobs and we'll both be all right."

And August drew to a close.

September. On a Labor Day Monday, 6,000 grim-faced fans straggled into Downing Stadium to watch the Stars play the Bell.

"It's going to be rough," said John Elliott to a reporter before the game. "We can't take a day off. We'll be practicing on Tuesday to get ready for Florida on Friday, and then Saturday to be ready for next Wednesday's game in Portland."

"Yeah," added Gerry Philbin, "and then we play in Hawaii four days later. Oh, I sure will *hate* going to Hawaii," he said, grinning.

Bill DeFlavio arrived at the stadium on crutches, with a cast cutting into his upper thigh. An operation at Lenox Hill Hospital in Manhattan a day after the home game against Portland successfully repaired the ligament damage to his right knee, but DeFlavio would never play for the Stars again. He painfully struggled to a seat next to Greg Lens in the nearly deserted stands. Lens, smiling weakly, had been deactivated after the Houston game. The big tackle's ankle was a swollen mess, puffed and purpled by a network of broken blood vessels.

"I'll be ready to go this Friday," Lens said to DeFlavio.

"Are you kidding? Your ankle looks horrible. How can you play on it?"

"Easy. Philbin says he'll carry it for me if it starts hurting."

The wounded players sat under the same lighting conditions that existed the week before and the week before that. Both sides of the end zone area were submerged in shadow, while the two high-powered stanchions produced a glaring, unnatural effect at midfield and partially blinded the press-box corps across the way. In their canary-yellow booth, a skeletal force of daily reporters clacked out pre-game copy without much enthusiasm. Some even cursed the weekly diet of limp ham, cheese, salami and liverwurst sandwiches.

"When are we going to have some decent food up here?" complained one writer to Vince Casey. "You should thank God you're eating," retorted the PR director. Moments later the national anthem was played on a record. There was no marching band or even a bugle corps to do the honors.

Just before the start of the game a season-ticket holder by the name of Jay Chasin went over to DeFlavio for an autograph.

"I hope you come back," said Chasin. "You've given me a lot of enjoyment, and so has the whole team. I just want you to know that."

Somehow, it came out like a prayer for the dead. DeFlavio almost cried as he signed his name.

The Stars went on to beat the Bell. Barely.

Rain swept the entire East Coast. In New York it beat against the steel and glass of Manhattan, flooded the parkways of Westchester and Long Island, drenched the streets of the Bronx and Brooklyn, inundated the gingerbread houses of Staten Island, and soaked Downing Stadium on Randall's Island. Despite an advance ticket sale of 14,000, less than 3,500 customers braved the elements to watch the Stars swim against the Florida Blazers on September 7.

All through the deluge, Blazer players in red ponchos and Star players in yellow rain gear stood like so many lighthouse keepers looking for ships in a storm-tossed night. Photographers gave up their sideline vigil at the half in order to prevent cameras from being water-damaged, and the field officials seemed anxious to flee from their tasks. Therefore, Tommy Reamon's game performance matched the best water ballets ever produced at Cyprus Gardens. The rookie Florida back, in his first start of the season, broke loose from the bubbly turf long enough to stutter-step and wriggle his way to a WFL-record-breaking 179 yards. In the end, less than 1,000 fans remained to witness Reamon and the Blazers clinch a spongy victory.

Dusty Rhodes caught up with a thoroughly disheartened Babe Parilli in the dressing-room tunnel after the game. "Schmertz hasn't come through with any cash. I don't even know if we can pay the electricians," she told him.

"Gee, Dusty," moaned Parilli, "don't tell me that now. I have enough problems trying to keep the team from falling apart."

Lou Angelo, scowling bitterly while holding his tongue, dallied at a JFK newspaper stand until the last possible minute. Then he boarded the team charter to Portland. The Star safety had been deactivated by Parilli at midweek. The coach told him he was making too many mistakes, that Ike Thomas, who had joined the team in late August, was going to get a chance to prove himself.

163

Angelo was furious. On the cross-country flight, he slouched in his seat, hardly spoke to anyone, not even to Philbin, whom he thought so much of.

Before meeting him for the first time at camp, Angelo thought Philbin was a sorehead. It was all over the papers that Philbin tore his name from his Jet locker after a salary dispute with Weeb Ewbank, wasn't it? But now Angelo felt a lot different about the guy. As far as he was concerned, Philbin was the best friend he had ever had; an all-AFC superstar who had "personally" invited him on a boat trip to Fire Island—and treated him like an equal. It was something he'd never forget.

Nor would he forget the Banana Man. That's what Angelo called George Boutselis, and would always call his defensive backfield coach, who strutted around in his banana-colored windbreaker and put him down during agility drills and threatened more than once to cut him in his first days at camp. Well, thought Angelo, the Banana Man is an asshole. Somehow, he'd get back in the lineup again. If not, he'd just take another long vacation, forget about everything. Maybe Portland and Hawaii would be a good start.

George Boutselis felt the hot flash of anger in Angelo's eyes all through the flight. In his seat, sensing the defensive back's implacable rage, he sighed and scratched his scalp—like one who has been flooded with poisonous thoughts and suddenly recovers reason.

It seemed ironic. In those first weeks of camp Boutselis was filled with pious ideals and values. He saw nothing but demons and other irrational horrors in an open society of personal liberty. Hence, his heavy-handed treatment of John Carlos and Manny Brown. But he was forced to change his tactics as the danger of complete alienation spread within his unit soon after their departure. He eased up on his players, even Lou Angelo, whom he considered paranoid and almost impossible to teach. And yet, as he sat in his seat high above the clouds and thought of all the adjustment he still had to make, an uneasy feeling swept through him and left him strangely meditative. Slowly, he closed his eyes, searching the darkness for a sign that would light his world again. He saw a man, neatly dressed and smiling, walk across a familiar street, the tips of his fingers fixed on his elegant hat.

In Harrisburg, Pennsylvania, John Boutselis walked to his bar and grill and tipped his hat to every woman on the street. "Good morning, good morning, nice day, isn't it?" Then he'd open his bar and grill in the rundown Hill section of Harrisburg. In the afternoon Amos Grant, handyman and helper, came in and said, "Hello, Mistuh Boots, how are you today?" In the evening the bar swelled with tired young men who drowned their failures in beer and whiskey. That's the way it was when George Boutselis grew up and worked his way through college in his father's bar and grill.

But at home everything sparkled. At home George discovered the simplicity of courage. At home, far from the swinging doors and brass spittoons and whiskey breaths, he found faith and spiritual renewal in the teachings of his father and mother, who raised three children under the law of Almighty God. "Go to school, Georgie," his father said one day. "Go to school for thirty-eight years. Go to college. Learn." His father was an uneducated Greek.

He died in 1960, and over three hundred people came to his funeral, which was held in the Orthodox Church. When the pallbearers lifted his father's coffin, his mother said, "Carry him softly. Don't hurt him." And George smiled through loving tears at his mother, and exulted to the triumphant paean that filled his heart with understanding. His father was a gentle man. He appreciated the worth of every human being. He loved God and family above everything. And his son would always remember these things that John Boutselis believed in.

He opened his eyes, no longer disillusioned, released from his terrible period of doubt. For George Boutselis had spent his most beautiful moment in the bosom of life, revering a little old man whom he called Papa. Before he dozed off into a dreamless sleep, he reminded himself that one day, soon, he'd have a long

165

talk with Lou Angelo. Somehow, he would get through, make him understand that the whole world wasn't against him. And certainly not his defensive backfield coach.

The players unwound in Portland. There were many fine seafood restaurants to eat in, nice shops to browse in, flowery parks to stroll through; and everywhere they looked, Portland smiled back in friendly welcome.

Under the lights of Civic Stadium on September 11, a squad of fifty cheerleaders, known as the Storm Spirits, exhorted a crowd of 13,000 to cheer their Western Division cellar-dwellers to victory. Instead, running back Jim Ford, subbing for an injured Harpo Gladieux, scored two touchdowns, tight end Ray Parson caught a Tom Sherman pass for another, Jimmy Sims intercepted a Storm pass for a fourth touchdown, and Moses Lajterman kicked the longest field goal of his pro career—a forty-two-yarder. The game was a laugher.

In the locker room, Parilli told reporters his defensive line played the way he knew they could, and that he was proud of his defensive backfield, especially Jimmy Sims, whose interception was a big break for the team.

A few yards away, Lou Angelo sat fully dressed on a wooden chair, his deep brown eyes boring holes into the wall. Right then, he wouldn't have cared if Civic Stadium and everyone in it blew sky-high.

The chartered jet rises high above the cloud line, coasting easily toward Hawaii, occasionally vibrating as it cuts through minor turbulence. The players shuffle cards, browse through paperbacks, eat tasty dishes served to them by smiling stewardesses, doze, watch a Woody Allen movie, laugh, yawn, go to the bathroom, fasten their seat belts—and suddenly, almost magically, they are in the brilliant sunlight of Hawaii, feeling the gentle touch of trade winds, scanning the magnificence of jagged green hills and the splendor of blue water and whitecaps that roll up to the beach of Waikiki. They are in Hawaii, *malihinis* all, strangers in a land of tropical paradise. It is the players' finest hour . . . their last full measure of peace as New York Stars.

For six days, from the time the team left Portland to the moment of kickoff against Hawaii in the Hula Bowl, the players earnestly tried to follow an orderly schedule of practice—and eagerly looked forward to relaxation and fun. Somewhere in between, most of their desires were realized. And yet there were some goals that could never be reached.

At night, with the lights of the city at his back and a golden moon rising from the sea, Moses Lajterman stood on his Holiday Inn balcony and wondered how God could have invented such a beautiful place as Hawaii. With white speckled waves breaking at his feet and someone playing a guitar farther up on the deserted beach, George Sauer wondered why he couldn't find an answer to all his dreams. Under a black sky sprinkled with Pacific stardust, Greg Lens focused his eyes on the neon lights of a discotheque and wondered when he'd be able to settle down to have a family of his own. They were only three of thirty-seven players who watched and wondered and waited for a sign to reveal the full secret of their existence. But when daylight filled the sky with brilliant red streaks, they all woke up no closer to the secret than they had been the night before.

One afternoon, when practice was over, Babe Parilli hailed Bill Crespinel on the beach and suggested they take a stroll. For more than an hour the pro football coach and the free-lance photographer walked along the sand, observing the pink stucco walls of the famed Royal Hawaiian Hotel, catamarans that pushed out into the foam, bronzed vacationers who rushed into the warm, invigorating water; and then, under a flaring sunset, the two men sat on a low embankment and watched the surfers ride in on pounding waves. After a while, as he looked out to the sea, Parilli told Crespinel a little about who he was and where he came from:

"My father is eighty-five, strong as an ox. But he spends most

167

of his time nowadays puttering in the garden or tinkering in the house. I'll tell you, though, he still has a twinkle in his eye. . . .

"My father worked in a mill. So did my older brother. And after I got out of grade school I worked as a bricklayer during summer vacations. Hell, if it wasn't for football I might still be laying bricks in Rochester, Pennsylvania. Not that it was bad, mind you. Honest work never hurt anybody . . .

"I guess Bear Bryant has been the strongest influence in my life. He was always able to get one hundred percent out of his players, and I was no exception. I remember one time, when I was quarterbacking Kentucky in 1950, we had a so-called breather against North Texas State before playing LSU the following Saturday night. Well, we beat North Texas, 25–0, but a big defensive end of theirs, kid by the name of Bishop, kicked me right in the nuts. The next thing you know I'm in the infirmary with a blood clot. Bear came in to see me. He threw a play book down on my bed and said, 'We're playing LSU Saturday night. Be ready to go.' What could I do? At that time I would've run over nails if Bear told me to. Anyway, Bear moved me into his house so that we could go over our game plan against LSU while I rested up. Meanwhile, the trainer devised a chastity belt for me to wear over my aching balls. That Saturday night Bear sent me into the game with these instructions: 'Okay, we're going with the shotgun formation. Start throwing until I tell you to stop.' I'll never forget it. I threw fifteen passes in the first sixteen plays, and we went on to beat LSU, 14–0. I even scored one of the touchdowns on a quarterback sneak. And my balls never hurt me once throughout the whole game. Maybe because Bear was watching me from the sideline . . .

"When I was in Green Bay I met my wife, Priscilla, whose father was a veterinarian. She was a Miss Wisconsin and I was a hotshot number one draft choice of the Packers at the time. But things didn't go too well for me while I was in Green Bay, so I wound up playing in Canada in 1959. We were married by then, but our home was still in Green Bay. When the AFL was founded in 1960 I refused to report to Ottawa, and signed with the Oakland Raiders. That season we had a child, a boy, and we

named him Vance. When the season ended, I packed up the family to drive back to Green Bay. Well, we had a Peugeot roadster, a blue one with a sun roof, and we started the trip in January. I tell you, it was cold. It was supposed to take us three days to get home, but it took us five. To tell you the truth, looking back, I still wonder how we came out of it alive. It must've been ten below when the heater went out. The snow was all around us and not a motel in sight. It was like a bad movie. Then we ran out of gas. Well, there was a gas station about a mile or so down the road, so I left my wife and baby in the car and walked in the snow to get gas. The guy gave me a can, took a ten-dollar deposit, and I went back to the car with my fingers frozen to the handle. When I got there, after about an hour from the time I left it, my baby looked blue. Somehow, I got my hands unstuck from the can, poured the gas in, then drove to the station to fill the car with a full tank. I mean, we barely made it to a motel. In another hour or so we would've frozen to death. And on the way I kept thinking, what the hell am I doing this for? Look at me, hotshot football player. Boy, how I wished right then that I was laying bricks in Rochester and coming home every night to a warm house. You want to know something, Bill? Every once in a while, I still think that."

Before the largest crowd of the season at Honolulu Stadium (12,169), Moses Lajterman kicked two field goals for the New York Stars. But when he kicked off to Hawaii early in the fourth quarter, Lajterman felt a sharp pain run down his right leg. He limped to the bench, praying that Parilli wouldn't have to call on him again. A few minutes later R. A. Coppedge cleared the crossbar with an Hawaiian field goal. It won the game.

On the long plane ride home, Parilli seemed more dejected than at any time since taking over the head coaching job. "We played a lousy game," he said to Stew Barber. "Our defense didn't play up to its potential. They just didn't put out one hundred percent, damn it!"

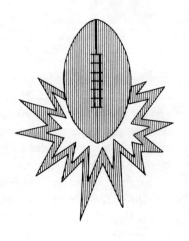

FIFTEEN

*"Here we go here we go here we go move
your hands move your hands move your
hands gimme a good hand and shoulder
block don't set so high get a good body lean
hurry hurry hurry quick quick quick do it
again set hike hut here we go hurry hurry
hurry bring that arm up gimme a better fake
than that goddamn that's horseshit don't butt
it pull it to the outside hurry hurry hurry
gitta gitta gitta . . ."*

LAMAR LEACHMAN

On September 18 the World Football League transferred the
debt-ridden Houston franchise to Shreveport, Louisiana. From
his office in Newport Beach, Commissioner Gary Davidson said
the team would operate under WFL administration until the end
of the season. Meanwhile, Texan coach Jim Garrett was sus-
pended by Davidson for imploring his players to boycott the
move.

On September 21 quarterback Bubba Wyche of the Detroit

170

Wheels sent out a distress signal to Davidson. "The situation here is desperate," said Wyche. "We haven't been paid in weeks. We've been calling off practice sessions because we can't afford the laundry service. And, in case you didn't know, if the Johnson & Johnson rep in Philadelphia hadn't supplied us with free tape we couldn't have played the Bell. And that was a month ago! Please, give us some relief, will you?"

Davidson assured Wyche that he would act on the problem within a couple of days.

On September 24 the World Football League took over the debt-ridden Jacksonville franchise. From his office in Newport Beach Commissioner Gary Davidson gathered up $65,000 in escrow funds to partially satisfy Shark players who had threatened a strike action at Anaheim Stadium, where they were scheduled to play the Sun on September 25. The Sharks had gone without paychecks for five weeks. When Davidson brought the money over on the morning of the game the players' militancy ebbed.

"The Jacksonville players have been wonderful," said Davidson after he had dispersed approximately one-fifth of the back pay. "We will continue to do whatever has to be done for them."

The September air filled with thunder, leaves dropped, gusty winds blew across Great South Bay, and the New York Stars made sweeping lineup changes. Cornerback Wendell Wilson, wide receiver Bob Hermanni, running back Andy Huff, safety Lou Angelo, and kicker Moses Lajterman were dropped; defensive tackle Joey Jackson, linebacker Marty Huff (Andy's brother), running backs Lee Bouggess and John King, wide receiver Al Barnes and cornerback John Dockery were added.

A homecoming of sorts was also prepared for Pete Rajecki, reactivated by Parilli as a replacement for Lajterman. The Argentine-born kicker had returned from Hawaii with a slight muscle pull—yet serious enough to keep him out of action for perhaps a week or two. Dr. Cowan reported his findings to Parilli.

"I'm going to bring Rajecki back," Parilli told Lajterman three days after the Hawaiian game. "You've done a good job for us, but we have financial problems and can't afford to carry two

171

kickers." Lajterman listened to his coach, heard his halting summation of passionless facts, then answered, "It isn't fair."

"Probably not. But I have to give Rajecki a chance now. I'm sorry, Moe. I wish it could be different."

The following week, Moses Lajterman went to work for the Metropolitan Life Insurance Company. He was still earthbound.

George Boutselis approached Lou Angelo on the day of the Turk with infinite composure, though his mind raced with a thousand things to say and so little time to say it in. Angelo had packed his things; season ended, flight booked to Youngstown; to face his father, who had coached at Chaney High for twenty-three years. He would tell his father it was just a question of bodies, not ability, that he could do it again, that he would somehow come back. What else could he say? Nothing. Nor would he have anything to say to the Banana Man, whose soft words fell on his ears as drumbeats in a far-off parade. But just before the two men drew apart—their final warfare waged in the grip of disillusionment and bewildering frustration—Angelo said, "Coach, I think you're the most insincere person I've ever known."

Boutselis allowed a sigh to escape. "If that's the way you feel, Lou, I can't help it. But I want to wish you luck, anyway."

They didn't shake hands.

Between the founding days of the World Football League and the thirteenth week of its inaugural season, a young man, not yet thirty-seven years old, worked assiduously, ofttimes around the clock, to own a major league professional football team. Initially his sights focused on Tampa, Florida, an announced expansion site of the NFL. Unable to raise the $16 million required to float a team in Tampa, he turned to Charlotte, North Carolina, a drawing board site for WFL games. In June he arrived in Charlotte, looked around and said to himself, "This is it. I want to be here." Three months later he returned as president of the WFL Charlotte Hornets—even though he wasn't the team's legal owner. The young man was Upton Bell.

Born to wealth and power, puckish by nature, a charming host and witty story teller, schoolboyish-handsome and steel-nerved, Upton Bell's greatest asset was what Leon Batista Alberti, the 15th-century Universal Man, once said of his own strongest point. Alberti, a Florentine architect, described himself as one who "could endure pain and cold and heat . . . showing by example that men could do anything with themselves if they will." For Bell, it all began in Mainline, Philadelphia.

Upton's grandfather, John Cromwell Bell I, played football at the University of Pennsylvania, and then went into the business world. He bought property in downtown Philadelphia when land was cheap, bought the Ritz-Carlton Hotel, sat on the board of trustees of his alma mater, and attended almost every meeting held by Walter Camp's football rules committee. John Cromwell Bell I believed in college football almost as much he did in money.

Upton's uncle, John Bell III, played tennis at the University of Pennsylvania, became a lawyer, a chief justice of the Pennsylvania Supreme Court, and a governor of the state.

Upton's mother, Frances Upton, sang for Flo Ziegfeld and co-starred with Eddie Cantor in a Broadway show called *Whoopee*.

Upton's father, DeBennville Bert Bell, attended Haverford Prep School. When Bert was eighteen, undecided about college, he asked his father, John Cromwell Bell I, what he should do. "You will go to the University of Pennsylvania or you will go to hell," said John Cromwell Bell I. In 1919 Bert Bell captained Penn and threw the first forward pass in the Rose Bowl. Twenty-seven years later he became commissioner of the NFL.

In mid-July of 1974, Gary Davidson granted Upton Bell a six-month option to put together an investment group in Charlotte in order to establish a WFL team there. Davidson also informed the former New England Patriot general manager that the Detroit Wheels franchise was in serious financial jeopardy. "I'll switch the club to Charlotte," said the commissioner, "if your group can take over its assets." Bell was intrigued with the possibilities, feeling he could build a powerful team around Detroit quarter-

173

back Bubba Wyche. He contacted Erwin Ziegelman, the club's attorney and one-thirty-second owner, who thought he could induce his associates to play at least one game in Charlotte as a test for fan reaction. However, after six weeks of frustrating negotiations, Bell was unable to obtain a final figure from Ziegelman as to how much the Detroit owners would take to unload their turkey. And by then the Wheels had lost ten out of their first eleven games. "Who needs a loser?" grumbled Bell's disenchanted backers. All contact between Charlotte and Detroit was broken off.

On Friday, September 20, receiving a tip from Howard Baldwin that the New York Stars were definitely up for sale, Bell placed a phone call from his home in Boston to Bob Schmertz in New York City. During their twenty-minute conversation, a verbal agreement was struck that would permit Bell to move the Stars to Charlotte after the Detroit game at Randall's Island—four days hence. In return, Schmertz was to receive $1.4 million from Bell's group, to be paid in increments over a three-year period.

"The creditors are banging on our doors," said Schmertz. "How soon can you come up with the first payment?"

"I don't know," replied Bell, "but I'm sure I can tie up the loose ends within a couple of weeks."

Bell's most significant prospect was Charlotte mayor John Belk, a country-styled politician who owned the largest department store chain in the South. "Now, Upton," said the mayor when Bell informed him of his deal with Schmertz, "I can't say exactly what I'm prepared to commit until y'all come back with a team. Then we'll see. But don't worry; I'm behind you one hundred percent."

With Belk's hedged guarantee as his only collateral, Bell then phoned Gary Davidson. The commissioner asked very few questions and offered no legal opinions.

"Do what you have to do," said Davidson from Newport Beach, "then call me so we can make a league statement."

On Tuesday morning, September 24, Bell flew to New York. Three hours later he arrived at the Stars office on Madison Avenue. With the exception of Bob Keating, no other team employee had knowledge of the impending franchise switch, not even Dusty Rhodes. Still she suspected the worst as soon as her former boss walked through the outer office.

"Hello, Upton." She blanched. "I was expecting you . . . sooner or later." Bell gave her a perfunctory nod.

It was noon, eight hours before Parilli and the New York Stars were to play their last game at Randall's Island. Bell felt exhilarated, almost drunk with excitement, but he needed to put his best foot forward with Keating.

"I know you must be disappointed, Bob," he said after shaking hands. "You've done a terrific job under trying circumstances."

"Thanks," said the Stars general manager, seeing the handwriting on the wall. "I always thought you were tough with the Patriots. Now I know *why* you had to be tough."

"I appreciate that. And, I need your help. Everything here has to be transferred to Charlotte. The quicker the better. I'll need documents, contracts, salary statements . . . the whole works. Can you start on it today?"

Keating agreed. All he knew about the deal was what Schmertz had told him the day before—that Upton Bell had the team, and that nothing should be said to anyone until Bell arrived from Charlotte in the morning. But Keating told his wife. She shrugged and said that somehow everything would work out for the best, as it always had in the past. More than at any time in his life, he hoped she was right.

They went into the outer office, where Bell informed the staff what had taken place. For the rest of the afternoon, in shocked silence, they began to remove seven months of accumulated treasure from files and desks for immediate shipment to a cold dark place somewhere in the labyrinths of North Carolina. Dusty spent an inordinate amount of time studying some glossies of the players during practice at La Salle. At one point during the afternoon she fled into the sanctity of her office and didn't come out again for an hour.

Bell had no plans to show up at Randall's Island that night, but he knew he had to inform Parilli about the move. After that he

would try to relax a bit in his room at the Essex House and prepare for his press conference the next morning. From Bob Keating's desk, he dialed out to La Salle.

"Babe? Upton here. How are you? . . . Yeah, I'm in New
York. I just want to tell you I'm taking over the team from
Schmertz and bringing it to Charlotte. I want the coaches to be
told, but it seems to me you shouldn't tell the players until after
the game. It might affect their play."

A long pause followed. "Hello, hello, Babe . . . ?"

"Yeah, I'm here, Upton. What does it mean?"

"It means I want you to come with me. We have a chance to
make it in Charlotte. The people there are great. Just relax."

"Jesus. I can hardly believe it's happening."

"Babe, just go out and play the ball game. We'll talk later at
the Essex House."

A crisp night. A good night for football. About 4,000 people
were in the stands. Maybe a little more. Rumors flew.

Bob Keating walked into the Downing Stadium press box ten
minutes after the game started. He was pounced on by a dozen
reporters. "Come on, give us a break," said Pete Alfano of
Newsday. "We already know an AP guy has talked to Gary Davidson, and that Davidson says the Stars are being sold. So why don't
you just tell us . . . to whom?"

"There'll be a press conference at the Essex House in the
morning. I can't tell you anything else. I don't want to break a
confidence."

"In other words," said Lew Fishman of the *LI Press*, "that's a
confirmation, right?"

"Look, fellows," said Keating vacantly, "let's wait awhile
longer. I'll make a phone call."

Vince Casey let the story out at the half. And the generally
unflappable New York writers gulped, as if they had learned of
a death in the family. Then Norm MacLean, stringing for the
Post, jumped up from his seat. "The Wheels have just filed for
bankruptcy!"

Down the line, Larry Ambrosino of the *Staten Island Advance* moaned, "Frankly, Charlotte, I don't give a damn."

Bell met with Keating, Parilli and Baldwin around midnight. They sat around in Bell's suite at the Essex House and talked until three in the morning, drinking beer and Cokes, sorting out the past, pointing toward the future. Keating, unsure of his position, was necessarily vague; Parilli was in a daze; Baldwin was confident; and Upton Bell was positively euphoric. He would finally own a football team.

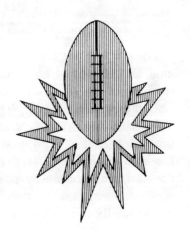

SIXTEEN

Everybody, it seemed, had been rendered punch-drunk by the incredible change in WFL fortunes during the past few weeks. In Chicago, Bob Markus filed a story for the October 3 morning edition of the *Tribune,* the day the new Charlotte Stars were to play the Fire. His column topped the sports page, above the section heading and a baseball lead story which reported the wrap-up of the National League East pennant by the Pittsburgh Pirates. The column head was emphatic:

DAVIDSON WILL GO,
BUT WFL TO SURVIVE: ORIGER

"Gary Davidson will be out as commissioner of the World Football League by next year," reported Markus, "and possibly sooner." Neither the prediction nor the quote was his. According to the *Tribune* scribe, they were the utterings of Tom Origer, the youthful owner of the Fire, who had just returned from a summit meeting in California with Davidson. The column went on to state that Origer's mission to Newport Beach was to convince

Davidson that a crisis point in league affairs had been reached, that Origer blamed all of the league's financial ills on Davidson and the other organizers who "did not take the trouble to line up sound investors. Anybody who could scrape up $250,000 for a franchise was in. All they were interested in was getting the front money. They cared more about that than they cared about the league."

The Fire owner was obviously steamed enough to risk the disclosure to Markus in order to bring the whole sorry mess out into the open. Besides, he had made an assessment of his own problems at home. Three straight Fire losses had caused the fans to think twice before shelling out the price of a ticket. Origer realized that a bad season, coupled with negative league publicity, could quickly erode the gate receipts at Soldier Field and choke off the enthusiasm that had given Chicago one of the few healthy franchises in the staggering WFL family.

On top of everything, key injuries to quarterback Virgil Carter, wide receiver Jim Scott and league-leading kickoff returner Charlie Reamon had flattened the Fire offense. Origer expected a turnout of less than 20,000 for the Thursday-night nationally televised game against the transplanted Stars.

The moment was ripe for Origer to publicly rake Davidson over the coals, at a time when gloomy forecasts were oozing in from almost every town harboring a WFL team. The Markus column freely quoted his displeasure with everything Davidson had done since the season opened.

Origer advised the columnist that the commissioner had already been relieved of his authority in the area of finding fresh buyers for some of the more troubled franchises, and that league offices would be moved from Newport Beach to New York in 1975. "And," added the Fire executive, "New York will get an expansion franchise in 1976, when Yankee Stadium will be ready for occupancy."

Indeed, Origer may well have been whistling through a graveyard when he issued those disclosures. Chicago newspapers had been ominously devoid of WFL news in recent days, even to the point of silence about the upcoming game between the Fire and the Stars. This singular fact brought about a rather laughable incident that would certainly become part of the growing WFL folklore.

Originally, the Fire was booked for a game on Wednesday, October 2, but a rescheduling change, in order to place the Fire in the national television slot, pushed the contest to October 3. Nonetheless, a good number of fans were unaware of the switch in dates. Nearly 5,000 of them trooped out to Soldier Field one evening too soon!

"Come back tomorrow night," shouted a stadium guard, who had trouble convincing one incredulous ticket holder the date had been changed.

"Yeah, baby," the fan answered, "but with all the fuck-ups going on in this league, I hope the *teams* show up."

The Stars arrived at Chicago's O'Hare Field on schedule late Wednesday afternoon after an hour-and-a-half flight out of LaGuardia Airport. Lines of communication failed in their case, too. Everybody on the squad except Coach Parilli thought they were going to bed down at the Regency Hyatt Hotel. However, the Regency was somewhat dubious about accommodating a team that had been unceremoniously swept out of New York with a trail of debts and a vacuum of information about its ability to satisfy screeching creditors. *No room at the inn* was the late-hour explanation tossed off by a Hyatt office manager. Back in Charlotte, Dusty Rhodes placed hurried calls to other Chicago hotels in order to find shelter for the Stars. The Sheraton Chicago on North Michigan Avenue came up with the rooms—as soon as a $1,500 deposit was wired to them from Upton Bell in Charlotte.

As the players were deposited from two airport buses to the sidewalk in front of the Sheraton, Greg Lens looked at the scrawled letters which identified the hotel. He nearly froze in his tracks.

"Shit!" he honked at John Elliott. "I thought we were going to the Regency Hyatt. What happened?"

Lens's consternation was soon cleared up by Lamar Leachman,

who was told of the change by Parilli on the flight out from New York.

"Just one of those things, darlin'," Leachman offered. "Some crossed signals over reservations, that's all."

"Well, I sure as hell better get them *uncrossed,*" said Lens. "I'm expecting someone at the Regency, and it ain't a *fella!*"

Lens's half-moon eyelids closed slowly, like a curtain going down at the end of *Othello.*

For the first time on the road, there was no Dusty Rhodes to take care of the room assignments, meal tickets and all the other details the players and coaches had taken for granted in the past. Vince Casey was now in charge of that thankless task, from the moment the team stepped off the plane at O'Hare Field. Dusty was struggling with her own grief in Charlotte.

At the Sheraton Chicago, Casey handed out the room keys at the registration desk, and, gratefully, the Stars lugged their bags into the elevators, closed the doors to their rooms, and made ready for another bus ride—to remove the rust from their muscles in a fifteen-minute workout at Soldier Field. Before leaving his room, Greg Lens furiously spun the dial of his phone, then grunted as soon as he reached the front desk of the Regency Hyatt: "Listen, I'd like to leave a message for a young lady who may be in the lobby waiting for me. Yup . . . that's right . . . my name is Greg Lens, and I'm with the New York . . . aah . . . Charlotte Stars . . ."

Babe Parilli came down to the Sheraton lobby with optimism painted on his face and with as much courage as he could muster, even though the franchise jugglers had drained away some of the concentration he needed to carry out his coaching duties. In the lobby, waiting for the bus to pull up to take the team to the stadium, Parilli looked like any other out-of-towner who might have shown up for one of the many seminars, sales meetings or coffee klatches going on in the hotel. Still tanned from his week in Hawaii, he watched his players emerge from the elevators— sleepy-eyed combat troops on their way to the loading zone.

Could he keep their morale going, relate to their needs—their silent hunger for acceptance? Their basic lust for the game itself? He could; he would. Winning against the Fire was all that mattered, after all. Events outside his control would dictate further contingencies, but defeat would only accelerate the smoldering fear, and panic had never been part of Parilli's makeup.

"Okay, fellows, let's get moving," said the Kentucky Babe. His troops trudged into the bus, never looking anywhere except at the open door leading into the vehicle. When they were all seated, Lens glowered heavily and cursed his luck. He had plumb forgotten the name of the girl he was supposed to meet in the lobby of the Regency Hyatt!

She was a blind date who had been set up for him by one of the stewardesses aboard the homecoming flight from Hawaii. A knockout, the stewardess had assured him.

"Hey, John," Lens asked Elliott, who was sitting alongside him, "do you think she might be waiting for me at the Sheraton when we get back?"

Elliott grinned. Lens had been anxiously looking forward to his forthcoming Chicago rendezvous in between practice breaks at La Salle, and Elliott had been listening dutifully to Lens's plans ever since the team loaded bag and baggage onto the plane taking them to the Windy City.

"What happened?" he asked his crushed-and-beaten friend.

"The Regency said they couldn't leave a message for a tall blonde with big tits. They said there were a million of 'em all over Chicago."

It was approximately four o'clock in Chicago and five o'clock in New York City. As the Stars bus chugged up North Michigan Avenue, traffic going out of Manhattan at that hour had built up with automobiles dragging off the suburban commuters. Central Park South was at its usual pace—clogged. Shut off from the noise, high above the congestion, Bob Keating and Ken Knigen faced Gary Davidson in the commissioner's suite at the Park Lane Hotel. Davidson had arrived in the early-morning hours after a long flight from Los Angeles to Kennedy Airport. He was anxious to sound out the crumbling New York situation before leaving for Chicago the next day to see the Stars play the Fire.

As far as Davidson was concerned, his hardnosed discussion with Origer in California had convinced him that he would have to take immediate steps to neutralize the adverse publicity that was snowballing all over the WFL map.

If this was to be a constructive meeting, the mood and direction of the ensuing conversation hardly suggested that possibility. It began with limp handshakes and a five-minute wait while Davidson testily completed a long distance call, obviously boiled over something or other in one of the bombed-out franchise cities.

A tall, heavy-set man in his late thirties, Ken Knigen was a crackerjack attorney. His strong-willed, abrupt personality underscored a previous stint as a city councilman in Mayor John Lindsay's administration. Now out of government, Knigen's sphere of influence in and around City Hall prevailed as a member of the prestigious firm of Ballon, Stoll and Itzler, specialists in bankruptcy law.

Knigen had fenced with men like Davidson before. Applying his wits against the WFL commissioner was a challenge he looked forward to. As all three men got directly down to business concerning the Stars transfer to Charlotte and the problem of filling the void, Knigen emphasized the importance of his firm's wire-pulling abilities in New York politics.

"It's just a simple matter of cash," said Knigen. "Now, the combined personal net worth of our people is about sixty-five million. Most of them are in the garment trade. The chief executive officer of my firm, Fred Ballon, was once the treasurer and general council for Yonkers Raceway and chairman of the board of Sunshine Park race track in Florida . . ."

No response.

"Well, it stands to reason that Mr. Ballon has funneled a lot of tax revenue into the city through track income. The city recognizes this and is willing to cooperate with him if he wishes to field a team in New York. Of course, Yankee Stadium is the place we want to play, so we've been talking to city officials about negotiating a lease to open pro football there in 1976. If we get the stadium, and we've been assured we can, then we're prepared to supply the proper backing for a first-class WFL operation in New York."

Davidson's reply was terse. "Anybody can get in if the money is right."

Keating tried vainly to mask a grimace. It pushed its way around the corners of his mouth.

"I think you've missed the point," continued Knigen. "The thing is, we've got the means to secure the stadium without a lot of red tape. It seems to me this is exactly what you're looking for. The question is . . . how much are you asking for a franchise?"

"We're asking four-point-two million," replied Davidson.

Knigen's eyes widened. He looked at Keating, who was by now halfway off his chair, finding it impossible to stay in one place after hearing the incredible figure.

"Look, Gary," said Knigen, "let's be realistic. If the league were a big success—which it isn't—and if New York were still in the picture—which it isn't—I wouldn't be here in the first place. Now, let's look at what's really happened to the WFL. The Detroit Wheels are bankrupt, the Houston Texans are out of business, Jacksonville has laid an egg, Florida is almost down the drain, and New York has taken a powder to Charlotte. Hardly an encouraging record, I'd say."

"Nevertheless," Davidson answered, his boyish smile hidden somewhere in the recesses of his cold blue eyes, "that's the figure I have to stay with."

"Well," persisted Knigen, "I just don't think your asking price is realistic. Or, for that matter, fair."

The commissioner never wavered. "We've been having ongoing conversations with other people who think we *are* realistic and fair. I'm afraid I'm going to have to hold the line somewhere around that price. If your people can handle it, we can reach some sort of understanding—as long as we're around that ball-park figure."

"Maybe so, maybe not," said Knigen. "I'll have to discuss this further with Fred Ballon. One way or another he'll get back to you before you leave for Chicago."

Keating made an effort to stir up a positive breeze in the fetid atmosphere. "All I can add, Gary, is that Mr. Knigen and Mr. Ballon have the means to cut through the bureaucracy and departmental roadblocks in a hurry. They can deliver Yankee Stadium, and I think that's the real issue here."

Davidson smiled, got up, and hunched his shoulders forward, indicating there was nothing more to add. After a few mumbled goodbyes, both Keating and Knigen left the Park Lane Hotel less happy than when they first entered the building.

Morning broke bright and clean for Tom Beer. Outside, Chicago began to warm up after setting a record low of twenty-eight degrees Wednesday morning. But now, on this crisp, comfortable Thursday morning, Beer could look down from his seventh-floor room at the Sheraton and see Chicagoans scurrying along North Michigan Avenue to their office buildings and other depositories of employment. Only a few of them were dressed in heavy outerwear.

It was Beer's kind of weather. He had carried along a slip of paper with the names of a few bookstores penciled in by his publisher, Houghton Mifflin. The Marshall Field department store, Brentano's, and a couple of other major outlets were on the list. *Sunday's Fools* would be in stock at those locations, his publisher said, and Beer was anxious to find out if his appearance on the NBC *Today* show the previous Thursday had helped sales. Gene Shalit, one of the *Today* hosts, had given him eighteen minutes on the program. Even Daniel Ellsberg, the man who turned the Pentagon Papers over to the *New York Times,* hadn't received that much time as a fellow guest.

In the hotel drugstore, Beer ordered up a hearty breakfast of orange juice, hash and eggs, a side order of bacon, toast, and steaming coffee. Hungrily, he went to work on his breakfast plate, all the while thinking about something Parilli had told him just before he made bed check at eleven o'clock the night before.

185

Parilli was in the lobby and had called him aside. They stood quietly and talked in an area where prints and watercolors were being sold to the public. At that late hour, only a desultory salesman, counting up the day's receipts, was around, although far enough away not to overhear their conversation.

"Tom," Parilli had said, "I know how much the book means to you. But I just called Upton about a few things, and he mentioned that he had read *Sunday's Fools*. Frankly, he said he didn't like some of the references you had made about him."

"Tough shit," Tom said defensively.

"Well, he said more than that," Parilli went on. "Upton doesn't feel you should publicize it in Charlotte. I guess he's thin-skinned about the whole thing. Now, I don't give a damn if you decide to go on every radio and television station in Charlotte to promote the book, but I'm telling you how he feels about it."

Beer realized that his book could become a thorn in his side. Written during his last miserable year as a tight end for the New England Patriots, it contained allusions to Upton Bell that were far from complimentary. One passage in particular stuck out:

> During the season Bell would occasionally stroll out onto the practice field to watch us in workouts. Some assistant coaches would sneer to one another, "Here comes Napoleon," and, "I wonder where his white horse is today? Maybe he left it on Broadway." There was clearly no love lost between Bell and any of the coaching staff. It was a case of mutual disrespect.

Of course, Beer had no inkling that Upton Bell would turn up again in his life, and this time in an even more powerful position than the one he'd held in Boston. Now that Upton Bell had become the new owner of the Charlotte franchise, there was no telling how he would feel about him.

But while sipping coffee dregs from his cup the following morning, he thought about it all over again. And the anger returned. He paid his bill and walked out of the hotel. Without hesitation, he strode over to the doorman.

"Could you tell me how I can get to Marshall Field?"

"Sure," replied the doorman, a red-nosed fellow with wide, happy cheeks. "Just walk four blocks this way"—he pointed— "and make a right turn on Wabash."

Beer thanked him and threaded his way into the crowd, feeling grateful that a brilliant sun was on his back and that Chicago had never looked any prettier than it did at that moment.

It was approximately ten hours before game time. Most of the players and coaches were either lazing about in their rooms or hanging around the drugstore or other lobby shops in the Sheraton. A few of them even ventured out to do some window shopping. But for Tiger and Mike Ferraro the late morning and early afternoon were anything but a lark.

Father and son were in search of one hundred decals. The old logo on the Star helmets—all thirty-seven of them—would have to be altered for the game against the Fire. Bell had called Parilli about it, said the *NY* on the helmets was to be replaced by a temporary *C*. Okay, said Parilli, it would be taken care of.

At the same time that Tom Beer crossed North Michigan Avenue to reach Marshall Field, the Ferraros rounded a corner that led them to a row of lithography shops on Clark Street. Surely, they surmised, one of the shops would have exactly what they were looking for. After two frustrating hours, however, they came away empty-handed. Not one of the stores had a *C* to fit over the *NY*. Either the decals were too narrow or too wide, or there simply weren't any in stock. Then Mike had an idea.

"Why don't we call the Chicago Bears?"

Tiger placed a call to Soldier Field, where the Bears were practicing for their Sunday game against the Saints. He knew the Bears' equipment man, who he hoped could help the Stars out. The equipment man said how the hell are you, Tiger, and, sure, his supplier, a Wilson Sporting Goods representative, probably had quite a few decals on hand. Why don't you come over? said Tiger's friend. He'd get right on the stick in the meantime. Within minutes, the Ferraros were in a cab heading for the stadium, and within an hour the Wilson salesman arrived at the stadium with the one hundred decals—the official Chicago Bear letter that identified the team helmets. A bright orange—perfect for television. Tiger held one over the *NY* on a Star helmet he had carried with him in a leather bag from the Sheraton. The *C* covered the *NY* almost perfectly, requiring just a little cutting at the edges to lie squarely inside the five-pointed star.

"Perfect!" Tiger chortled.

"Perfect!" echoed Mike.

"That'll come to one hundred and fifty dollars," said the Wilson salesman.

Coexistence was achieved for the first time between the NFL and the WFL.

At three o'clock that afternoon in the crowded lobby of the Sheraton Chicago, powdery-faced women in mink wraps sat on sofas and chairs, clucking happily about this show in town and that specialty shop on the avenue. At the head of the staircase leading to the front entrance, enthusiastic business men shook hands, discussed merchandising gimmicks, and laughed uproariously over new jokes that had filtered into the territory.

Ten floors up, in room 1063, Greg Lens lay on his bed and stared dumbly at a soundless television rerun of an old movie. Only sleep would diminish the disappointment of love's labor lost. His blind date never showed up at the Sheraton, or as much as left a message or a clue that she actually existed. Thinking about it, Lens vowed to take out his frustration on the Chicago Fire. Yessiree, he swore, maybe he *did* miss out on a piece of tail . . . *but* he sure in hell was going to have a piece of Leroy Kelly's leg that night. And the idea of it—of meeting Kelly under a pileup at Soldier Field—spun Lens off on other tangents. Before long, he drifted into a deep, smiling sleep.

Down the hall, in room 1057, Gerry Philbin came out of the bathroom with a towel draped around his waist. It was as though a white, cold curtain had dropped out of the sky, encircling Philbin's muscular body, surrounding his manhood. Quickly, he moved toward his bed, sweeping into it without a sound.

188

Stretched out, with his hands locked behind his head, he idly thought of a LeRoy Neiman print he had purchased in the lobby shop the night before—a Kentucky Derby scene with horsemen and horses and the smell of roses in the paint. He already owned three Neiman originals, including a portrait of himself in a Jet uniform—a present from the artist. Well, he figured, why not? Neiman always painted the superstuds, didn't he?

He let his eyes wander over to the window, where the afternoon light of Chicago's sun flooded the room and washed over George Sauer's yellow-brown hair. Philbin's roomie was sitting in a wing chair, engrossed in a paperback book, pulling thoughtfully at his mustache.

"Hey, George, what are you reading?"

"Oh, it's about Vincent Van Gogh. An excellent book called *Dear Theo.*"

"Irving Stone wrote it, right?"

"No, he edited it. It's an account of Van Gogh's letters to his brother."

"Tell me about his ear, George . . ." Philbin laughed, mimicking one of the characters in a John Steinbeck novel.

Sauer placed the paperback face down on his lap and crooked up his mouth in a half-smile.

"I take it you have read *Of Mice and Men,*" he said. "Or . . . did you see the movie?"

"I saw the television version, the one with George Segal playing George. I forget who the hell Lennie was . . . you know, the dummy who keeps asking, 'Tell me about the rabbits, George' . . ."

"Lon Chaney, Junior, played Lennie in the movie, and Burgess Meredith was George."

"You really dig movies, don't you?"

"Sure. As long as it's a good story."

"Yeah," said Philbin, "I get what you mean. Something with Linda Lovelace . . ."

"Well, hardly. I would say something on the order of Laurel and Hardy."

"Huh? Oh . . . I can see that . . . yeah."

Philbin allowed a low cackle to fall from his lips. He didn't know what the hell George was trying to lead him into, although the idea of testing his buddy's intellectual and philosophical theories always appealed to him. Philbin had met all kinds of people during his pro football career, and George Sauer had to be one of the smartest guys he ever knew—maybe *the* smartest. But he wasn't prepared to deal with the symbolic meaning of Laurel and Hardy at the moment. Not now, at the time of his last hurrah . . . when to be properly roguish, carefree, and well-heeled meant more to him than the examination of his own sensitivities—and the painful processes that might be involved in his discoveries.

"Hey, George, do you know the three most damaging words to a man's ego?"

"No, what are they?"

" 'Is it in?' "

Twenty-four hours had passed since Bob Keating and Ken Knigen met with Commissioner Gary Davidson to discuss a new franchise for New York. Now, as he sat at his desk in the nearly deserted Stars office on Madison Avenue, Keating resented the isolation imposed on him by the conditions of economic collapse. Since most of his administrative staff had been let go, the office plunged into eerie silence, which shrouded every square foot of the expansive quarters. The silence exasperated his patience. It played havoc with his nerves.

To make matters worse, the stillness was occasionally interrupted by the piercing ring of the switchboard phone, then another ring on Keating's phone when Lois Cohen, his secretary, signaled that an irate caller demanded to speak with only the general manager. A pause; then Keating would pick up and listen in apparent discomfort to the voices of creditors who hammered at his ear for payment of long-overdue bills.

"Mr. Keating," incanted one hollow-sounding attorney, "this is Mr. Meyrowitz of Simon, Meyrowitz and Jobrack. My firm represents Champion Stationery and Printing Corporation. We've been advised by our client that you are currently indebted to them for the sum of $1,485.85. Of course, Mr. Keating, in view of recent events concerning the Stars, we'd like to know what you intend doing about this debt . . ."

Another: "Mr. Keating, my name is Betty Maloney. I represent The Saints Drum and Bugle Corps in Fords, New Jersey. Well, you may recall that our organization was hired by the Stars management to perform before and during halftime at a game on August 28 at Downing Stadium . . ."

"Yes, Miss Maloney, I remember . . ."

"Since we are a nonprofit organization, and since the children did perform and were well accepted by the attending fans, the five hundred dollars agreed upon for their services is urgently needed by the Saints Corps. We expect that you'll meet your obligation to the agreement . . ."

Still another: "Mr. Keating, this is Campus Coach Lines. . . . Now, about your account . . . a matter of something over three thousand dollars past due on using our coaches to and from Randall's Island to play your games . . ."

It was only the tip of the iceberg. Keating had no conclusive evidence that nearly a million dollars in accumulated bills would ever be paid. Hell, he knew about as much as his creditors where the money was coming from.

And now, sitting at his desk in the late afternoon on the day the Charlotte Stars were getting ready to play the Fire in Chicago, another call came in. At first he hesitated. It was enough, he thought. He'd go home, try to spend a quiet evening with his wife and kids in Connecticut, even turn on the television set that evening and watch his former team perform on Channel 9. But he decided to answer on the fourth ring.

"Hello, Mr. Keating, this is Bob Kurland of the *Bergen Record*."

"Yes?"

"I just thought I'd get an update. Can you tell me what the situation is at the moment . . . ?"

"Yeah," Keating sighed, "I'm just putting the body into the ground."

Under high-intensity lights, Soldier Field awakened to the rites of autumnal amusement. Massed Army, Navy, Air Force and

191

Coast Guard bands played "God Bless America" and "You're a Grand Old Flag" to a nation no longer interested in Irving Berlin and George M. Cohan. On one side of the stadium, lights glimmered between the triangle and abacus of an ersatz Greek temple; mocking antiquity, bowing to modern vanity, to the gods of sport who sat across the way in a long narrow bunker. Up there, above the customers and contestants, press and media dwelled in sanctified seclusion, warmed by the flame of a phantom visionary in their midst—Gary Davidson.

And down below on the near sideline, TVS announcer Alex Hawkins held up a book while Tom Beer, in his yellow New York Stars windbreaker, talked about his sojourn through the NFL as a Sunday Fool.

"The ball is up. Ike Thomas has it. He's hit . . . downed on the Charlotte Stars thirty-five-yard line. Okay, first and ten . . ."

After the game, Larry Butler led the players in prayer and thanked the Lord for bringing them through a hard-earned victory over the Fire; team captain Gerry Philbin presented the game ball to cornerback Larry Shears, who ran in a sixty-four-yard interception for a key touchdown; Greg Lens whooped it up and proclaimed he had taken a bite out of Leroy Kelly's leg; Al Barnes said he was happy to be playing with the best group of guys he had ever met and spoke modestly about his three catches for 108 yards—and Babe Parilli introduced the team's new owner.

"I think you all did a helluva job out there tonight," said Upton Bell. "So, rather than keep you with a long-winded speech, I just want to add two things: you'll be playing before the most enthusiastic fans in the world in Charlotte . . . and you'll be getting your paychecks on time." There was a hollowness in the cheers.

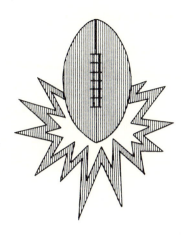

SEVENTEEN

By late Sunday afternoon, October 6, the last vestiges of pro football at La Salle Military Academy were reduced to mundane samplings: a crumpled sock in the dressing room, cleat marks on the deserted practice field, the stub of Babe Parilli's cigar in an ashtray—on a desk he would no longer use—and a black-and-yellow NEW YORK STARS sign on the dormitory entrance. These were the visible facts—scanty reminders of a former presence that once filled every acre of the La Salle campus.

But all else—sounds and sensibilities—dissipated into the autumn breezes above Great South Bay. The jarring "gitta-gitta-gitta" of Lamar Leachman faded and died here, as did the yelping of Harpo's dog, Mr. Brown. Gone were the deep-chested laugh of Gerry Philbin, the rumbling wheezes of Greg Lens, and the jubilation of Moses Lajterman. The highly discernible tumult that had once wedded itself to mortality had now taken on the silence of the grave, lost forever in the currents of human endeavor.

At dusk the moving vans, U-Hauls and autos roared south, speeding along the highways and byroads to Charlotte, the largest

193

city in the Carolinas. The exodus began at two that afternoon, when Babe Parilli and sixteen other coaches and players caught a commercial flight from LaGuardia Airport. But the majority of migrants traveled overland, on a course that would take them 725 sluggish miles to the "Land of Textiles." Suitcases and shopping bags were stuffed into car trunks, furniture into moving vans— weary bodies into anything with four wheels and enough gas to carry the tonnage south.

Turbine difficulties temporarily immobilized the team's equipment van at the approach to the George Washington Bridge. Undaunted, Mike Ferraro snarled choice blasphemies at honking autos and screaming motorists while Tiger Ferraro wrestled with the cantankerous engine. After a six-hour delay the truck started, vomiting out black clouds of poisonous fumes as it lumbered over the bridge. In a little over an hour they had reached Trenton on the Jersey Turnpike. With Mike's foot pressed hard on the accelerator, the escaping noise from the exhaust produced a discordant howl, causing Tiger to stir in his seat alongside Mike. He squeezed open one eye, moaned, and then slipped back into unconsciousness.

Mike let up on the gas, deferring to his father's condition. The tremendous exertion of packing and moving had leveled Tiger's bones, puffed his eyes and cut fresh crevices into his face. Mike could see the change, and it worried him. He thought back to an earlier time when his father's cheeks were smooth and his eyes sparkled with youthful clarity.

The miles clicked off. Mike Ferraro rolled down the window, stuck his arm on the ledge of the window and gulped in the sweet-smelling air. He had to concentrate on something—anything—or fatigue would shortly overwhelm him and just as surely destroy them both.

Tightly packed cardboard cartons, containing helmets, shoulder pads and uniforms, rested in the van's sizable interior. The day before, Mike and his father had carefully checked each piece of equipment, handling them like precious antiques. One by one —pants, shoes, socks, surgical supplies, footballs—all sorts of gear were removed from cabinets and shelves.

As he drove, Mike heard an occasional shifting of the boxes—imperceptible at first, then more distinct. Almost hypnotically, he began to count off the pieces, as though he were actually in the back of the truck—looking into each box. He was comforted, convinced that he would now make it through the night—that soon he and his father would be able to slide under clean sheets and sleep away the miseries of the past ten days.

"Yeah," he heard himself bellow into the Jersey hills, "we'll get there, Tiger! Don't you worry about a thing!"

The sun dipped low in the Maryland sky, spreading shadows along the verdant countryside. Here and there, horses grazed in open fields close to the highway. Battered pickup trucks filled with produce carried suntanned farmers to candy villages hidden in the distant hills. All the while, Tommy Sherman gripped the wheel of his car and cursed the cruelties of the road. He had started his journey in a rented truck, with the family belongings lashed down in the rear. In a mishap similar to the one that disabled the Ferraro vehicle in the Bronx, Sherman's truck broke down near Elkton, Maryland. Fortunately, his wife and three children were up ahead in their car. Within an hour the truck and its contents were safely stored, and the Shermans were on the turnpike—headed for Charlotte. Tom would retrieve the truck after Wednesday's game against Memphis. Still, the ordeal turned his thoughts inward. Grim-faced and silent for a dozen miles or more, he drove by instinct alone, unaware of the beautiful Maryland landscape before him.

His wife sat at his side, knowing the extent of his unspeakable rage. Ruth Sherman had gone through so much with him in the past. Thinking about it all, she ran her fingers through the silken hair of Timmy Sherman, who sat quietly on her lap. Timmy was only nine months old but easy to manage. The two older children, Heidi and Tom, Jr., scrunched up in the back seat, fussing now and then as children do, unable to grasp the meaning of their father's private agony.

All through her married life, Ruth Sherman had rarely enjoyed a sense of permanency. Not in Boston, where Tom played his rookie season with the Patriots in 1968. Or in Buffalo, where he was released during the team's 1970 training camp. And certainly not in Hartford, where Tom spent the next four years with the semipro Hartford Knights of the Atlantic Coast Football League. It was in this period that Tom's emotions ran together in peaks and valleys of hope and despair.

She remembered how he would come home after a hard day's work at the transportation company, sit quietly in the living room and study his play book. She saw the hope in his face then. And also the despair, when letters from NFL clubs lay crumpled on the table; curt paragraphs that ended in a rejection of his talent. But while he practiced twice a week in the evening, while he played with passionate frenzy on ruined ballfields in the Atlantic Coast circuit, she managed to raise three children and settle for the life that she had. It wasn't a bad life, she thought.

Their truck crossed the state line, under a red glow that signaled approaching nightfall. Speeding south on the turnpike, Tom Sherman listened to the sound of spinning wheels on smooth road, unmindful of the acceleration of time and distance in his own life. Instead, a stirring inside filled him with visions of long-ago Saturdays at Penn State, when he was perhaps the most underrated passer in the nation. In 1967, under coach Joe Paterno, he placed eighth nationally in total offense, broke the Penn State career passing record with 2,588 yards, shattered all the important quarterback standards of the school. Hurtling along into the enveloping darkness, he tried to concentrate on that glorious season, in which he masterminded victories over Miami, Boston College, West Virginia, Syracuse, Maryland, North Carolina State, Ohio and Pittsburgh. But, inevitably, all the golden moments wavered, then fell apart before a ghostly impression of tangled bodies thrashing about before thousands of screaming fans.

Now, seven years and three children later, he turned to his wife and released some of the hurt, if not all of the guilt.

"You know," he said, "as soon as things settle down, I'm going to have a talk with Parilli. I mean, here we are . . . driving to God knows *what* in Charlotte, and I don't even have a contract beyond this season. As it is, Ruthie, we're losing six hundred dol-

196

lars in deposit money on the house, not to mention the cost of
moving. I tell you, I don't even know if I'll have a job next
year . . ."

"Everything will be all right, Tom," said his wife. But she
didn't have the courage to look into her husband's eyes.

"It's getting dark," said Tom after a while. "I better turn on
the headlights . . ."

Dave Richards and Al Young rolled past the city of Wilmington, Delaware, and saw the silhouetted smokestacks of the E. I.
du Pont Company rising like stone cannons above the merging
Delaware and Christina rivers. Their eyes caught the faint out-
line of tankers standing in shallow water at the marine terminal.
Their hearts sensed the gloom and desperation of a prevailing
labor force in the ancient foundries, machine shops and paper
mills. In its Sunday-evening shroud, Wilmington slid by like a
terrible accident of life.

Richards glanced at his rear-view mirror, then flicked the left-
hand signal so that he could move into the speed lane. The car
zoomed past a laconic station wagon. With nothing but clear
highway ahead, Richards felt good—like he had just broken free
on a kickoff return.

Wilmington receded in the distance. Baltimore was less than
seventy miles away, a bulging glowworm under the long dark
skies of Maryland. While Richards drove, Al Young tilted his
chin down on his chest and closed his eyes. The purring motor
and whoosh of turnpike traffic made him drowsy, sent him skit-
tering along on the edge of a troubled sleep.

Only short months before, without direction or purpose, he had
retreated to his roots in Columbia, South Carolina, in order to
find salvation. It was there, in the spring of 1974, that Young
wandered through cool woods, gazed dreamily at his city's land-
marks, and watched black children play neighborhood games
with innocent celebration on their lips. One day, while he ob-
served his father polish marble in a dust-clogged shop, his eyes
watered for an instant. Once, his father's back was strong and
straight, and his hands could curl around the lower end of a bat

197

and whiplash a baseball out of sight. But Edwin Young was no Jackie Robinson, or even a Larry Doby, so he put aside his bat and glove, and polished marble until his back bent and the calcite crystals turned his hands white. As he looked at his father's hands, a deep sadness came over Al Young.

Now he was half-awake, squinting into a stream of lights that exploded on the windshield of the car.

"Where are we?" he asked.

"Comin' into Washington, Al," said Richards.

Washington. The seat of the American dream. D.C. *Dream City*. Al Young almost said it out loud, but suppressed the thought. Richards was into other things. Stevie Wonder was wailing on the car radio, and Young didn't feel like laying down any heavy philosophy while Richards was tapping soulfully on the steering wheel.

So he remained silent. A short time later, when the lighted Capitol dome came into view, he thought about a lot of things that shouldn't be—like the enormous egos of his leaders and the stress they placed on materialism, and all the frustrations that made the American way of life so vexing to him now. He wished more people would get into raja yoga; things would be different. He had studied the Upanishads and was convinced it had brought him nearer to serenity—to an understanding of eternal truth. But he could not have anticipated the shadowy terror that grabbed at his gut on Friday, shaking the very core of his newfound faith.

He had taken a physical exam, a simple matter of having his blood pressure and heart rate checked. He was used to the ritual, having gone through it many times since camp opened in June. Besides, Parilli had assured him he would be activated for the Memphis game in Charlotte if the doc gave him a clean bill of health. He looked forward to the examination without a thought in his head except to have it done with and return to camp with a report that his elbow separation had healed completely. But the doctor's voice was uncommonly flat when the rubber wrapping was removed from his arm.

"It could be nothing, Al, nothing to be alarmed about. But your blood pressure is way up. I'll have to take tests . . ."

At camp, Young told Parilli. The coach shook his head and said that he couldn't play until the tests came back. There was no sense in pushing it, the coach said. That was on Friday. For Al Young, it seemed an eternity had gone by.

He sat up, suddenly wide awake. A minute or two later he and Richards swept by the Quantico Marine installation on Interstate 95. Then he relaxed, turned his face toward Richards and smiled.

"Hey . . ." said his friend, somewhat puzzled by the expression on Young's face. "What's up, man?"

"Oh, nothing. I guess it's that I feel safe with you driving. Yeah . . . you drive real good, Davey . . ."

By mid-morning of October 7, all the moving vans, U-Hauls and autos had arrived. By 3:30 in the afternoon the old New York Stars were no more. Exhausted beyond words, the Charlotte Hornets staggered out to the Belmont Abbey College practice field to begin their first workout.

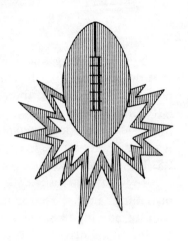

EIGHTEEN

Within a period of a few weeks, financial chaos had swept through the WFL. With the shifting of the Houston Texans to Shreveport, the collapse of the Detroit Wheels, and the displacement of the New York Stars to Charlotte, the inner structure of the entire league was in danger of imminent collapse. The fear was reinforced further on September 28, when Gary Davidson warned the Florida Blazers that he would revoke the franchise unless Rommie Loudd, Florida's managing general partner, was able to raise a reported $2 million to cover its outstanding debts. Phone calls and letters written to the commissioner by disenchanted Blazer players helped to move Davidson off the stick. But Loudd blamed the team's financial woes on Orlando motel owner David Williams, who also owned twenty-nine of the thirty-six limited partnership shares in the Blazers.

"Williams may be the majority investor," Loudd told Davidson, "but he doesn't have control over management. Anyway, under the terms of our agreement, Williams was supposed to put up $3.6 million for his shares, and so far he's invested only

$950,000. You're the commissioner. Go after him . . . not me."

Before the day was over, Loudd had entered a lawsuit in Orlando against both Williams and the league in an effort to block Davidson from taking over the franchise. Among other things, he accused Davidson and Williams of conspiracy and the WFL of discriminating against the Blazers by refusing to subsidize the team.

Apparently, Loudd's last-minute attempt to stave off the inevitable didn't faze Davidson at all. A week later, the WFL took over the Florida franchise.

"The Blazers have forfeited the right to operate the club because they have been unable to meet their financial obligations," intoned WFL public relations director Don Anderson from his post in Newport Beach. However, he was not prepared to say who *did* have the right to operate the team, or for how much. Nor did the commissioner. At this point the future of the league was, at best, murky.

The city of Charlotte was bathed in cool morning sunshine as the Hornets officially met their fans in public for the first time on October 8. At precisely ten o'clock, impressive-looking marching bands, pretty drum majorettes, buglers, dignitaries and a wide-eyed Hornet team gathered in the parking lot of the Sears department store for the start of a parade that would take Parilli and his men through South Tryon Street to the Union Plaza downtown. Although schools were still in session, a profusion of youngsters mingled with their elders, shouting and laughing, exhilarated by the thought of having an honest-to-goodness professional football team they could call their own. In the colorful, electric atmosphere, gaiety ruled.

Looking on unobtrusively, Bob Keating found it difficult, if not impossible, to get into a festive mood. He had arrived with an overnight bag, a headache and a taut stomach. From the time he left LaGuardia Airport at 7:00 A.M. until his plane landed in Charlotte an hour and a half later, his mind worked feverishly to sort out all the unanswered questions: Does Upton Bell really own the team? If not, who does? The league? Schmertz? Who?

And suppose an actual sale had not yet been completed? If so, was the transfer of files, records and equipment from New York to Charlotte legal? Who's liable to pay the $150,000 in back taxes? Who's going to make good on over $100,000 in refunds to the New York season-ticket holders? And finally . . . why the hell am I going to Charlotte in the first place?

But he was there, in the Sears parking lot with everyone else. Only, this time not as general manager of the New York Stars. On this sparkling October morning, Bob Keating was just another out-of-towner gawking at some people he knew—every member of the Charlotte Hornets.

There were two open Cadillac convertibles on the edge of the lot. Behind the convertibles, three old-fashioned trams—painted bright yellow with red trim, and with "Welcome Charlotte Hornets" signs covering their sides—gleamed in the bright sun. The lead car was reserved for Parilli, Upton Bell, and Jim Whittington, the mayor pro tem of Charlotte. The second car was to be occupied by the assistant coaches—Moore, Barber, Leachman and Boutselis. As for the players, they were more than delighted to climb aboard the Gay Nineties trolleys for the ride downtown.

Keating was standing near the Cadillacs, watching Parilli sign autographs for a group of local boosters. Suddenly, he felt awkward, alarmingly uncomfortable in the surroundings. In another moment, he would have broken from the crowd. But Parilli saw him and walked over, grinning.

"Hey, Bob . . . welcome to Charlotte! You're just in time for the parade!"

Keating smiled back, genuinely relieved. But Parilli caught the hesitation in his handshake and the wistful expression on his face.

"Listen," said the coach, his arm now around his former general manager's shoulder, "why don't you jump on one of the trolleys? Jesus, we may never get another chance like this again."

Just then, Upton Bell, wearing a dark blue business suit, emerged from a throng of admirers.

"Hello, Bob, nice to see you," he said. However, the Hornet boss was visibly surprised. He hadn't really expected Keating's arrival in Charlotte. After the usual amenities, Keating stepped back and Bell sank into the rear seat of the Caddie. On signal, the North Charlotte High School band struck up a rousing march tune.

It was a triumphant two hours of pulsating music, generous applause from the multitude that lined the South Tryon Street pavement, flowery speeches by politicians, and a summing up by Bell and Parilli from a platform above an overflow crowd at the Union Plaza.

"I believe we have more people here today than we had at the last New York Stars game," Bell told the enthusiastic fans.

Parilli was next. Before introducing each player to the goggle-eyed audience, he remarked, "This is probably the greatest moment we've had in the WFL."

The observation was heartfelt. Parilli had been under such intense pressure during recent weeks that the outpouring of affection in Charlotte truly amazed him. Sure, he had been part of the Super Bowl Jets in January of 1969. He also remembered how it had been up in Boston, when he was Mister Big in the powerful Patriot aggregation of the early sixties. They loved him in Boston. But this was something else entirely. Here, in Charlotte, he was head coach of a confused, disillusioned team, a family man blundering farther and farther away from his home base in Acton, Massachusetts; a sensitive human being caught up in a power play engineered by highwire manipulators—and he was standing erect and *glorious* in the sight of thousands of strangers who hadn't even known his name a few days ago. Hell, he thought to himself as the Union Plaza crowd acclaimed him, this is probably the greatest moment of my life!

Surrounded by many of the players she helped recruit, Dusty Rhodes stared up at Parilli as he began to make a player-by-player introduction to the crowd. She knew there wouldn't be any acknowledgement of her presence from the platform. Upton Bell had made it a point to tell Parilli before the ceremony that only the coaches and players would take a bow. When the last of them stepped down, Dusty was convinced that nothing but hard times lay ahead of her in Charlotte.

Nevertheless, the excitement, the ecstasy that rippled over the Union Plaza obscured all other conditions and emotions. Cheerleaders jumped, bands played, choruses sang, players scribbled their signatures on scraps of paper and in autograph books, while normally reticent women ogled them, felt their muscles and smiled dreamily into their eyes. The local groupies were already at work—black beauties ready to sink their fingernails and teeth into black Hornet flesh; white honeys prepared to do the same to white Hornet flesh. In contrast, the majority of people typified the standard version of Anglo-Saxon goodness. Mothers with red or yellow or white gardenias pinned to chic, sedate dresses pointed out this or that football player to their children. Men in conservative business suits, with American Legion pins stuck in their lapels, grabbed Hornet elbows and slapped Hornet backs. Some gave out business cards. "Look me up," one said with a wink. "I'll take good care of you. Used to be a jock myself, you know. . . ."

Then it was over. The Union Plaza emptied, the Caddies and trolley cars rolled back to the Sears parking lot, and the Department of Sanitation combed and brushed away everything but the memory of a parade that had once passed by on South Tryon Street.

Another parade of sorts began when the players reached the Sears lot. They sped off in their cars to the training site at Belmont Abbey, a Roman Catholic liberal arts school nestled on rolling hills near the Catawba River. In the rush of things, Bob Keating wandered about the lot calling out to this one or that, "Are you going back to the motel?" He was staying at the Holiday Inn South, the temporary home and headquarters of the Hornets. No, they answered, they had to pick up their gear at Belmont Abbey. Coach is holding a two-hour practice session that evening at Memorial Field, they said. Sorry.

Sitting contentedly in his slick, expensive sedan, Jim Whittington noticed Keating, sized up his difficulty, then cupped a hand to his mouth.

"Are you with the team?"

"No, not exactly. I'm just down for the game."

"Where from?"

"New York. I used to be the general manager of the New York Stars."

"In that case, hop in. I'll drive you to where you're going."

During the short ride, Keating sat in insulated comfort on a soft-leathered rear seat, staring mindlessly at the back of Whittington's head while the mayor pro tem drove and spoke glowingly of a private developer's plans for expansion of Memorial Stadium.

"We had our city council meeting just yesterday," said Whittington, a tall, robust, thin-crowned man of sixty or so whose soft Southern inflection suggested a college education and an unerring instinct for the good life. "One of our leading realtors, man by the name of Fred Godley, says he can expand the stadium from a capacity of 25,000 seats to 60,000. Of course, it would take a lot of money, something like $13 million to do it, but that would also include the construction of a parking deck with space for over 3,000 cars. Quite a project, I'd say."

"Sure is," said Keating.

"Just goes to show you what can happen when Charlotte gets involved in something big, like the World Football League. All you have to do is bring in something that the people can relate to—like professional sports—and everybody gets excited. But I'll tell you," confided Whittington with lowered voice, "if the product turns out to be inferior, there's no way for it to survive.

"Some years ago, as a matter of fact, I helped to bring a pro hockey team into Charlotte. What happened was, the team originally played in Baltimore, in the Eastern Hockey League, but the arena burned down. Well, the community pitched in, and the next thing you know we brought the team here. Called them the Charlotte Clippers. But as soon as they started losing, you never saw so many ex-hockey fans in all your life. That's the trick; you gotta win in Charlotte . . . or you're dead."

At the entrance to the Holiday Inn, Whittington extended his hand, gave Keating his card, then eased his sedan around the driveway and out onto route I-77, fading into the traffic whence he had come. In the solitude of his room, Keating sat down heavily on his bed, sighed, and wondered what he would be doing next. Lazily, he held Whittington's card in front of him and saw the raised letters:

FUNERAL DIRECTOR

The American Legion Memorial Stadium in Charlotte shares a common background with New York's Downing Stadium. Both were built during the Great Depression; both were inadequately lighted for modern-day viewing; both stadiums contained less than the required seating capacity for professional football games; and, like its counterpart in New York, Memorial Stadium was an infinitesimal speck in the vast configuration of national sporting events. Its most heralded extravaganza, until the coming of the Hornets, matched the best North and South Carolina college football players in an annual Shrine Bowl game.

But unlike the barren wasteland that swallowed the Stars at Downing Stadium, a sellout crowd was expected for the Memorial Stadium debut of the Hornets on Wednesday, October 9. Throughout the week, ticket locations all over town were jammed with people who eagerly ordered $5.50 and $7.50 seats for the game. Nearly 12,000 season tickets (there were four home games left on the schedule) were sold by Tuesday afternoon.

"It hasn't been this active since the *Disney on Parade* was here," said Mary McCommons, one of the ticket sellers at the Coliseum, Charlotte's Madison Square Garden. As she spoke, a fleet of special buses was put into service to deliver the fans, round-trip, to the stadium from behind Belk's department store on College Street, and from Church and 4th streets downtown— at twenty-five cents a head.

Working almost around the clock, Vince Casey developed incredible ink in the *Charlotte Observer* and the *Charlotte News,* saturation coverage on radio and television, and a glittering showcase for the potential backers of Upton Bell's new windup franchise—the Charlotte Hornets.

That Tuesday evening at 7:00, with 2,000 rubber-necking free-bies on the scene, the team practiced under the myopic lights of Memorial Stadium; running scrimmage plays, loosening muscles, testing the sod (slightly dry) and getting the feel of things. Sauer, Elliott, Philbin and Parilli drew the most attention. They had the credentials, the stamp of NFL PRIME on their hides. And when Sauer made a fast cut to snare a Sherman bullet, his choreography brought them up with a standing ovation. But right after the catch, Sauer pirouetted inches away from a row of temporary wooden seats beyond the player benches, thereby sidestepping disastrous injury.

Parilli shook his head, then tramped over to Bell, who seemed to be all over the place at once, observing, checking, talking—shaking hands with this one or that. Pointing to the obstruction, Parilli spat out his disgust.

"We better get rid of those seats, or someone is going to get killed around here. And another thing . . . look at those stone walls!"

Rough-surfaced stone and gravel sheathed the grandstand wall from end zone to end zone—strong enough to withstand anything from Greg Lens to a howitzer shell.

"Maybe we can put up some blankets," offered Bell.

"Blankets?" snorted Parilli.

While Bell pondered the problem, a number of youngsters ran on the field, whooping and hollering, weaving in and out of the practice area in wild delight. The commotion distracted the play-ers and irritated the assistant coaches. Suddenly, Dusty Rhodes flew into the center of the pack, ordering them off with loud-voiced authority. The kids scattered into their seats as quickly as they had vacated them. Smiling broadly, Dusty brushed back a wisp of hair and winked at Tom Moore, who formed an "o" with his thumb and middle finger.

Bell forgot about the stone wall. Anger jolted through him. He clenched his fists, broke off his conversation with Parilli, and within a moment or two cornered Dusty behind the deserted end zone section.

"I don't want you to *ever* go out on the field again," he said.

"Listen, Upton, those kids were screwing up the practice. I only . . ."

"I don't care about that. I'm running this team . . . not you. And, I repeat, I don't want you on the field."

"Why?"

"Because it's not your job."

After he walked away, Dusty sat down on an end zone seat, held a yellow legal pad to her chest and let the tears spill undisturbed from her eyes. Her whole life seemed to be crumbling into the parched grass of Memorial Stadium.

The practice continued. At 8:30 P.M. a cab drew up to the front gate, letting out its only passenger, Bob Keating. He was glad that he had worn his topcoat, as the night air had turned chilly. He made a beeline to the field, avoiding one of the wide receivers, who whizzed past with outstretched arms, mouth agape. He smiled when one of the cornerbacks clapped his shoulder and said, "Way to go, Bob," and the top of his skull throbbed painfully when he located Bell, who stood with arms folded at the fifty-yard line, staring into the lusterless lights above the stadium, like a warrior king seeking divine inspiration. Keating interrupted his soliloquy.

"Just so you know exactly why I'm here, it's because I think somebody might be in trouble."

"Trouble? What do you mean?"

"To get to the point, Upton, Schmertz is involved in this transaction, Baldwin is involved, Davidson is involved, and you're involved. So, what I simply want to know is—who the hell is going to pay off the New York debts, which are now running close to two million? I mean, Upton, I don't even know if Schmertz has a piece of paper with you!"

"Calm down, Bob. Gary will be holding a press conference at the Manger tomorrow morning at ten, so why don't you call him there? I'm sure he'll be able to answer all your questions. Meanwhile, I don't think this is the proper time or place to discuss the situation."

There wasn't anything more to say. Keating hung around the field for a while, glumly watching the athletes go through their drills, desperately wishing he could be part of it again. By the time he hailed a cab at the front gate, he felt disconnected and totally alone.

One small footnote closed the book on the evening's workout. Gerry Philbin had decided to grow a beard. There was no particular reason for his decision. It was just something he thought he'd like to do two days before he drove down to Charlotte in his new Cadillac. After all, Parson had a beard. So did Sims, Ford and Ellison. Well, he'd grow one, too. At the parade, he thought Upton Bell looked at him peculiarly, then quickly discarded the idea as nothing more than a baseless aberration. But during a break on the field, as he stroked his budding whiskers, feeling raw and funky in his football livery, his musings were interrupted by the man now responsible for signing his biweekly paychecks.

"Hey, Gerry," said Upton Bell, his words sliding out thin through an icy smile, "when are you going to shave?"

Philbin cocked his head to one side. He felt the turbulent rumble deep inside, as though cannon balls were rattling around in his gut.

"Harr-harr-harr . . ." he laughed before trotting off to his assignment in the defensive line, leaving Bell standing there scratching the back of his head and wondering what Gerry Philbin was all about, anyway.

In the dressing room after practice, Philbin tore at his shirt, pulled it over his shoulder pads, flung it against the door of his locker, and spewed out a single word:

"She-ii-tt!"

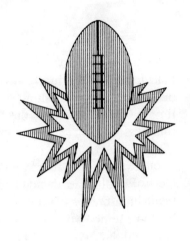

NINETEEN

"I have reared a monument more enduring than brass, and loftier than the pyramids' royal structure; which not the wasting shower, nor the raving North-wind can have power to overthrow, or the countless successions of years, and the ages' flight."

Thus wrote Horace, one of the most admired of the ancient Roman lyric poets. There was a time, in July of 1974, when Horace's ode to his own creative genius could conceivably have been written by the creator of the World Football League. If not more enduring than brass, at least his monument shone as brightly during those early Wednesday- and Thursday-evening games around the league. In July, Philadelphia, Jacksonville, Birmingham, Memphis and other WFL teams found clicking turnstiles the most pleasing poetry of all. And the creator, Gary Davidson, surveyed his domain and said . . . *"It is good."*

Now it was an October morning in Charlotte, short hours away from the Memorial Stadium battle between the Hornets and the

Southmen. No longer did Davidson's monument shine. Like sand-castles at high tide, the superficially constructed franchises began to collapse around his head.

On that singular Wednesday morning, news hit the wire service desks stating the games of the Detroit Wheels and the Jacksonville Sharks were being postponed. Unless new investors for the troubled teams were found, said the reports, the franchises would be folded by the league. It marked the first time the weekly schedule had been diluted—from six games to five.

On still another front, an attorney for the Florida Blazers demanded a full investigation of WFL finances. Robert Deutsch, a Boston attorney representing the team, emphasized he would go to court if necessary to open WFL books for inspection. "There have been a lot of things going on that no one really understands," said Deutsch.

While the Blazer lawyer brandished his legal sword under Davidson's nose, Atlanta businessman David Pendley was also active. He filed suit in U.S. District Court in Orlando, seeking $150,000 in damages from the Blazers because he hadn't been repaid a $40,000 loan he had made to the club.

With legal artillery firing at him from every direction, Davidson wiped his mouth with a napkin, pushed back from his table in the coffee shop of the Manger Motor Inn, and nodded to his associate, Max Muhleman. The commissioner was ready to meet the press.

Life in the Holiday Inn South was pleasant, if not altogether rewarding. The players lounged quietly in their rooms, or sat on sofas in the lobby, or breakfasted casually in the coffee shop; reading, stretching, talking, daydreaming. The pageantry and trappings of the parade and the surprising turnout at their evening practice had revitalized the team, restored their confidence in themselves and each other. Even Gerry Philbin felt better about things. He was still unshaven, and his infectious laugh could be heard above the tinkling, droning sounds of coffee shop existence.

At a corner table, Gary and Kristy Danielson poked vacuously at their breakfast plates, saying little but communicating all the same. His father was dying—slack-jawed and gray in a Dearborn hospital—dying slowly of emphysema.

In the early light of his hotel room Gary had placed a phone to his ear and listened to his mother's voice—flat and strained—saying that his father had lapsed into a coma. Tears came to his eyes as he sat on the edge of the bed with Kristy still asleep. After many pauses, strangled words, and the sound of someone saying, "Are you finished with your call?" he hung up and slipped under the covers, pressing his wet face against Kristy's until she awoke. Later, they rode the elevator down to the lobby in numbed silence.

Now, skimming through the sports pages of the *Charlotte Observer,* sipping coffee, glancing at Kristy, he could still hear his mother's voice . . . *It's only a matter of time . . . all we can do is hope and pray . . .* over and over again.

He was reading a Bob Quincy column—a humorous account of Hornet history past and present in Charlotte, with a photo of Babe Parilli and Tom Sherman in their New York Stars jackets above Quincy's byline.

"Listen to this, honey," he said, as the echoes faded under the vibration of his own voice. *"The Hornets are already one-up on most of the WFL entries. What kind of a football player wants to be known as a Philadelphia Bell? Or a Wheel? Wheels run off. A Bell is to be rung. A Hornet stings, and his calling card is a swollen red blotch."*

"That's about the way I feel," he said. "Like one big swollen red blotch. I guess you might say that I've been jinxed by the Stars and stung by the Hornets."

Babe Parilli was seated at a table near the cash register, in guarded conversation with Dusty Rhodes. Gary looked over. He would have to inform his coach about his father's condition. He might have to go home at any minute, and the thought of it made him feel sick in the pit of his stomach.

"It just doesn't seem right," he suddenly blurted out to Kristy. "I mean, my dad wanted so little out of life. Jeez, he worked his butt off in that lithography shop, six days a week, year after year, putting in all kinds of hours . . . overtime, doubletime . . . just so he wouldn't have to work a hundred years and die without having a decent burial. Can you imagine that . . . ?"

"Gary . . . don't . . ." Gary didn't say anything more until the waitress came over, and then he asked for a check. When the waitress left, he took Kristy's hand in his.

"You know, I remember when I was a little guy . . . oh, maybe ten or eleven years old . . . and my dad would get up every Sunday morning at six in the wintertime. Sometimes it was so cold you'd think he'd never want to get out of bed. Anyway, he'd drive me to Essex, forty miles away in Ontario, Canada—to the indoor ice rink—just to watch me practice for junior hockey games. That's the way I remember him most. Standing off to one side while I skated . . . looking so proud . . . like I was the most important thing that ever came into his life. I guess I felt the same way, too. To me, he was the greatest guy who ever lived."

A few minutes later Gary and Kristy walked over to Parilli's table.

"My dad's dying, Babe. I talked to my mom this morning, and she told me it was just a matter of time. I wanted you to know . . ."

Parilli's dark eyes blinked. "If you have to go home, just take off. Football can wait."

He followed them with saddened eyes until they opened the door that took them into the lobby.

"Nice kid," he whispered hoarsely.

"Sure is," said Dusty.

A few miles away, Bob Keating met Gary Davidson in the lobby of the Manger Motor Inn. With Max Muhleman at the commissioner's side, they talked for ten minutes. According to Davidson, everything about the New York-to-Charlotte franchise switch was legal. The league took the franchise away from Schmertz because he couldn't meet his assessments. Bell had the franchise, but Schmertz was still the legal owner. Either the league or Schmertz would get paid off when Bell got his backing.

"That's all well and good," said Keating, "but what about the debts, the back taxes . . . and what do we do with all those season-ticket holders who were left holding the bag?"

"We'll look into it, Bob. Make a note of that, Max." Then the commissioner excused himself to attend his press conference, leaving Keating with a pained expression on his face. There were no other moves to make. He'd watch the game and the next morning he'd fly back to New York, knowing nothing would be looked into, knowing that his mission to Charlotte had failed.

Twelve batches of helium-filled balloons floated above Memorial Stadium that night as a capacity crowd of 25,000 sprang to their feet. Bands blared, and frozen-smiled dignitaries, including Gary Davidson and Mayor John Belk, honored Upton Bell for bringing a new professional World Football League team to Charlotte. And as Bell looked out at the congealed mass, listening to trumpets in the chilled night, the speechless rhythms of a stadium unchained, he saw the bright hope of tomorrow in the long laborious days of his past. Charlotte bloomed in the land. The earth was whole. His finest hour had tolled.

With one minute and ten seconds remaining in the fourth quarter, his team down by four points, fighting back, with the crowd screaming GO, HORNETS, GO!, Tom Sherman went to the air on third-and-ten. The ball floated up in the night, into the lights, lost for one-tenth of a second in the glare, spiraling orange-striped toward the end zone. It was slightly underthrown. Left cornerback David Thomas jumped in front of wide receiver Al Barnes at the twelve-yard line and fell to the turf with a Southmen victory in his grasp.

The crowd filtered out, hollow, hoarse-throated, disappointed that Charlotte had lost, but feeling as if they had rooted for the Hornets all their lives. Empty beer cans by the thousands were swept up, car motors started, the lights dimmed, and, within an hour, Memorial Stadium was as silent as a tomb. But across the way, a gymnasium woke to the wicked sounds of a rock group. Upton Bell and most of the Hornet coaches and players moved

214

about in a sea of well-wishers, helping themselves to a buffet of cold cuts, nodding and smiling, convivial, relishing the attention given them after having gone through a painful defeat. And Gerry Philbin, acting as spokesman for the team, struck a perfect keynote to bring the Hornets even closer to the genteel citizens of Charlotte.

"When I first came down from Buffalo to play with the Jets," he began, "I roomed with a Southern boy from Clemson. His name is Bill Mathis, a helluva running back. Well, Bill would say the South was a great place to be, but I never believed him. But in the short time I've been down here, I've met the friendliest, most loyal fans of my entire professional career, and I know that all of my teammates feel the same way. So thanks again for your support. I hope we can justify your faith in us and be a winning team for the people of Charlotte."

Glowing, Upton Bell couldn't have cared less at that moment if Gerry Philbin decided to grow a beard down to his ankles.

Babe Parilli started out enjoying the party as much as anyone. He was fawned over by quietly dressed women and men who hungered for his words and radiated in the aura of his benign grace. But as the evening wore on, Parilli began to think of fumbles and dropped passes and interceptions. It erased some of the pleasure.

George Boutselis was happier than he could ever remember. In the agony of movement and change, he kept himself going with a growing belief in his own worth as a professional football coach and human being. Now he was sure he had found his groove, was relating to his unit as never before. Only that morning Jeff Woodcock, a bright, open-faced red-headed Kentuckian with a habit of addressing everyone as *sir* and *ma'am,* had thanked him for his help and wished him luck in the game. He felt absolutely smashing after that, because Woody had developed into one of the best safeties in the WFL.

"You know," Boutselis told trainer Lew Cohen in a sudden burst of elation, "this is some life. I love it. . . . I love it!"

Al Young loved life as much as the next one. And now he'd

be able to enjoy it to the fullest. Three hours before game time Doc Cowan had told him he was okay, that his high blood pressure was down to normal. He was fit again and would be activated by Parilli against the Fire the following week.

"It'll be good to start catching a few again," he said to Davey Richards at the party.

"No sweat," said Davey. "It was meant to be, man, y'know what I mean?"

Young reckoned he did.

And the night went on. And Upton Bell's bright hope passed into the next day. And the next.

On Friday, October 11, Gary Danielson felt a dreadful shifting of something vital and eternal in the depths of his soul. For he knew that as long as he would live, no matter triumph or tragedy, he could never again lift a phone or walk through a door or reach out a hand and say, "Hi, Dad." On that final day of his father's life, he and Kristy flew home to Detroit.

And the clock of human existence ticked on.

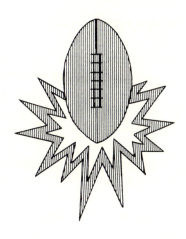

TWENTY

LOUISIANA SHERIFF SEIZES HORNETS' UNIFORMS

By Richard Sink
Charlotte Observer Sportswriter

SHREVEPORT, La., Nov. 7—The Charlotte Hornets returned home this morning from their World Football League game, but their equipment did not. It was confiscated by Caddo Parish Sheriff Jimmy Goslin in compliance with a lawsuit against the Hornets by plaintiffs in New York.

The suit charges the Hornets with failure to pay $26,216 it accumulated in debts while the club was located in New York for the first half of the season. Although the club has changed management, the plaintiffs, believed to be a security firm and a cleaning establishment, feel new president-general manager Upton Bell remains liable for the money.

The World Football League season ended with a whimper. And the men who spun the money wheel around, what of them?

For some, calamity resulted from the irresistible urge to promote themselves into the inner councils of Gary Davidson's vainglorious empire without commitments to ideals or action.

For others, who hid behind venetian blinds and doctored

217

ledger accounts, for whom the playing field was alien ground, the players isolated hulks of bought flesh—without physical, biological, psychological or cultural identities . . . mere objects to be analyzed, categorized and reduced to cold assets—in the end, they also fell by the wayside.

Before the long, devastating season was over, a wretched litany of events illustrated the collapse of the league.

• Jacksonville Sharks owner Fran Monaco, unable to meet his payroll for a month, borrowed $27,000 from head coach Bud Asher, whom he then fired. Then Monaco and the Sharks went under.

• Southern California Sun owner Larry Hatfield pleaded guilty in a United States District Court to submitting a false financial statement when negotiating for a $365,000 bank loan for the team.

• Florida Blazers managing general partner Rommie Loudd was indicted by a Federal grand jury for tax fraud.

• The Internal Revenue Service claimed Birmingham Americans owner Bill Putnam owed the government $160,000 in personal back taxes.

• The IRS lodged a tax lien of $168,000 against the Portland Storm.

• The University of California entered a judgment against the Hawaiians, claiming a $9,062 check it had received from the team for training camp facilities had bounced.

• A $1.5-million check, displayed on national television as a down payment for the purchase of the Florida Blazers, later bounced. The check was issued by a convicted felon who had served a year behind bars for transporting stolen cars across state lines.

From the formless jumble, the picture of misfortune surfaced like so many splotches on a Jackson Pollock canvas. Heartbreaking tales—of WFL players in Portland being fed and clothed by

218

charitable citizens, of WFL players in Hawaii being cut and left stranded without funds thousands of miles from home, of WFL players in Charlotte and Shreveport unable to be compensated for transportation and housing losses, of WFL players in Orlando being turned away from stores and banks while trying to cash personal checks—were like the murmurings of desert sand in the path of a raging windstorm. Everyone in the WFL felt the pressure, but few could withstand the turbulence.

On October 29, an emergency meeting of WFL owners was held in Chicago—ostensibly to dissuade Fire owner Tom Origer from pulling his team out of the league. What had happened was this: Origer did contemplate the action. His team had dropped eight games in a row, and a series of economic and attendance problems had thinned his cash reserves. Now that his Fire home schedule was completed, with no possible source of new income, Origer plunged into a lonely period of self-examination. Finally, he decided to take a giant step.

First, he informed Commissioner Gary Davidson that he was going to abort his remaining three games. Then he told Memphis owner and league executive committee Chairman John Bassett, "Either Gary goes or I go, because there's no way for me to coexist with him." But if Origer thought he was in for a knock-down battle with Davidson he was mistaken—on a number of counts.

Essentially, the commissioner was caught in a web he could not escape. At an earlier time he was able to wriggle from entrapments, explain his way out of serious setbacks, leap from crisis to crisis and still maintain a firm grip on his WFL throne. But now his franchises were collectively around $20 million in debt, his own office in Newport Beach owed close to $1 million in accounts payable, personal damage suits had seen served against him, his reputation was under attack by press and media, and his wife had filed for divorce. Sensing only imperfectly the collapse of his power base and the reasons behind his personal misfortune, Davidson nonetheless realized he had outlived his usefulness as commissioner. Rather than continue his battle against a gathering

219

tide of dissent, he used the Chicago meeting to announce his resignation.

Afterward, with bitter defeat veiled in a camouflage of cool detachment, Davidson said he would stay on as a member of the league's executive and expansion committee, and serve on the board of governors of the California Sun. "I prefer to be on the selling end of the game rather than at the administrative end," he told reporters at the conclusion of the two-hour session.

For Larry Hatfield, appointing Davidson to a nebulous post with the Sun was his way of softening Davidson's ignominious fall from power. "If I had to fault Gary," said Hatfield of his California crony, "it would be for his honesty. He freely admitted he expected to make a lot of money out of the WFL. He might have been better off if he'd kept his mouth shut."

Dan Regan found little solace in Hatfield's statement. Removed from his position as legal and general counsel of the league, reduced to the role of a puppet executive director, Regan reluctantly agreed to carry out orders, knowing he and his law partner were all but finished in the palace guard revolt of October 29.

As for Upton Bell, who attended the macabre proceedings, it was a time for privately giving the devil his due and publicly moving on to practical considerations. Bell had benefited from Davidson's despotic benevolence during the lightning-fast negotiations to move the New York franchise to Charlotte. He was able to swing the deal primarily because he had promised Davidson he would promptly send along team assessment fees to Newport Beach—an obligation Bob Schmertz never got around to while operating the Stars. Bell followed through on his commitment by turning over a $100,000 check to Davidson out of gate receipts from Charlotte's first two home games.

Now Davidson's reign as WFL czar was over; there would be no more binding ties, and Bell used the moment to direct a few psychological broadsides at Mayor Belk and other potential Hornet backers.

"I look upon Gary's resignation as a very positive thing," said Bell. "Most people felt, myself included, that the responsible owners of the league should take over and run it until the end of the season. People in Charlotte should already be aware of solid men like John Bassett, Tom Origer and Bill Putnam. They're a big plus. After all, a lot of things had to be settled, and I think we got over the hump today in many ways."

The Hornet season ended seventeen days later. It ended on a lovely practice day at Belmont Abbey College in Charlotte as the players scrimmaged in a celebration of juvenescence and sang praises to simple pleasure in exquisite abstractions:

> *Start your weave*
> *square cut*
> *clear deep*
> *quick release*
> *bingo bingo bingo!*

This was the unchangeable passion of their profession, and they gave it full devotion; waiting for a whistle to start another game, daring time to bring their careers to an end—while the world fell away from them.

At exactly 3:30 P.M., Saturday, November 16, John Bassett placed a phone call from Memphis to Upton Bell in Charlotte. Acting officially as WFL executive committee chairman, he informed the Hornet chief that his team's scheduled Wednesday night playoff game against the Blazers in Orlando was being canceled for financial reasons. Bassett pointed out that fewer than one thousand tickets had been sold, that the players couldn't hope to receive more than a token one hundred dollars or so if they played, and that it would be an insult to their intelligence to ask them to go through with the game. Therefore, said Bassett, the Blazers would meet Central Division runner-up Birmingham in a more lucrative Thursday-night national TV game.

Bell was justifiably disappointed over Charlotte's elimination from the playoffs, but certainly not dismayed by the league ruling. It released him from the distractions of pure football matters and gave him precious time to wrestle with his considerable financial problems.

The facts were unshakable. After two months of tiresome meet-ings with Mayor Belk and others, he was no further along in his quest for Hornet funding than he was in September. Furthermore, Bob Schmertz was expecting a hefty down payment on the agreed selling price that permitted him to move the franchise. Also, the team had not received its regular biweekly paychecks since the third week in October, and John Elliott, the highest paid player, was owed approximately $14,000 before taxes. Another serious problem was the Holiday Inn South, which held around $13,000 in team debts. Adding to the strain, printing, advertising, trans-portation and utility firms were also getting restless. Therefore, in the relative peace and quiet of his Tryon Street office in Charlotte, Bell moved swiftly to dismantle his football team. He called Parilli at Belmont Abbey, cleared his throat and broke the news about the canceled playoff game.

It wasn't easy.

The following morning Bell spoke to the entire squad in the training room of Belmont Abbey. In moments such as this, he could always summon up an image of his father, who once told him never to lie, that the only thing he'd ever have in life was the truth. And now, while adversity buffeted his spirit, he told his players and coaches exactly where they stood.

"You'll be paid out of playoff receipts . . . there'll be an owners meeting in Memphis on Tuesday . . . decisions will be made about next year . . . there must be a new commissioner . . . fresh money must go into a fund for back salaries . . . I'm meeting with investors on Thursday . . . either I stay because I have the money or I will turn the team back to Schmertz . . . If I can't pay you, the league will . . . if there's no league you're free to go to the NFL . . . I can tell you on Saturday if there will or won't be a league . . . I can see the mess, but there's no way out of it. That's all I have to say."

John Elliott, the player representative, got up and asked one question.

"Upton, what the players would like to know is . . . can you guarantee the money if the league doesn't give us our back pay?"

"I can't give you a guarantee," answered Bell, "because I don't own the football team."

And Al Young got up and asked one question.

"What about our insurance?"

"I don't know if we're covered."

And when the silence seemed thickest, Babe Parilli slowly rose to his feet, thanked the team for their efforts, said he was proud of them, and then hurled a plaintive cry into the wilderness: "I know we could have beaten Florida."

And Lamar Leachman, while clearing out his things from the coaches' room a few minutes later, looked up at Tommy Beer with desperate sadness, knowing that he was in the midst of discovering an extraordinary truth.

"Goddamn, Tommy," he said, "my head is twirlin' like a knob on a shithouse door."

It was a time to say goodbye, a time for summing up, for viewing the end of warm friendships before the full ripening. So, Len St. Jean—a veteran NFL guard who had joined the team in September—gave a party in his garden apartment the next evening. And as the players and coaches drove up in their cars, some with wives, some with dates, they saw John Elliott turning hamburger patties on a charcoal grill outside and heard Greg Lens singing one of his funny songs inside the apartment, and everyone who came sat around in the living room or in the kitchen and talked about their long season in the World Football League.

George Boutselis couldn't make the party because a Charlotte doctor had taken lymph nodes from his neck after the Shreveport game and then sent him on to specialists at the Mayo Clinic and Duke University, who confirmed that he had Hodgkin's disease. So Boutselis said his goodbyes the day before at Belmont Abbey. He had swallowed hard when Jimmy Sims, in behalf of all the defensive backs, said that he was a good coach and that they had all learned something from him. Then he got into his car and drove up to Johns Hopkins Hospital in Baltimore for further tests that would determine whether he needed surgery, radiation or chemotherapy. Miles and miles from Charlotte, on the open road, Boutselis truly understood why he loved life, but understood far too little the ultimate *why* of his life.

Tiger Ferraro didn't show up, either. He went to bed early. The next morning he had to pack all that gear away at Belmont Abbey. So he turned the blinds down, shut off the lights, and wondered what it would be like never to see a football again. Legally blind in one eye from birth, Ferraro faced a cataract operation on his good right eye in December. It scared him. He wanted to be back the next year. He wanted to see the Hornets make it. But he knew nothing in life was sure, except that he did have some good times with the team—like when they were in Houston and rookie tackle Dana Carpenter ate twenty-six eggs for breakfast to establish a new team record. Yeah, that was one of the good times, all right, Tiger thought before falling asleep— before dreaming beautiful dreams in shining color.

While he slept, the party in St. Jean's apartment, filled with bursts of decent laughter, kindled with pleasurable conversation, drifted into the night air like a fading ray of joy; lost forever in the gloom of intemperate time.

But memories remained. Their names, their season together, the places they had seen, the fields they had played on—remained locked in their hearts and minds; in the lonely lingering years ahead, little would be forgotten.

And as phantasmagoric scenes of their vanished season slipped into place, Lloyd Voss remembered a beach party on the windward side of Oahu, where, under a tropical golden light, he had stared up at ochre and dark red cliffs—towering razor-edged mountains perhaps a million or more years old—and thought of dim-distant voyages he would take in the measureless dawns ahead.

"I guess I felt a little guilty," he said to his wife. "I wanted you to be there, to look at those incredible mountains with me. I knew I owed you."

Jane Voss smiled, prodded her husband in the ribs. "Now I

224

know why you brought back that gorgeous dress from Hawaii. I suppose you're getting soft in your old age, you big ape."

"Yeah. I guess that's it," he said, holding her around the shoulders, draining his can of beer, fumbling to say something more, then succumbing to a misty silence while others chattered lightly in St. Jean's apartment.

And, in the tantalizing reality of their spent season, fragmented images were seized by all the players and coaches who sat around and talked of home games and road games: of Larry Butler, Dick Hart and Lou Angelo getting their pictures taken in Philadelphia with tennis champion Billie Jean King, of Gerry Philbin and Bob Hermanni taking a riverboat ride at Disneyland, of Darryl and Marsha Bunge's wedding at the Unity Center in Charlotte, of Harpo Gladieux running Mr. Brown on the high grass at La Salle, of Gary and Kristy Danielson climbing to the summit of Diamond Head while Tom Sherman and Ike Thomas passed over the sunken hull of the USS *Arizona* at Pearl Harbor, of Jacksonville's cheerleaders and Portland's roses, of Houston's steaks and Chicago's pizzas, of a thousand laughs and at least one hidden tear in the wide bulge of their pro football season. And, at one point, Len St. Jean said to Stew Barber, "Maybe I enjoyed myself with these guys because most of them are young and unspoiled—trying to get somewhere—trying to find a way to relate to something important."

And Babe Parilli called out, "Hey, Woody, I saved something for you."

"Yes, sir?"

"Let me get it. It's in my car."

Outside, Parilli presented Jeff Woodcock, class of '74, with a Kentucky Wildcat doormat, one he had kept since his days with Bear Bryant. And Woodcock blinked, saying that he'd cherish it forever and would hang it on his wall. Greg Lens laughed and sang "For He's a Jolly Good Fellow," and everybody came outside to drown the long Charlotte night in song, which caused Woodcock to crinkle his nose while a crimson flush touched his cheeks. And Dusty Rhodes, immersed in the amusement, said, "It's a great party." But once inside, she bit her lips to keep from

225

crying, and whispered to Parilli, "It's all been worth it, hasn't it, Babe?" The coach nodded, his eyes trained on the far wall, a great fire blazing behind the stare.

And when the party had ebbed, when all the noble thoughts had been expressed, when the unforgiving clock could not further prolong their sad-happy hours together, George Sauer, in a velour cap and bow tie, looking so much like Little Boy Blue, walked over to a writer who had traveled with the team all season. The writer was with him on the beach of Waikiki, on flights to Los Angeles and Chicago and Memphis and all the other towns along the shattered WFL trail—and many times had watched him glide lazily in pursuit of a leather ball; always to remember the airy surge of his immortal flight.

"I have to go now," said Sauer. "But here, I've written something you might like. I want you to have it."

In a moment he was gone.

The next morning, on a jet ride back to New York, the writer once again read what George Sauer had written—and felt as if he had read it for the first time:

> The sky sighs deep with a bleak radiance;
> Fragile nervous clouds tremble short of breath—
> Warm, sweet breezes cool in doomed abeyance,
> The sun fades red like the drunken eye of death . . .